TEEN TITANS ACADEMY

VOL. 1: X MARKS THE SPOT

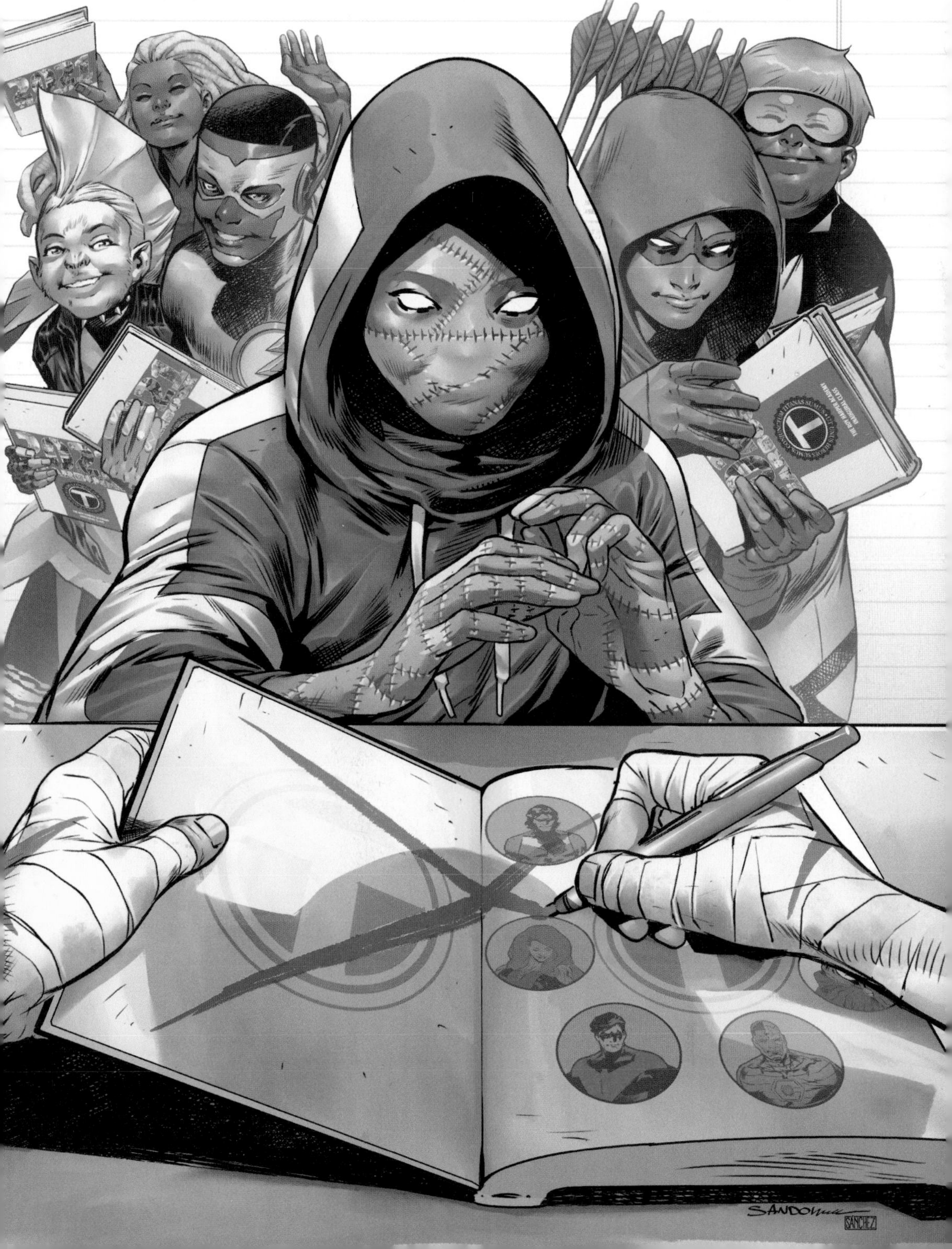

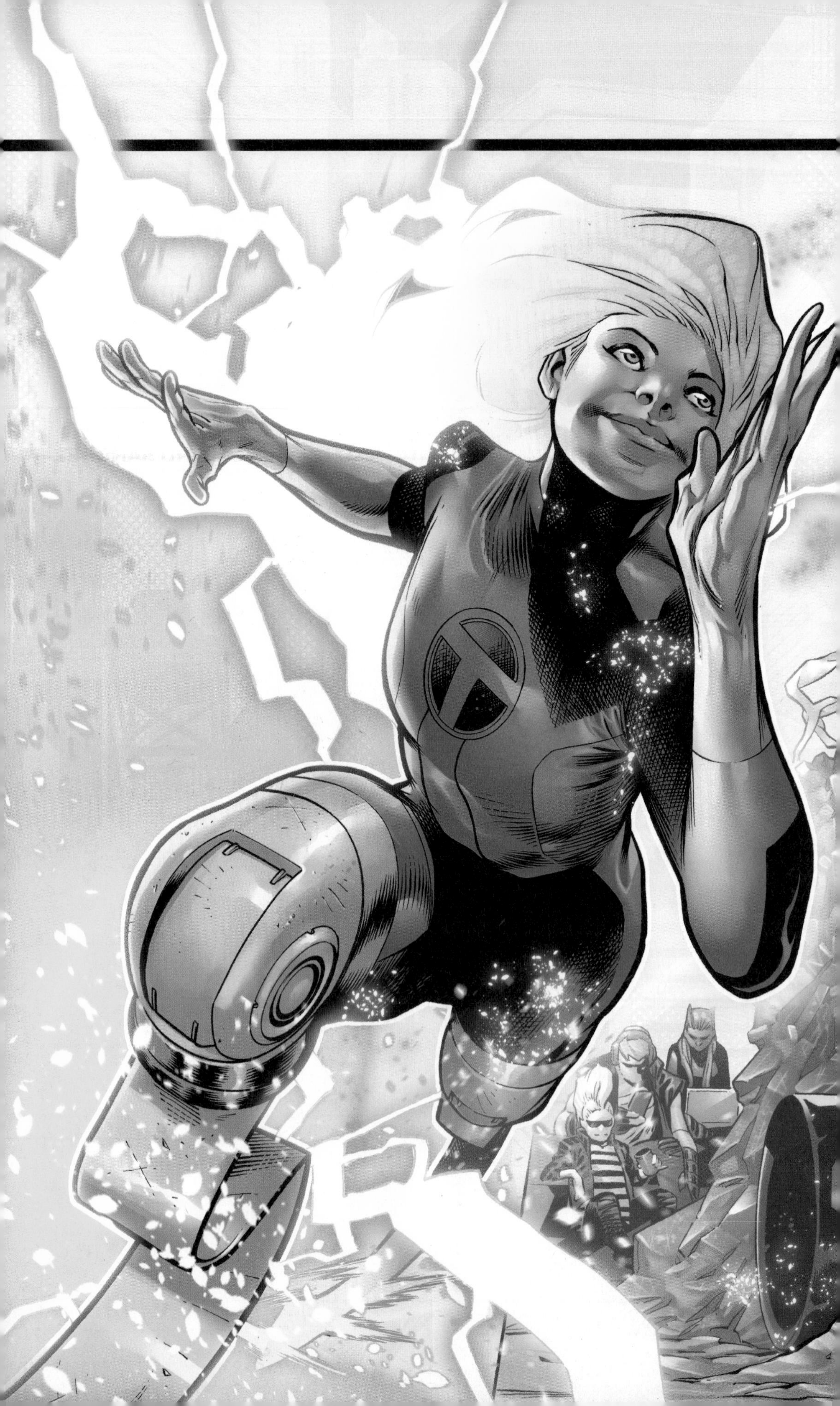

TEEN TITANS ACADEMY

VOL. 1: X MARKS THE SPOT

TIM SHERIDAN
ROBBIE THOMPSON
writers

RAFA SANDOVAL
JORDI TARRAGONA
STEVE LIEBER
EDUARDO PANSICA
JULIO FERREIRA
MAX RAYNOR
BERNARD CHANG
MARCO SANTUCCI
DARKO LAFUENTE
artists

ALEJANDRO SÁNCHEZ
DAVE STEWART
ALEX SINCLAIR
MARCELO MAIOLO
MICHAEL ATIYEH
MIQUEL MUERTO
colorists

ROB LEIGH
WES ABBOTT
letterers

RAFA SANDOVAL and
ALEJANDRO SÁNCHEZ
collection cover artists

SUPERBOY created
by JERRY SIEGEL
By special arrangement
with the Jerry Siegel family

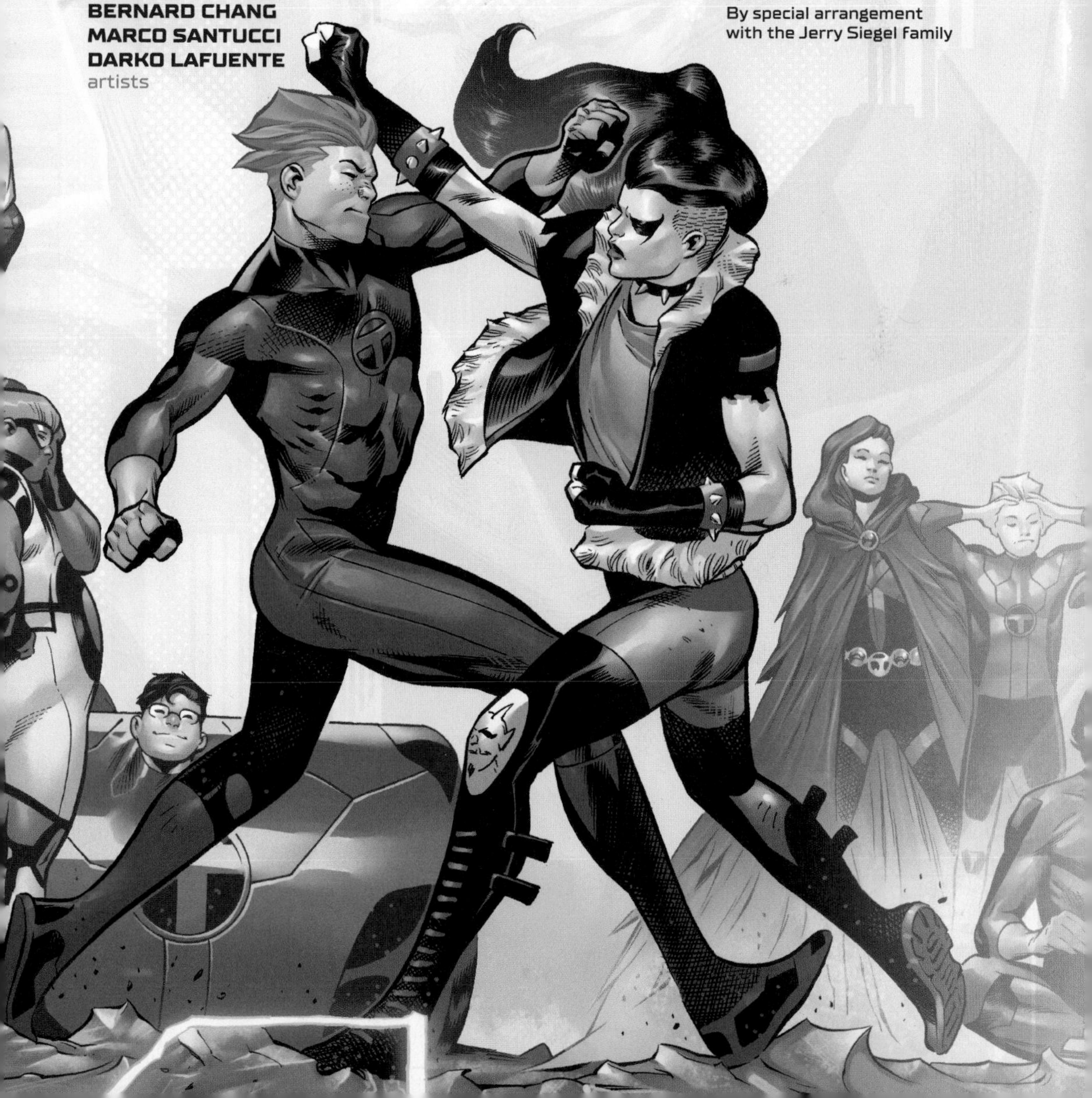

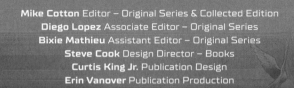

Mike Cotton Editor – Original Series & Collected Edition
Diego Lopez Associate Editor – Original Series
Bixie Mathieu Assistant Editor – Original Series
Steve Cook Design Director – Books
Curtis King Jr. Publication Design
Erin Vanover Publication Production

Marie Javins Editor-in-Chief, DC Comics

Daniel Cherry III Senior VP – General Manager
Jim Lee Publisher & Chief Creative Officer
Don Falletti VP – Manufacturing Operations & Workflow Management
Lawrence Ganem VP – Talent Services
Alison Gill Senior VP – Manufacturing & Operations
Jeffrey Kaufman VP – Editorial Strategy & Programming
Nick J. Napolitano VP – Manufacturing Administration & Design
Nancy Spears VP – Revenue

TEEN TITANS ACADEMY VOL. 1: X MARKS THE SPOT

Published by DC Comics. Compilation and all new material Copyright © 2022 DC Comics. All Rights Reserved. Originally published in single magazine form in *Teen Titans Academy* 1–5, *Suicide Squad* 3, *Teen Titans Academy 2021 Yearbook* 1, *Infinite Frontier* 0. Copyright © 2021 DC Comics. All Rights Reserved. All characters, their distinctive likenesses, and related elements featured in this publication are trademarks of DC Comics. The stories, characters, and incidents featured in this publication are entirely fictional. DC Comics does not read or accept unsolicited submissions of ideas, stories, or artwork. DC – a WarnerMedia Company.

DC Comics, 2900 West Alameda Ave., Burbank, CA 91505
Printed by Transcontinental Interglobe, Beauceville, QC, Canada.
1/28/22. First Printing. ISBN: 978-1-77951-281-9.

Library of Congress Cataloging-in-Publication
Data is available.

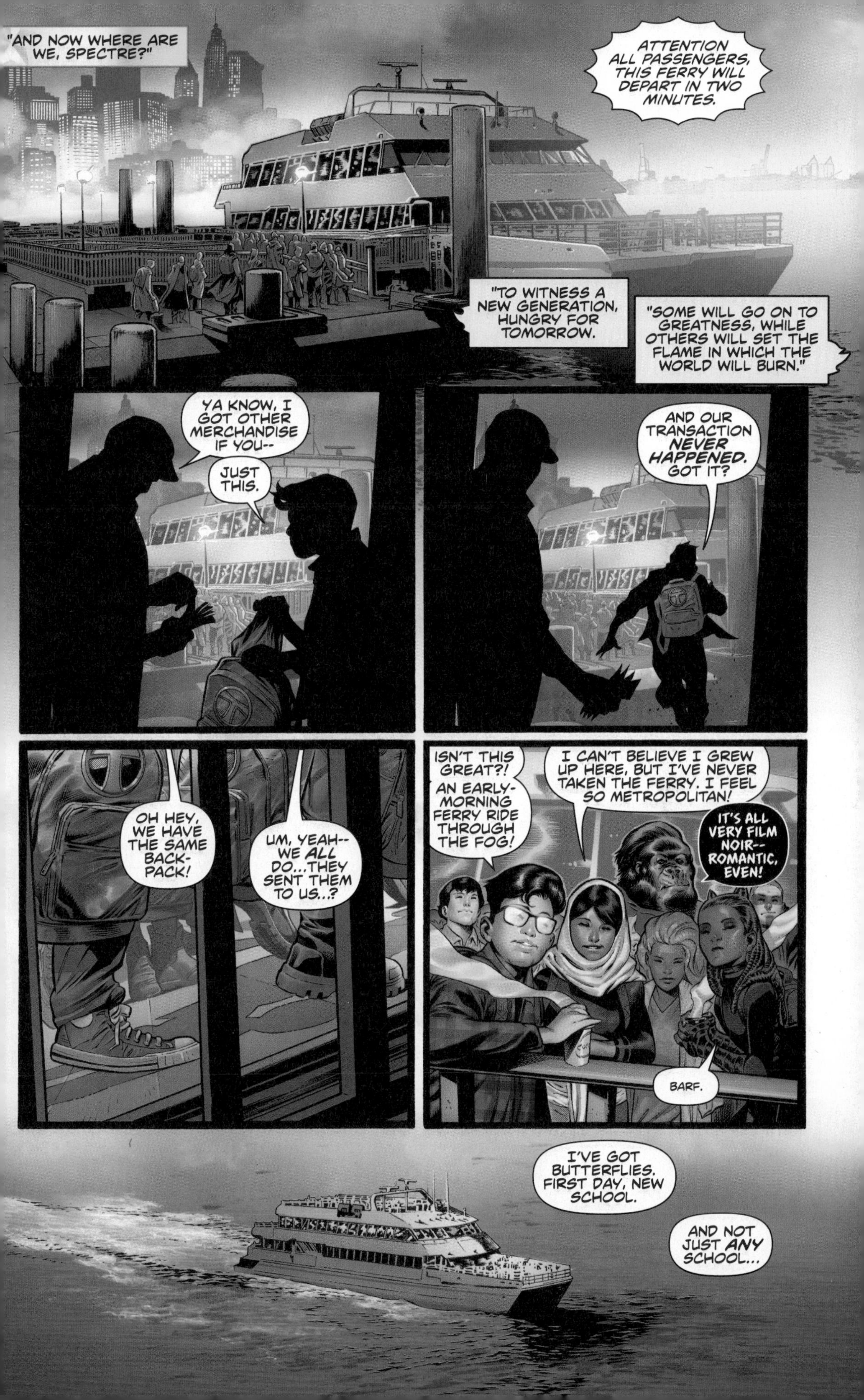
"AND NOW WHERE ARE WE, SPECTRE?"
ATTENTION ALL PASSENGERS, THIS FERRY WILL DEPART IN TWO MINUTES.
"TO WITNESS A NEW GENERATION, HUNGRY FOR TOMORROW.
"SOME WILL GO ON TO GREATNESS, WHILE OTHERS WILL SET THE FLAME IN WHICH THE WORLD WILL BURN."
YA KNOW, I GOT OTHER MERCHANDISE IF YOU--
JUST THIS.
AND OUR TRANSACTION *NEVER HAPPENED.* GOT IT?
OH HEY, WE HAVE THE SAME BACK-PACK!
UM, YEAH--WE *ALL* DO...THEY SENT THEM TO US..?
ISN'T THIS GREAT?! AN EARLY-MORNING FERRY RIDE THROUGH THE FOG!
I CAN'T BELIEVE I GREW UP HERE, BUT I'VE NEVER TAKEN THE FERRY. I FEEL SO METROPOLITAN!
IT'S ALL VERY FILM NOIR--ROMANTIC, EVEN!
BARF.
I'VE GOT BUTTERFLIES. FIRST DAY, NEW SCHOOL.
AND NOT JUST *ANY* SCHOOL...

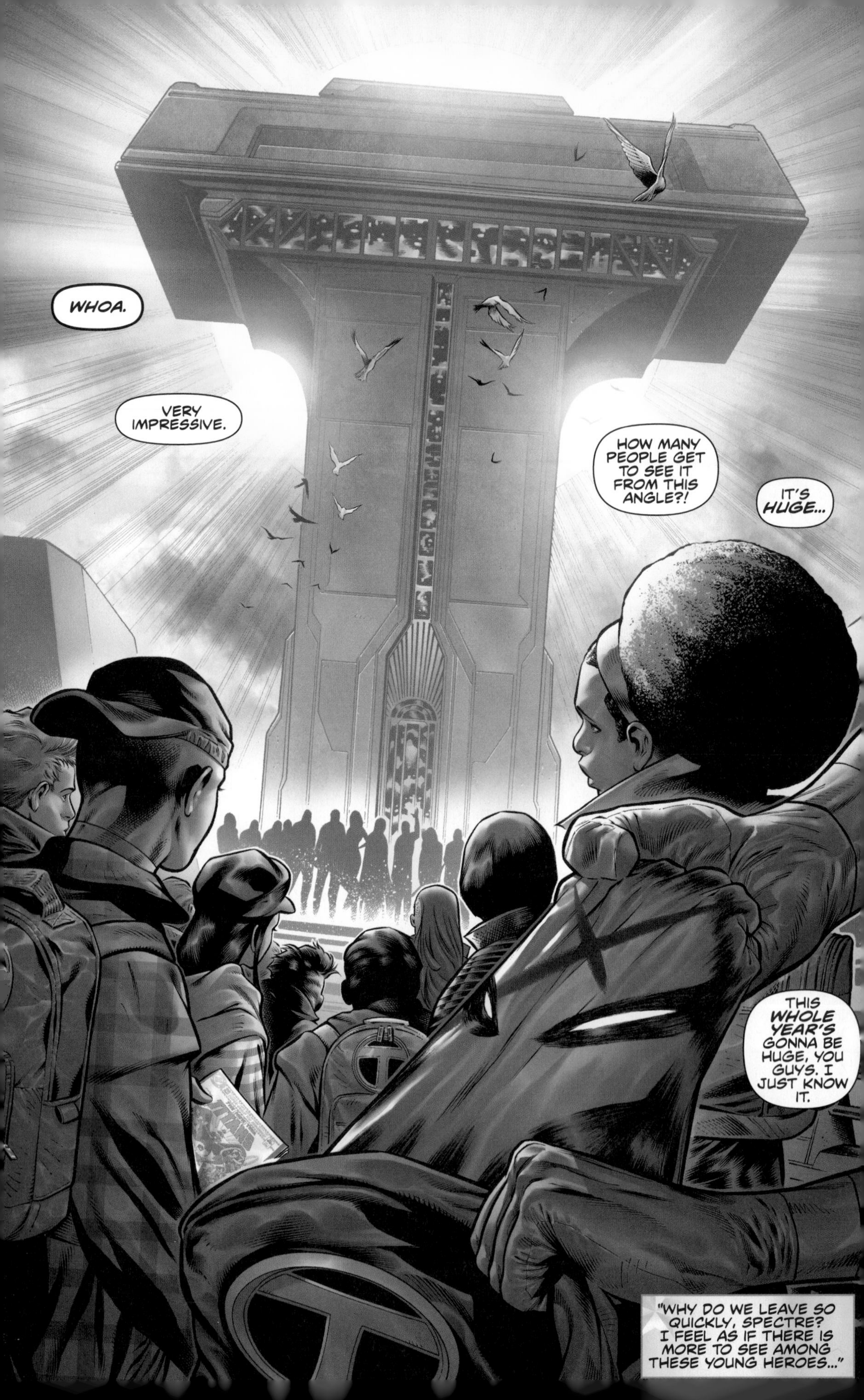
WHOA.
VERY IMPRESSIVE.
HOW MANY PEOPLE GET TO SEE IT FROM THIS ANGLE?!
IT'S HUGE...
THIS WHOLE YEAR'S GONNA BE HUGE, YOU GUYS. I JUST KNOW IT.
"WHY DO WE LEAVE SO QUICKLY, SPECTRE? I FEEL AS IF THERE IS MORE TO SEE AMONG THESE YOUNG HEROES..."

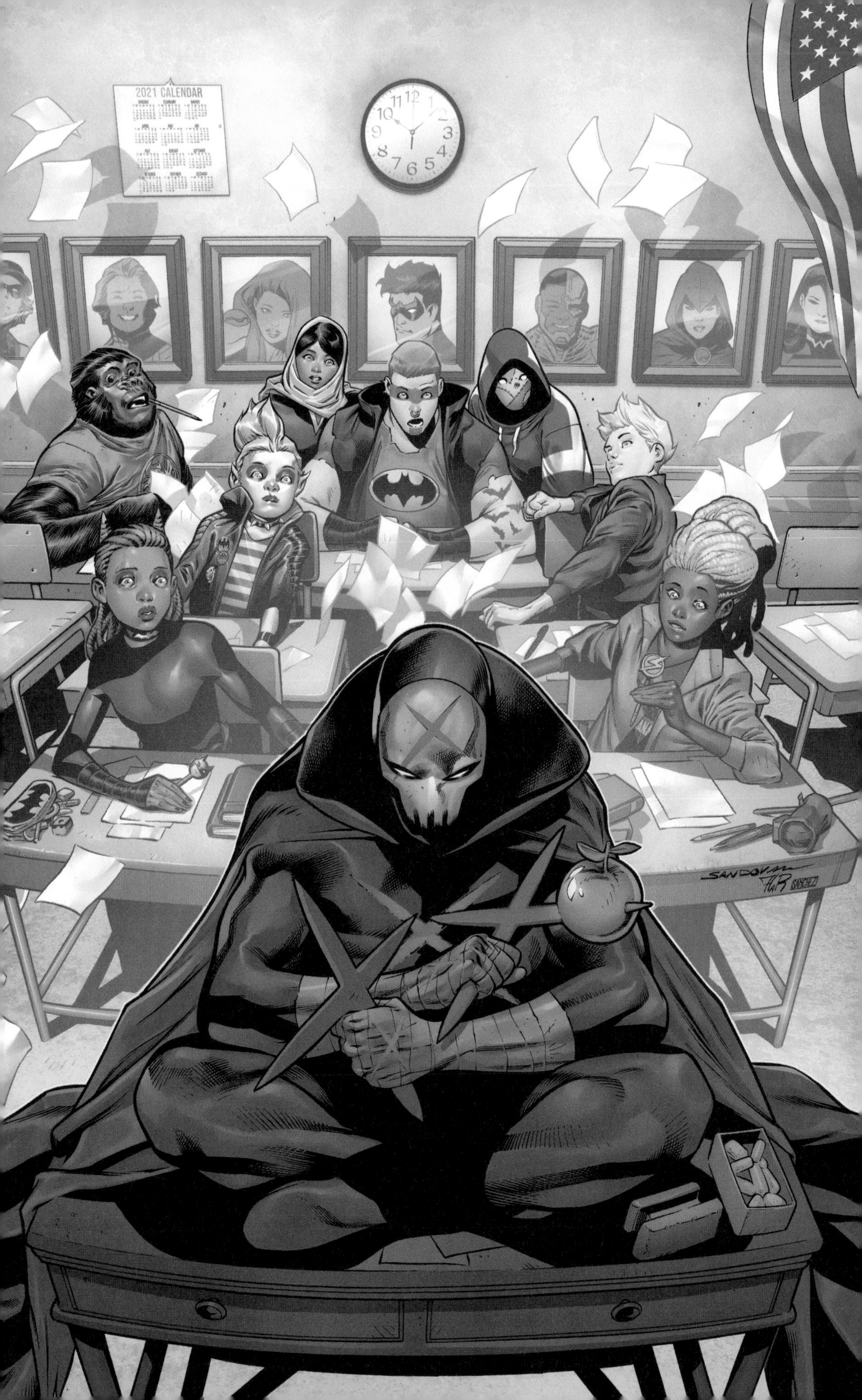
2021 CALENDAR

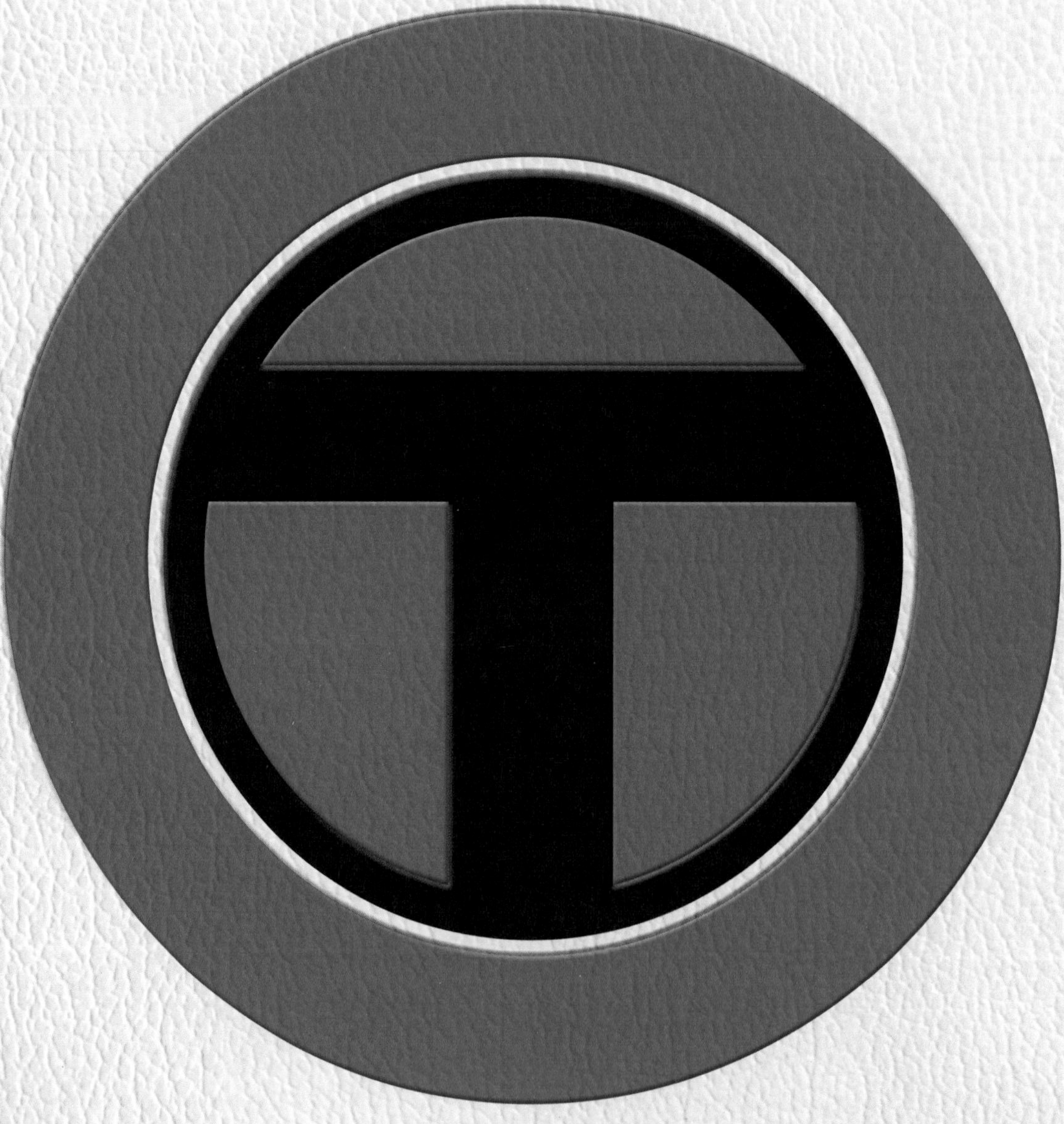

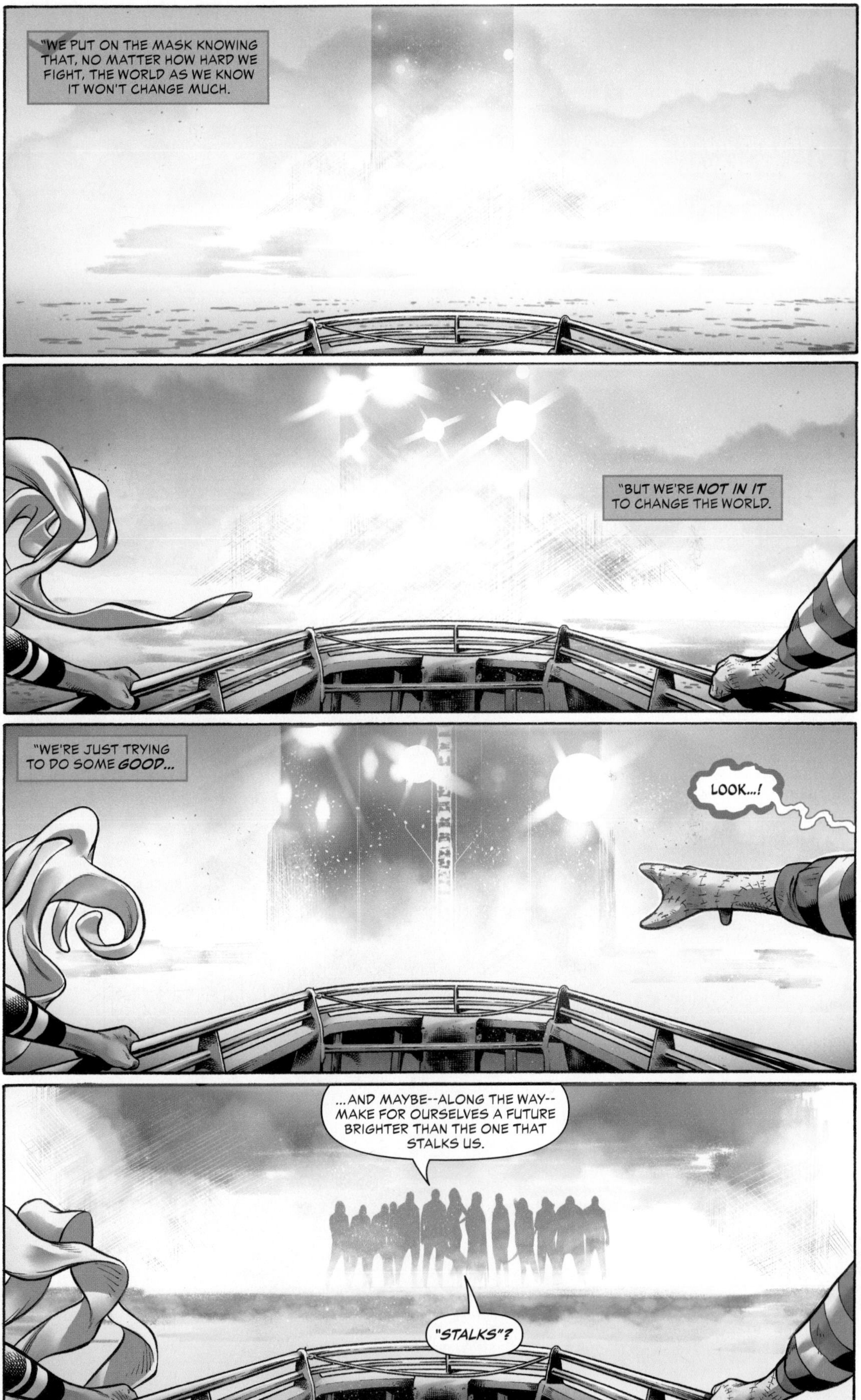
"WE PUT ON THE MASK KNOWING THAT, NO MATTER HOW HARD WE FIGHT, THE WORLD AS WE KNOW IT WON'T CHANGE MUCH.
"BUT WE'RE *NOT IN IT* TO CHANGE THE WORLD.
"WE'RE JUST TRYING TO DO SOME *GOOD*...
LOOK...!
...AND MAYBE--ALONG THE WAY--MAKE FOR OURSELVES A FUTURE BRIGHTER THAN THE ONE THAT STALKS US.
"STALKS"?

ADMISSIONS

TIM SHERIDAN WRITER
RAFA SANDOVAL PENCILLER
JORDI TARRAGONA INKER
ALEJANDRO SANCHEZ COLORIST
ROB LEIGH LETTERER
SANDOVAL, TARRAGONA
& SANCHEZ COVER
JAMAL CAMPBELL VARIANT COVER
DIEGO LOPEZ ASSOCIATE EDITOR
MIKE COTTON EDITOR
JAMIE S. RICH GROUP EDITOR

YEAH, *"STALKS"* IS TOO DARK.

SORRY-- MY BLÜDHAVEN'S SHOWING.

HOW ABOUT *"AWAITS US"*?

TEEN TITANS ACADEMY

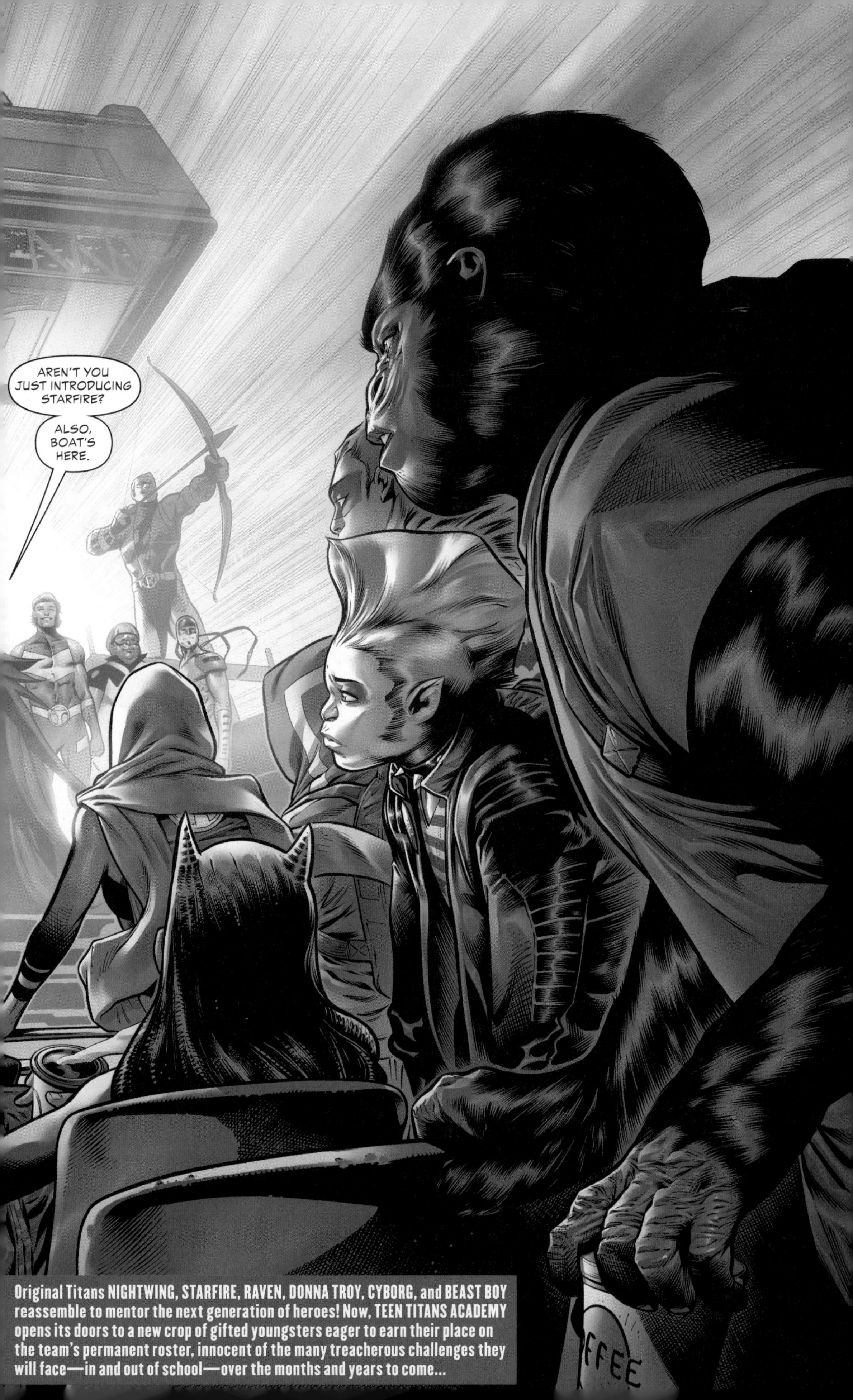
AREN'T YOU JUST INTRODUCING STARFIRE?
ALSO, BOAT'S HERE.
Original Titans NIGHTWING, STARFIRE, RAVEN, DONNA TROY, CYBORG, and BEAST BOY reassemble to mentor the next generation of heroes! Now, TEEN TITANS ACADEMY opens its doors to a new crop of gifted youngsters eager to earn their place on the team's permanent roster, innocent of the many treacherous challenges they will face—in and out of school—over the months and years to come...

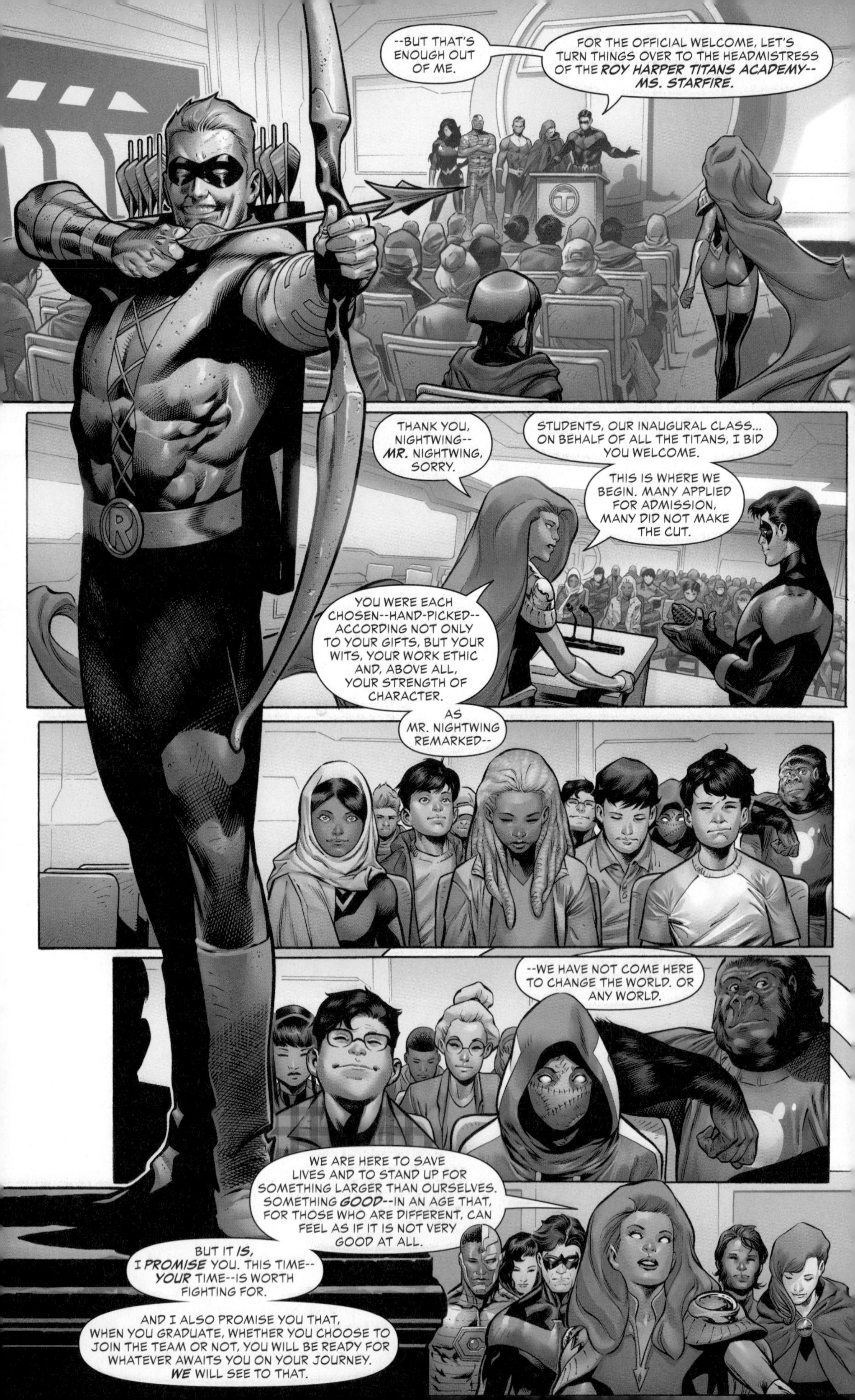
--BUT THAT'S ENOUGH OUT OF ME.
FOR THE OFFICIAL WELCOME, LET'S TURN THINGS OVER TO THE HEADMISTRESS OF THE ROY HARPER TITANS ACADEMY-- MS. STARFIRE.
THANK YOU, NIGHTWING-- MR. NIGHTWING, SORRY.
STUDENTS, OUR INAUGURAL CLASS... ON BEHALF OF ALL THE TITANS, I BID YOU WELCOME.
THIS IS WHERE WE BEGIN. MANY APPLIED FOR ADMISSION, MANY DID NOT MAKE THE CUT.
YOU WERE EACH CHOSEN--HAND-PICKED-- ACCORDING NOT ONLY TO YOUR GIFTS, BUT YOUR WITS, YOUR WORK ETHIC AND, ABOVE ALL, YOUR STRENGTH OF CHARACTER.
AS MR. NIGHTWING REMARKED--
--WE HAVE NOT COME HERE TO CHANGE THE WORLD. OR ANY WORLD.
WE ARE HERE TO SAVE LIVES AND TO STAND UP FOR SOMETHING LARGER THAN OURSELVES. SOMETHING GOOD--IN AN AGE THAT, FOR THOSE WHO ARE DIFFERENT, CAN FEEL AS IF IT IS NOT VERY GOOD AT ALL.
BUT IT IS, I PROMISE YOU. THIS TIME-- YOUR TIME--IS WORTH FIGHTING FOR.
AND I ALSO PROMISE YOU THAT, WHEN YOU GRADUATE, WHETHER YOU CHOOSE TO JOIN THE TEAM OR NOT, YOU WILL BE READY FOR WHATEVER AWAITS YOU ON YOUR JOURNEY. WE WILL SEE TO THAT.

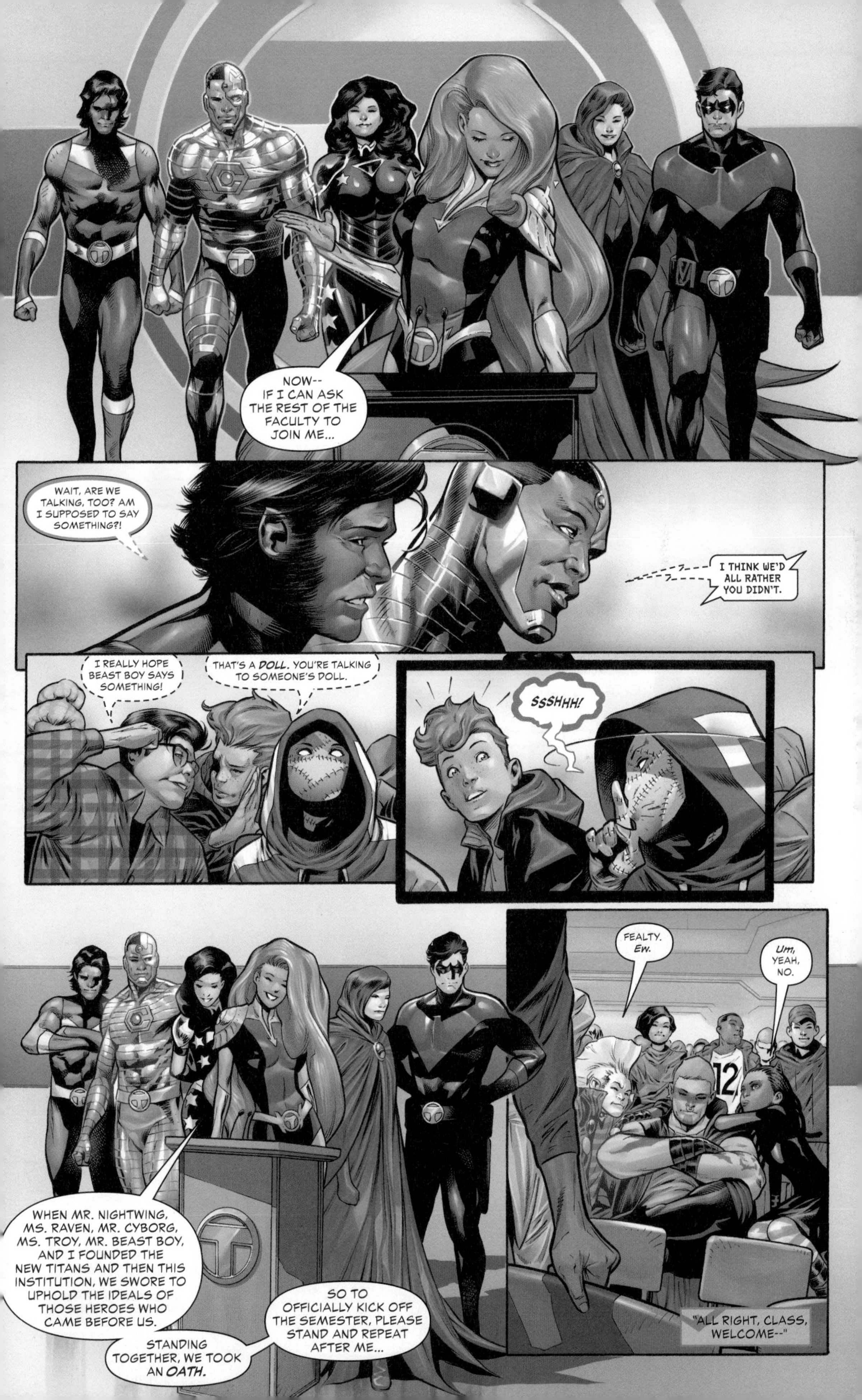
NOW-- IF I CAN ASK THE REST OF THE FACULTY TO JOIN ME...
WAIT, ARE WE TALKING, TOO? AM I SUPPOSED TO SAY SOMETHING?!
I THINK WE'D ALL RATHER YOU DIDN'T.
I REALLY HOPE BEAST BOY SAYS SOMETHING!
THAT'S A DOLL. YOU'RE TALKING TO SOMEONE'S DOLL.
SSSHHH!
WHEN MR. NIGHTWING, MS. RAVEN, MR. CYBORG, MS. TROY, MR. BEAST BOY, AND I FOUNDED THE NEW TITANS AND THEN THIS INSTITUTION, WE SWORE TO UPHOLD THE IDEALS OF THOSE HEROES WHO CAME BEFORE US.
STANDING TOGETHER, WE TOOK AN OATH.
SO TO OFFICIALLY KICK OFF THE SEMESTER, PLEASE STAND AND REPEAT AFTER ME...
FEALTY. Ew.
Um, YEAH, NO.
"ALL RIGHT, CLASS, WELCOME--"

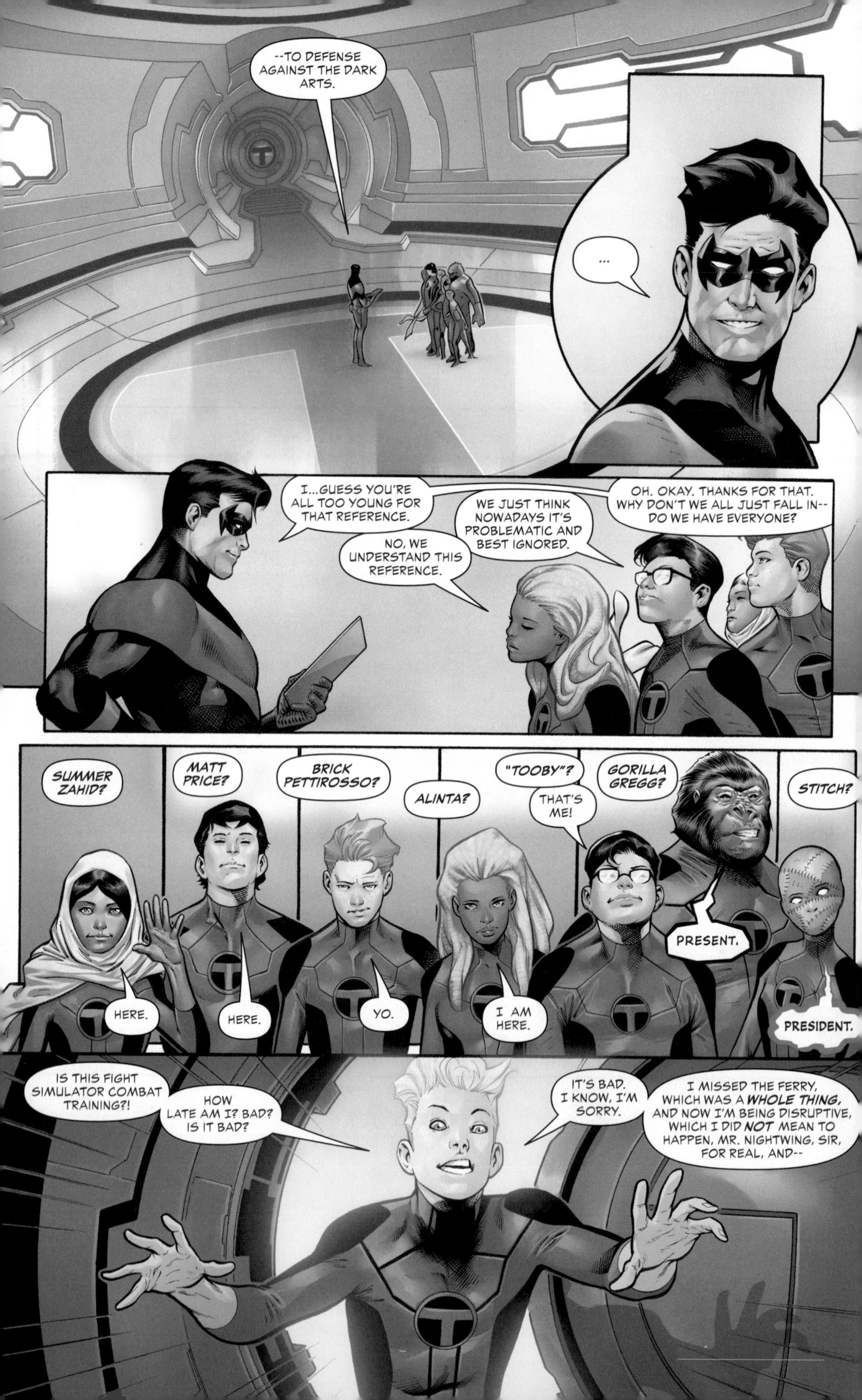
--TO DEFENSE AGAINST THE DARK ARTS.
...
I...GUESS YOU'RE ALL TOO YOUNG FOR THAT REFERENCE.
NO, WE UNDERSTAND THIS REFERENCE.
WE JUST THINK NOWADAYS IT'S PROBLEMATIC AND BEST IGNORED.
OH. OKAY. THANKS FOR THAT. WHY DON'T WE ALL JUST FALL IN-- DO WE HAVE EVERYONE?
SUMMER ZAHID?
HERE.
MATT PRICE?
HERE.
BRICK PETTIROSSO?
YO.
ALINTA?
I AM HERE.
"TOOBY"?
THAT'S ME!
GORILLA GREGG?
PRESENT.
STITCH?
PRESIDENT.
IS THIS FIGHT SIMULATOR COMBAT TRAINING?!
HOW LATE AM I? BAD? IS IT BAD?
IT'S BAD. I KNOW, I'M SORRY.
I MISSED THE FERRY, WHICH WAS A ***WHOLE THING,*** AND NOW I'M BEING DISRUPTIVE, WHICH I DID ***NOT*** MEAN TO HAPPEN, MR. NIGHTWING, SIR, FOR REAL, AND--

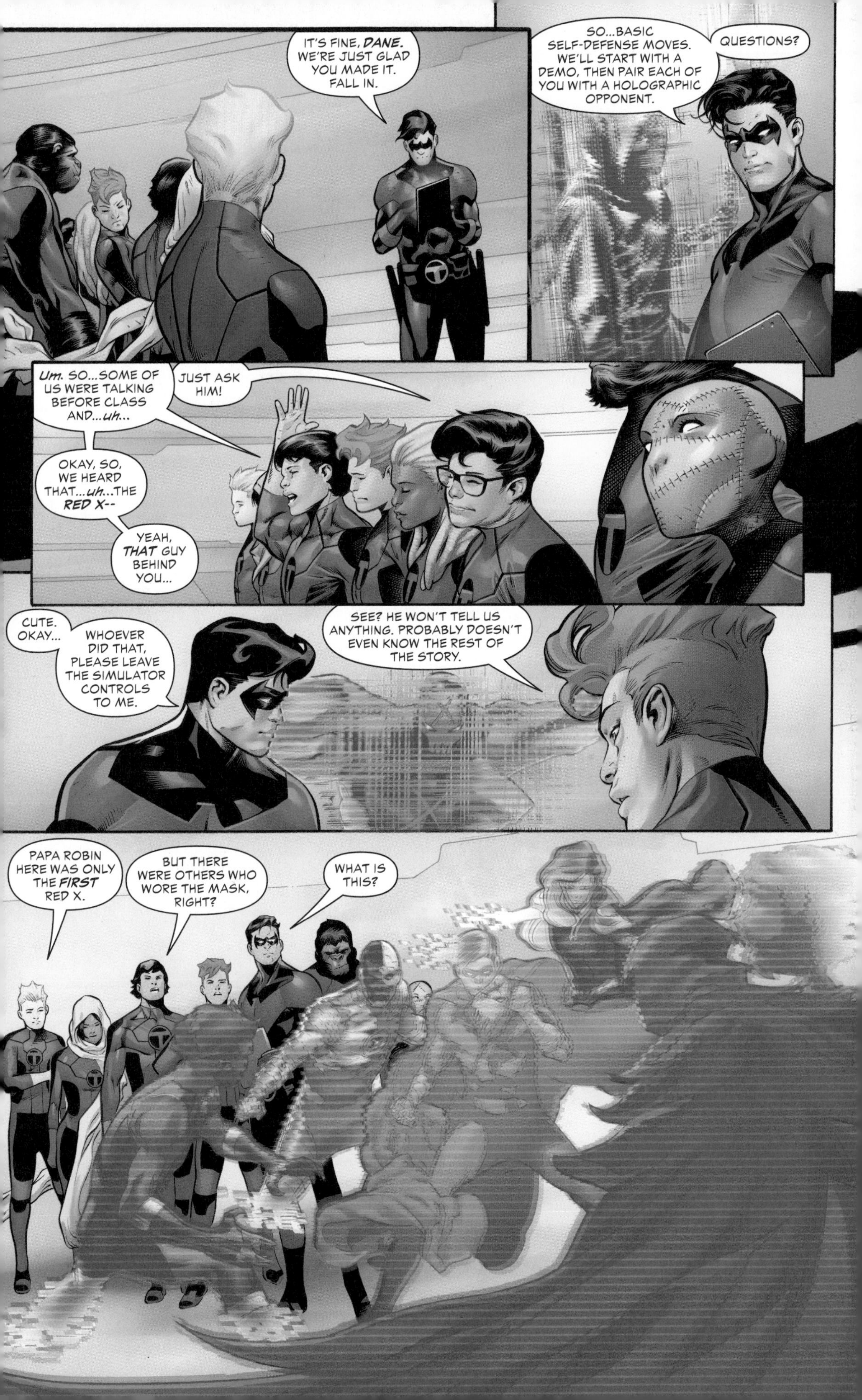

IT'S FINE, **DANE.** WE'RE JUST GLAD YOU MADE IT. FALL IN.
SO...BASIC SELF-DEFENSE MOVES. WE'LL START WITH A DEMO, THEN PAIR EACH OF YOU WITH A HOLOGRAPHIC OPPONENT.
QUESTIONS?
Um. SO...SOME OF US WERE TALKING BEFORE CLASS AND...*uh*...
JUST ASK HIM!
OKAY, SO, WE HEARD THAT...*uh*...THE ***RED X***--
YEAH, ***THAT*** GUY BEHIND YOU...
CUTE. OKAY...
WHOEVER DID THAT, PLEASE LEAVE THE SIMULATOR CONTROLS TO ME.
SEE? HE WON'T TELL US ANYTHING. PROBABLY DOESN'T EVEN KNOW THE REST OF THE STORY.
PAPA ROBIN HERE WAS ONLY THE ***FIRST*** RED X.
BUT THERE WERE OTHERS WHO WORE THE MASK, RIGHT?
WHAT IS THIS?

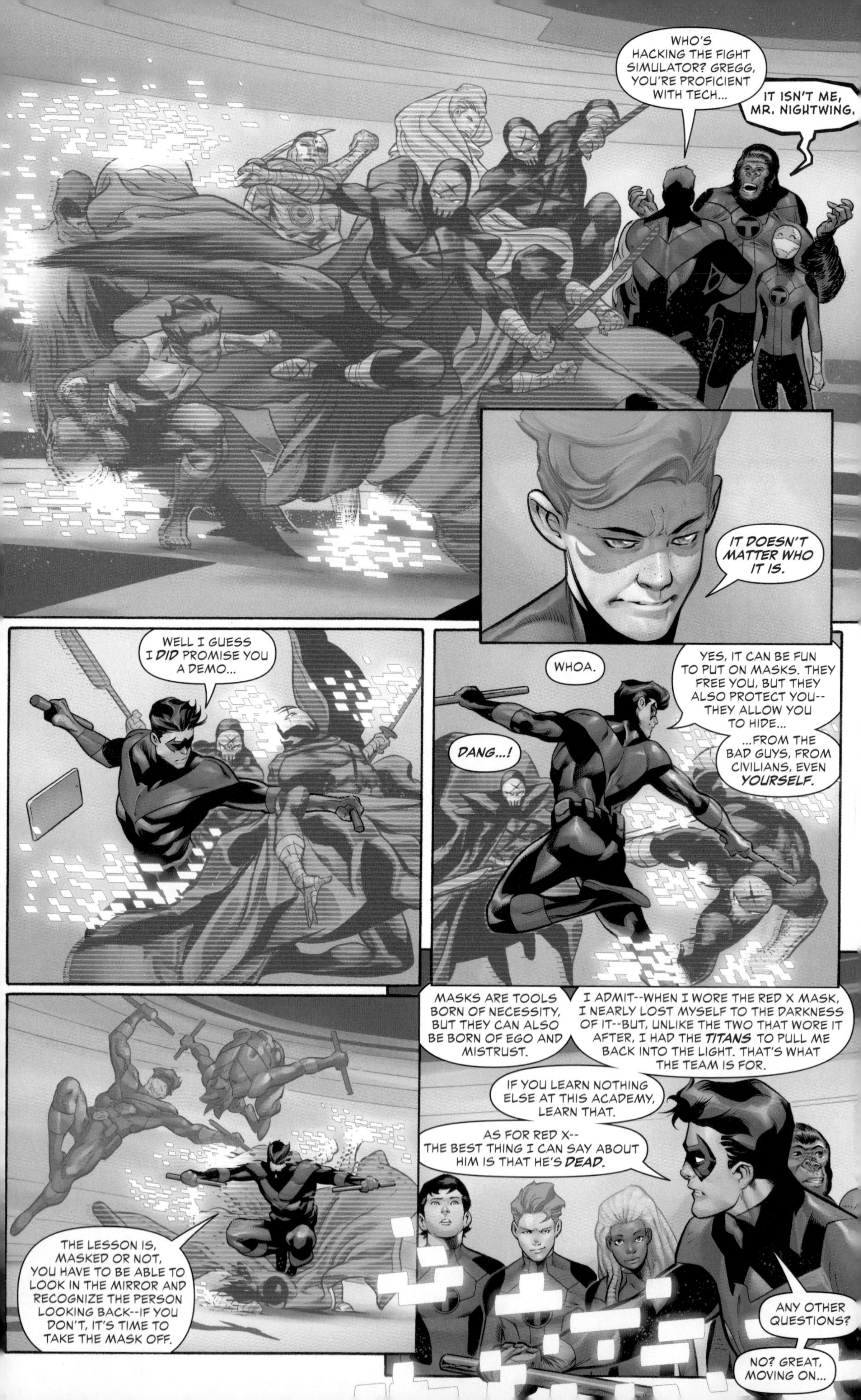
WHO'S HACKING THE FIGHT SIMULATOR? GREGG, YOU'RE PROFICIENT WITH TECH...
IT ISN'T ME, MR. NIGHTWING.
IT DOESN'T MATTER WHO IT IS.
WELL I GUESS I DID PROMISE YOU A DEMO...
DANG...!
WHOA.
YES, IT CAN BE FUN TO PUT ON MASKS. THEY FREE YOU, BUT THEY ALSO PROTECT YOU--THEY ALLOW YOU TO HIDE...
...FROM THE BAD GUYS, FROM CIVILIANS, EVEN YOURSELF.
THE LESSON IS, MASKED OR NOT, YOU HAVE TO BE ABLE TO LOOK IN THE MIRROR AND RECOGNIZE THE PERSON LOOKING BACK--IF YOU DON'T, IT'S TIME TO TAKE THE MASK OFF.
MASKS ARE TOOLS BORN OF NECESSITY, BUT THEY CAN ALSO BE BORN OF EGO AND MISTRUST.
I ADMIT--WHEN I WORE THE RED X MASK, I NEARLY LOST MYSELF TO THE DARKNESS OF IT--BUT, UNLIKE THE TWO THAT WORE IT AFTER, I HAD THE TITANS TO PULL ME BACK INTO THE LIGHT. THAT'S WHAT THE TEAM IS FOR.
IF YOU LEARN NOTHING ELSE AT THIS ACADEMY, LEARN THAT.
AS FOR RED X--THE BEST THING I CAN SAY ABOUT HIM IS THAT HE'S DEAD.
ANY OTHER QUESTIONS?
NO? GREAT, MOVING ON...

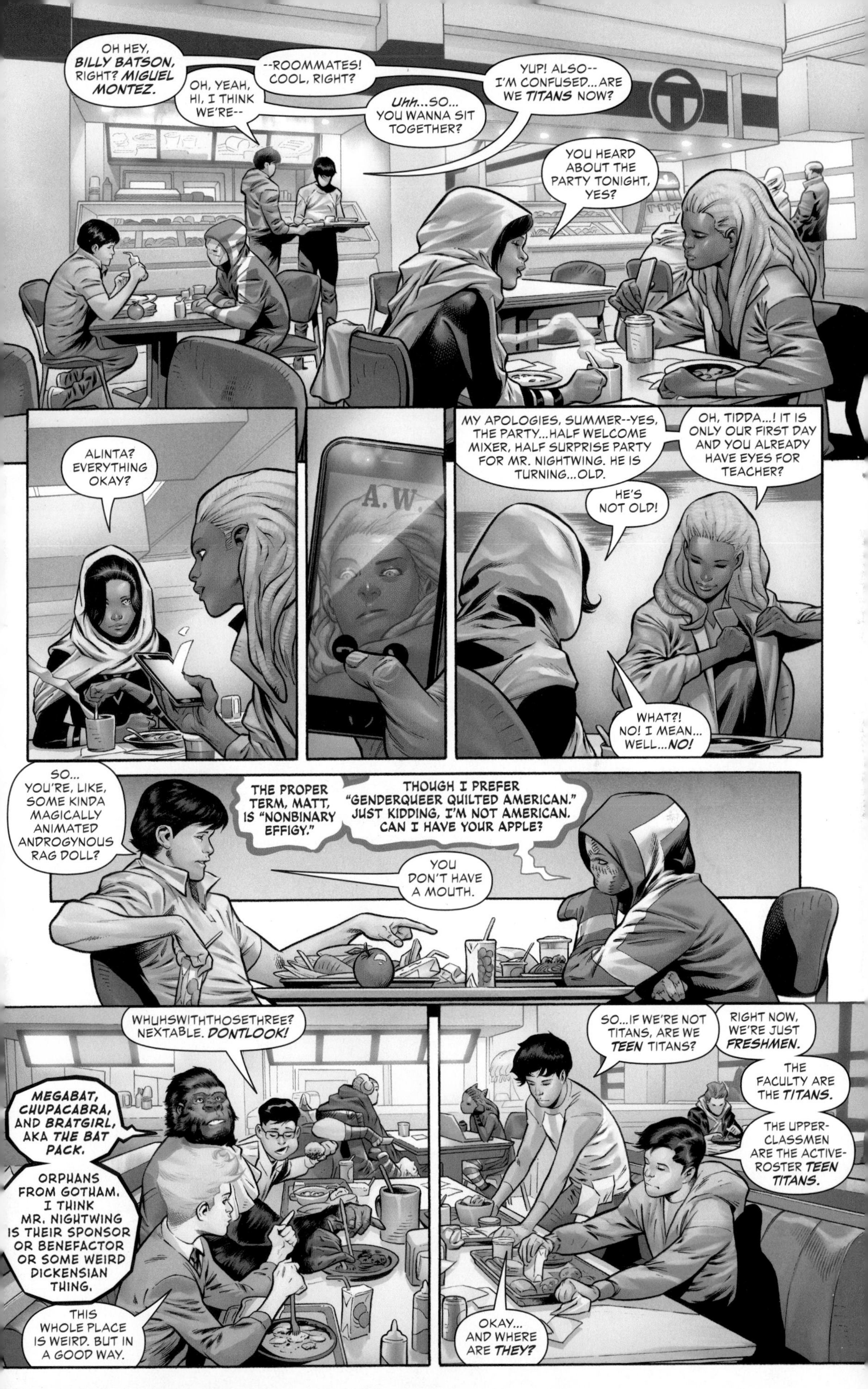
OH HEY, BILLY BATSON, RIGHT? MIGUEL MONTEZ.
OH, YEAH, HI, I THINK WE'RE--
--ROOMMATES! COOL, RIGHT?
Uhh...SO... YOU WANNA SIT TOGETHER?
YUP! ALSO-- I'M CONFUSED...ARE WE TITANS NOW?
YOU HEARD ABOUT THE PARTY TONIGHT, YES?
ALINTA? EVERYTHING OKAY?
A.W.
MY APOLOGIES, SUMMER--YES, THE PARTY...HALF WELCOME MIXER, HALF SURPRISE PARTY FOR MR. NIGHTWING. HE IS TURNING...OLD.
OH, TIDDA...! IT IS ONLY OUR FIRST DAY AND YOU ALREADY HAVE EYES FOR TEACHER?
HE'S NOT OLD!
WHAT?! NO! I MEAN... WELL...NO!
SO... YOU'RE, LIKE, SOME KINDA MAGICALLY ANIMATED ANDROGYNOUS RAG DOLL?
THE PROPER TERM, MATT, IS "NONBINARY EFFIGY."
THOUGH I PREFER "GENDERQUEER QUILTED AMERICAN." JUST KIDDING, I'M NOT AMERICAN. CAN I HAVE YOUR APPLE?
YOU DON'T HAVE A MOUTH.
WHUHSWITHTHOSETHREE? NEXTABLE. DONTLOOK!
MEGABAT, CHUPACABRA, AND BRATGIRL, AKA THE BAT PACK.
ORPHANS FROM GOTHAM. I THINK MR. NIGHTWING IS THEIR SPONSOR OR BENEFACTOR OR SOME WEIRD DICKENSIAN THING.
THIS WHOLE PLACE IS WEIRD. BUT IN A GOOD WAY.
SO...IF WE'RE NOT TITANS, ARE WE TEEN TITANS?
RIGHT NOW, WE'RE JUST FRESHMEN.
THE FACULTY ARE THE TITANS.
THE UPPER-CLASSMEN ARE THE ACTIVE-ROSTER TEEN TITANS.
OKAY... AND WHERE ARE THEY?

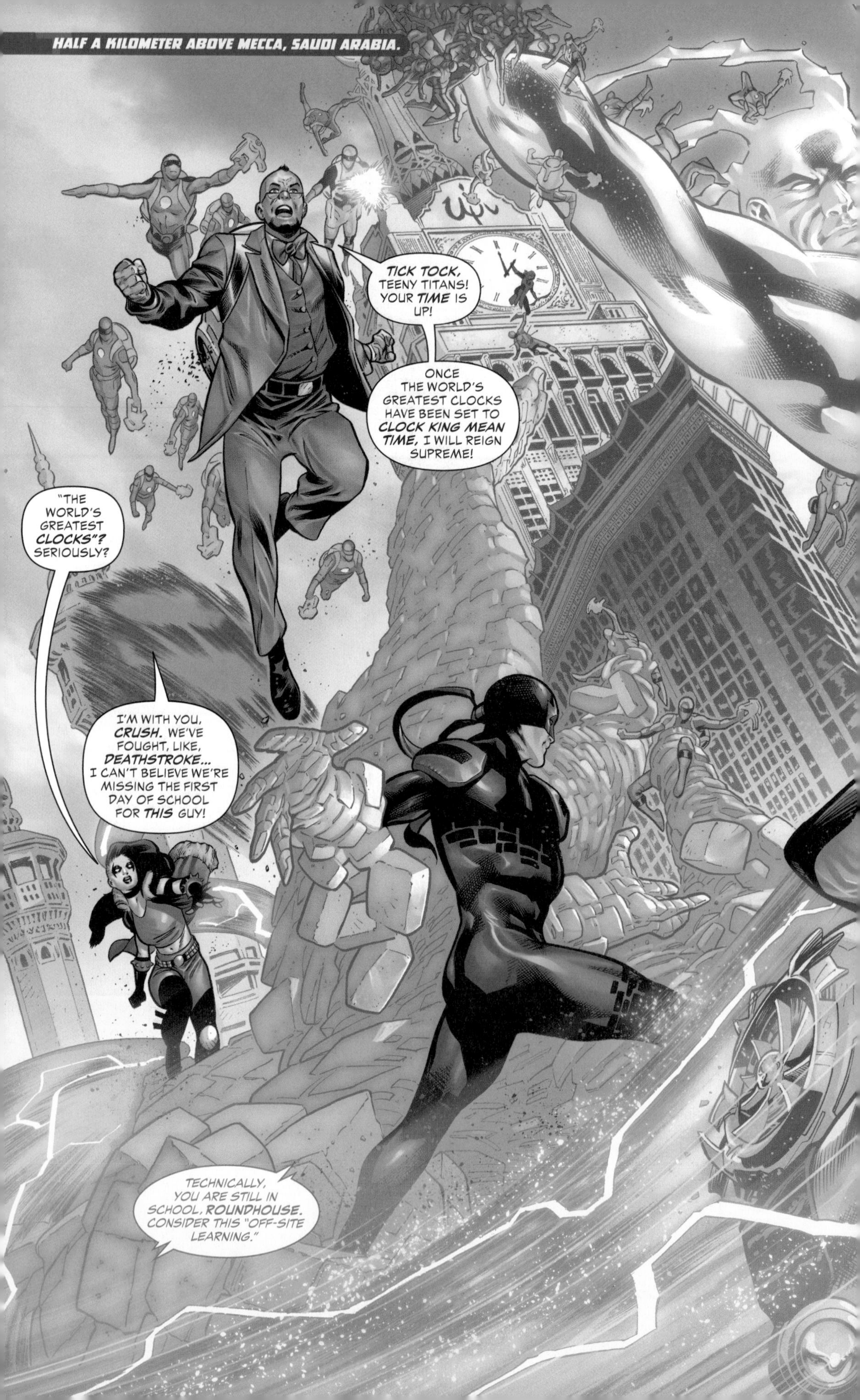
HALF A KILOMETER ABOVE MECCA, SAUDI ARABIA.
TICK TOCK, TEENY TITANS! YOUR TIME IS UP!
ONCE THE WORLD'S GREATEST CLOCKS HAVE BEEN SET TO CLOCK KING MEAN TIME, I WILL REIGN SUPREME!
"THE WORLD'S GREATEST CLOCKS"? SERIOUSLY?
I'M WITH YOU, CRUSH. WE'VE FOUGHT, LIKE, DEATHSTROKE... I CAN'T BELIEVE WE'RE MISSING THE FIRST DAY OF SCHOOL FOR THIS GUY!
TECHNICALLY, YOU ARE STILL IN SCHOOL, ROUNDHOUSE. CONSIDER THIS "OFF-SITE LEARNING."

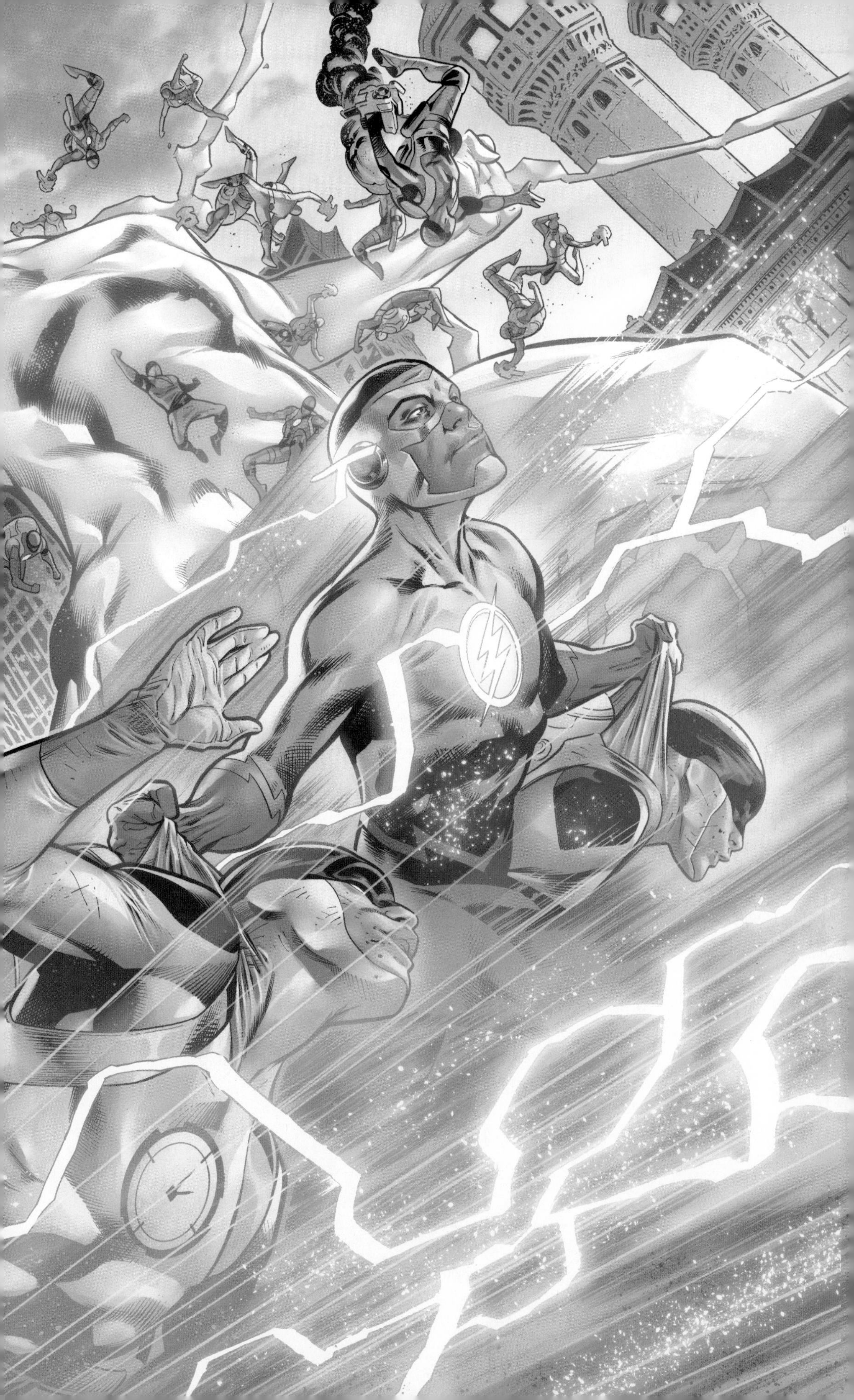

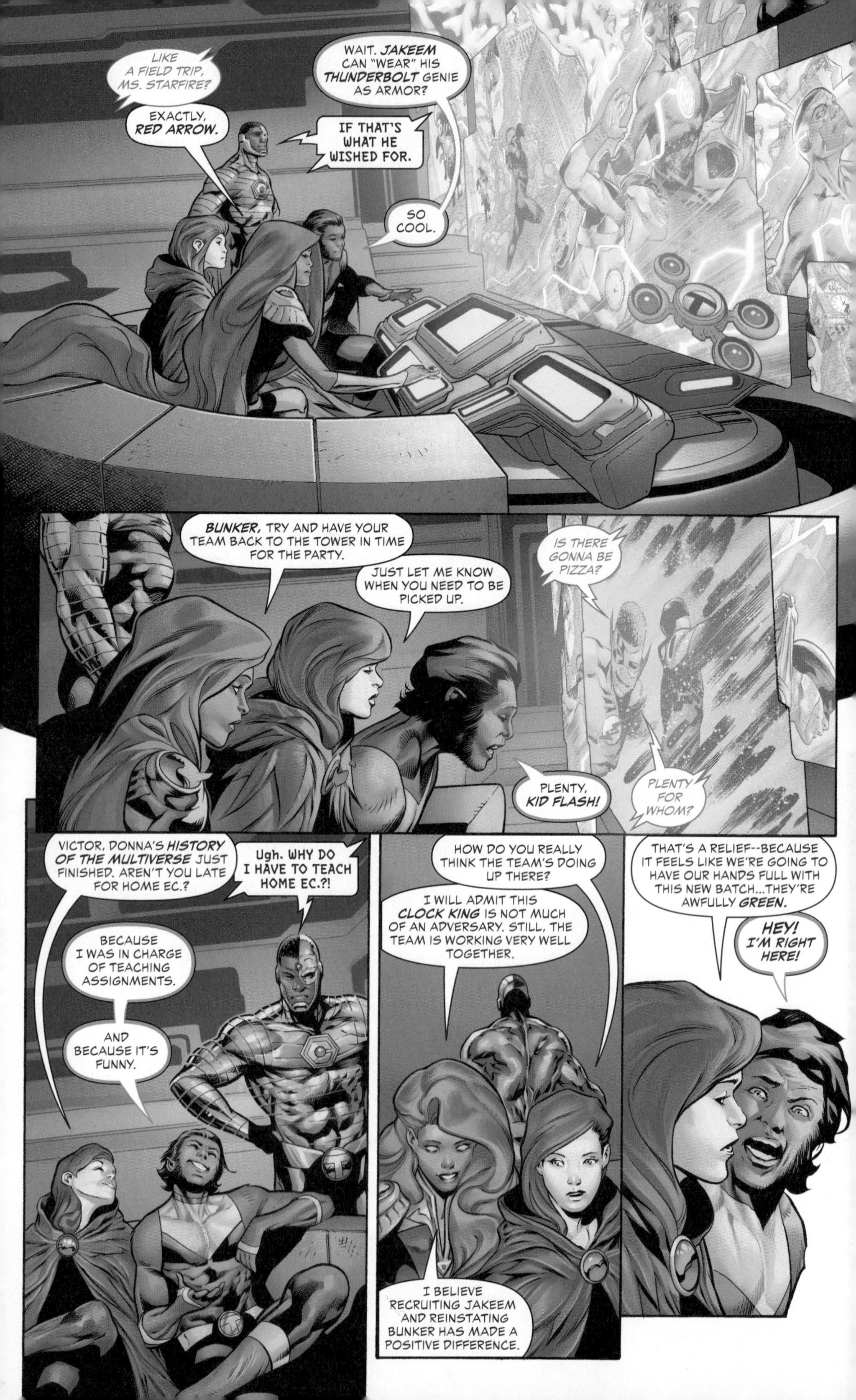
LIKE A FIELD TRIP, MS. STARFIRE?
EXACTLY, RED ARROW.
WAIT. JAKEEM CAN "WEAR" HIS THUNDERBOLT GENIE AS ARMOR?
IF THAT'S WHAT HE WISHED FOR.
SO COOL.
BUNKER, TRY AND HAVE YOUR TEAM BACK TO THE TOWER IN TIME FOR THE PARTY.
JUST LET ME KNOW WHEN YOU NEED TO BE PICKED UP.
IS THERE GONNA BE PIZZA?
PLENTY, KID FLASH!
PLENTY FOR WHOM?
VICTOR, DONNA'S HISTORY OF THE MULTIVERSE JUST FINISHED. AREN'T YOU LATE FOR HOME EC.?
Ugh. WHY DO I HAVE TO TEACH HOME EC.?!
BECAUSE I WAS IN CHARGE OF TEACHING ASSIGNMENTS.
AND BECAUSE IT'S FUNNY.
HOW DO YOU REALLY THINK THE TEAM'S DOING UP THERE?
I WILL ADMIT THIS CLOCK KING IS NOT MUCH OF AN ADVERSARY. STILL, THE TEAM IS WORKING VERY WELL TOGETHER.
I BELIEVE RECRUITING JAKEEM AND REINSTATING BUNKER HAS MADE A POSITIVE DIFFERENCE.
THAT'S A RELIEF--BECAUSE IT FEELS LIKE WE'RE GOING TO HAVE OUR HANDS FULL WITH THIS NEW BATCH...THEY'RE AWFULLY GREEN.
HEY! I'M RIGHT HERE!

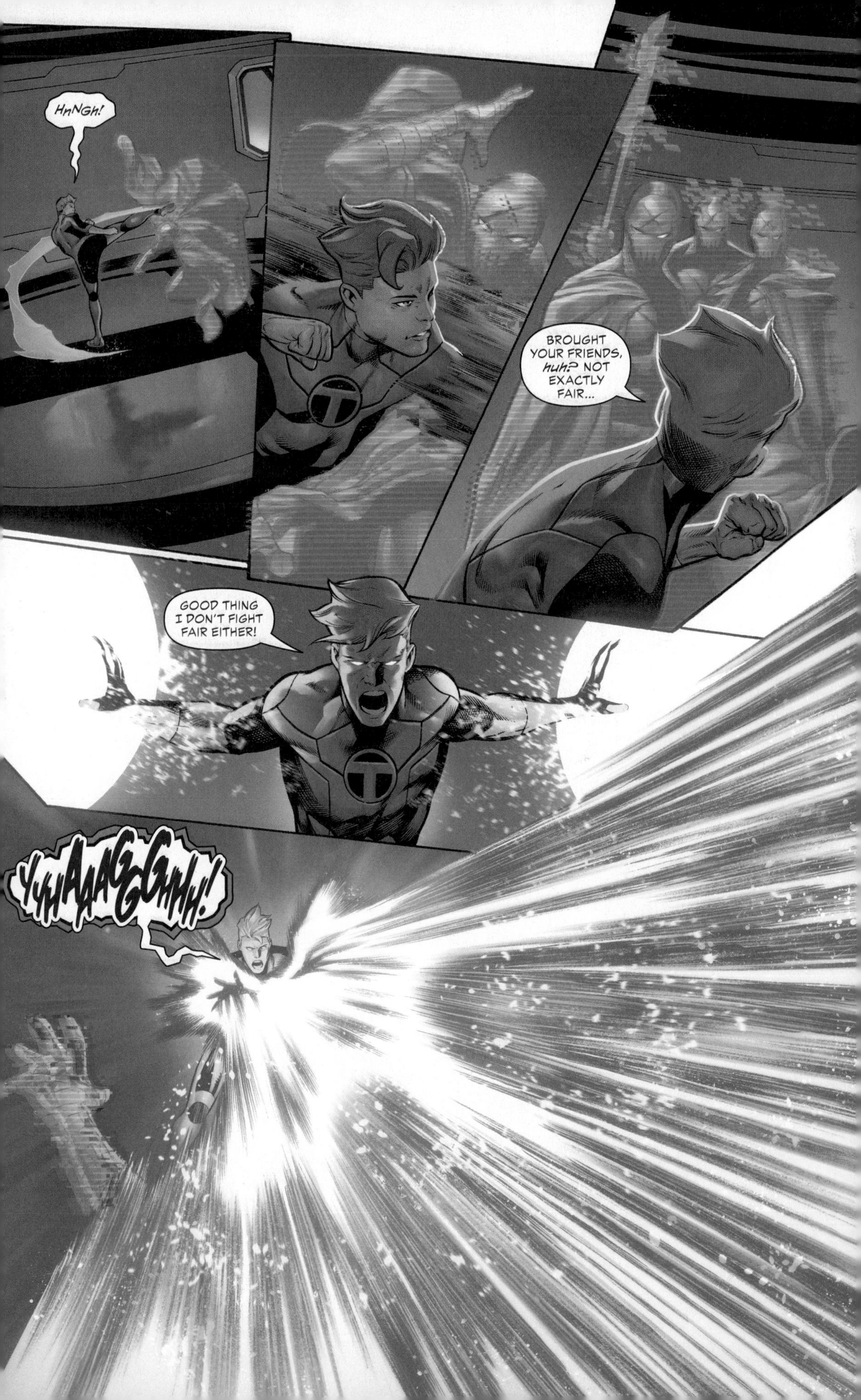
HnNGh!
BROUGHT YOUR FRIENDS, *huh?* NOT EXACTLY FAIR...
GOOD THING I DON'T FIGHT FAIR EITHER!
YYYHAAAGGGHHH!

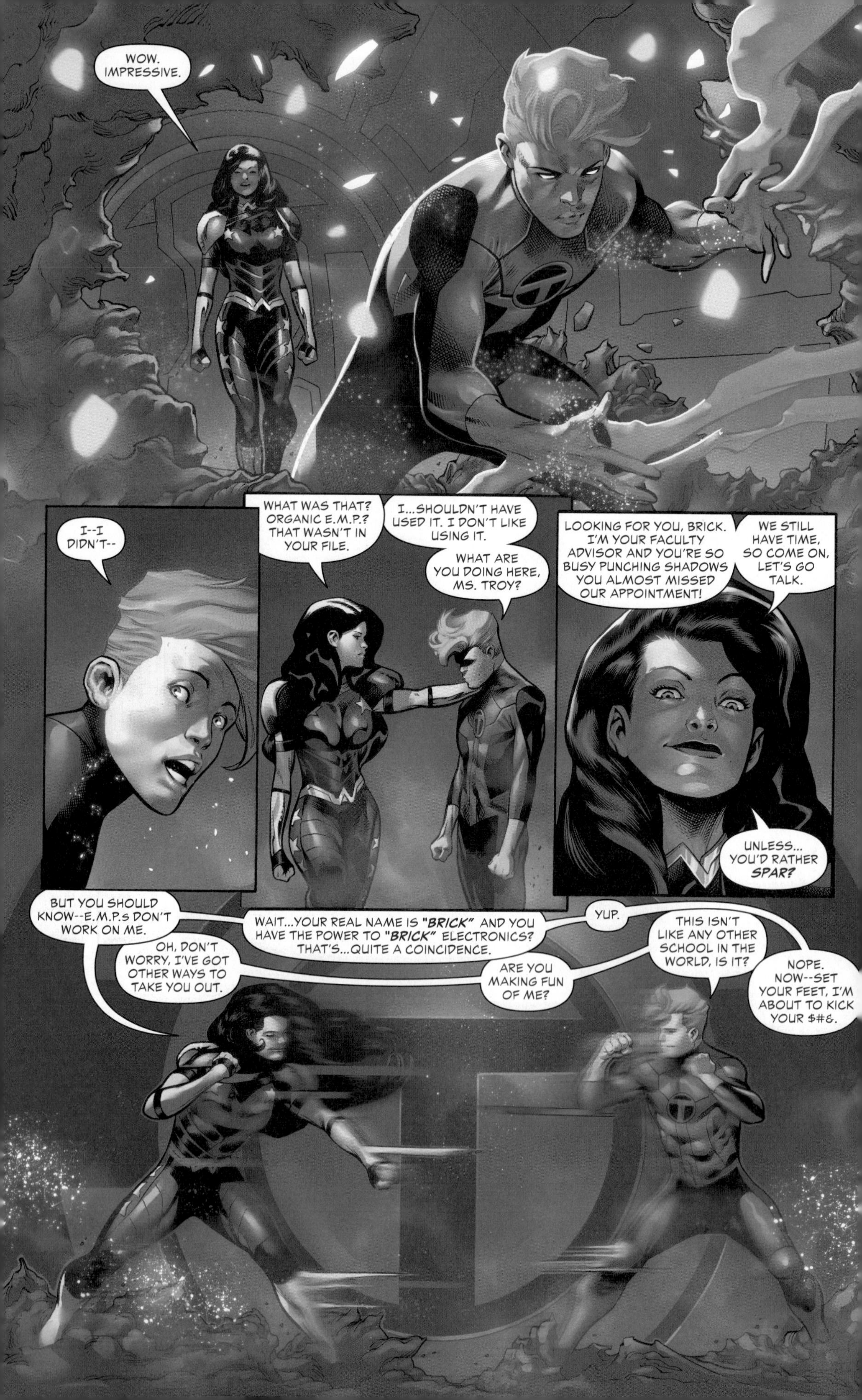
WOW. IMPRESSIVE.
I--I DIDN'T--
WHAT WAS THAT? ORGANIC E.M.P.? THAT WASN'T IN YOUR FILE.
I...SHOULDN'T HAVE USED IT. I DON'T LIKE USING IT.
WHAT ARE YOU DOING HERE, MS. TROY?
LOOKING FOR YOU, BRICK. I'M YOUR FACULTY ADVISOR AND YOU'RE SO BUSY PUNCHING SHADOWS YOU ALMOST MISSED OUR APPOINTMENT!
WE STILL HAVE TIME, SO COME ON, LET'S GO TALK.
UNLESS... YOU'D RATHER ***SPAR?***
BUT YOU SHOULD KNOW--E.M.P.s DON'T WORK ON ME.
OH, DON'T WORRY, I'VE GOT OTHER WAYS TO TAKE YOU OUT.
WAIT...YOUR REAL NAME IS "***BRICK***" AND YOU HAVE THE POWER TO "***BRICK***" ELECTRONICS? THAT'S...QUITE A COINCIDENCE.
YUP.
ARE YOU MAKING FUN OF ME?
THIS ISN'T LIKE ANY OTHER SCHOOL IN THE WORLD, IS IT?
NOPE. NOW--SET YOUR FEET, I'M ABOUT TO KICK YOUR $#&.

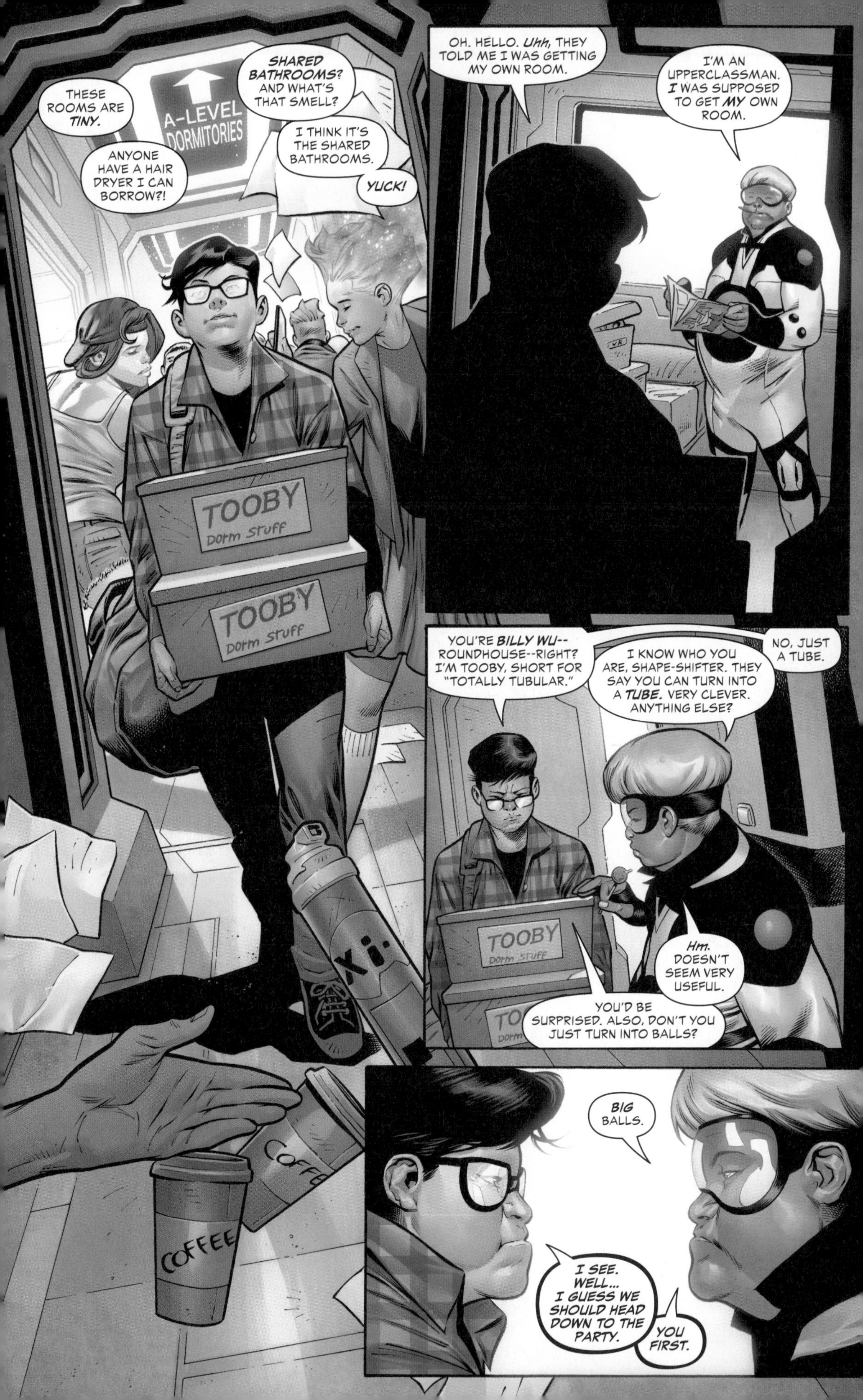
A-LEVEL DORMITORIES
THESE ROOMS ARE *TINY.*
ANYONE HAVE A HAIR DRYER I CAN BORROW?!
SHARED BATHROOMS? AND WHAT'S THAT SMELL?
I THINK IT'S THE SHARED BATHROOMS.
YUCK!
TOOBY Dorm Stuff
TOOBY Dorm Stuff
OH. HELLO. *Uhh,* THEY TOLD ME I WAS GETTING MY OWN ROOM.
I'M AN UPPERCLASSMAN. *I* WAS SUPPOSED TO GET *MY* OWN ROOM.
YOU'RE *BILLY WU--* ROUNDHOUSE--RIGHT? I'M TOOBY, SHORT FOR "TOTALLY TUBULAR."
I KNOW WHO YOU ARE, SHAPE-SHIFTER. THEY SAY YOU CAN TURN INTO A *TUBE.* VERY CLEVER. ANYTHING ELSE?
NO, JUST A TUBE.
TOOBY Dorm Stuff
Hm. DOESN'T SEEM VERY USEFUL.
YOU'D BE SURPRISED. ALSO, DON'T YOU JUST TURN INTO BALLS?
COFFEE
COFFEE
BIG BALLS.
I SEE. WELL... I GUESS WE SHOULD HEAD DOWN TO THE PARTY.
YOU FIRST.

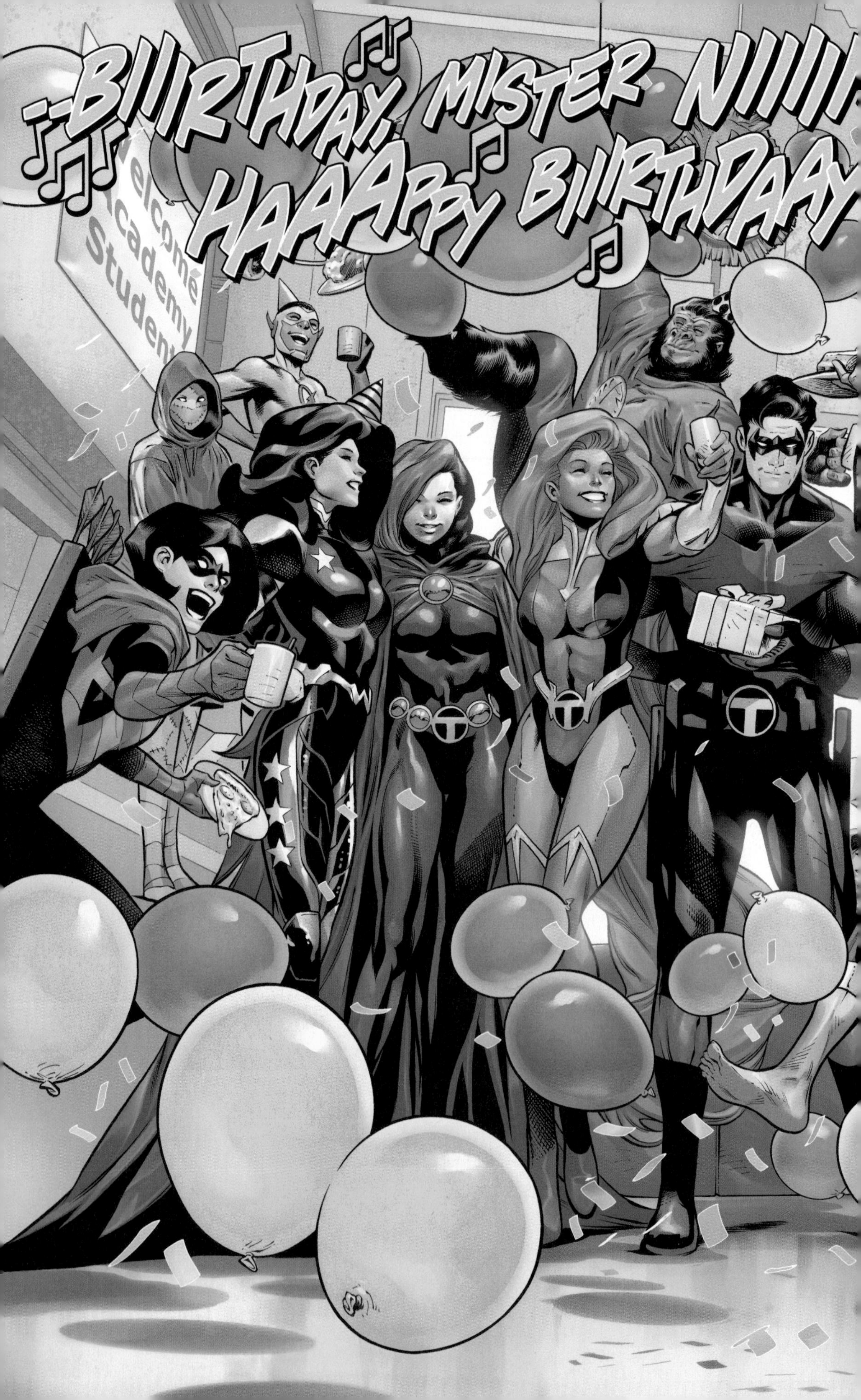

Welcome Academy Students
♫ --BIIIRTHDAY, MISTER NIIIII ♫
♫ HAAAPPY BIIIRTHDAAAY ♫

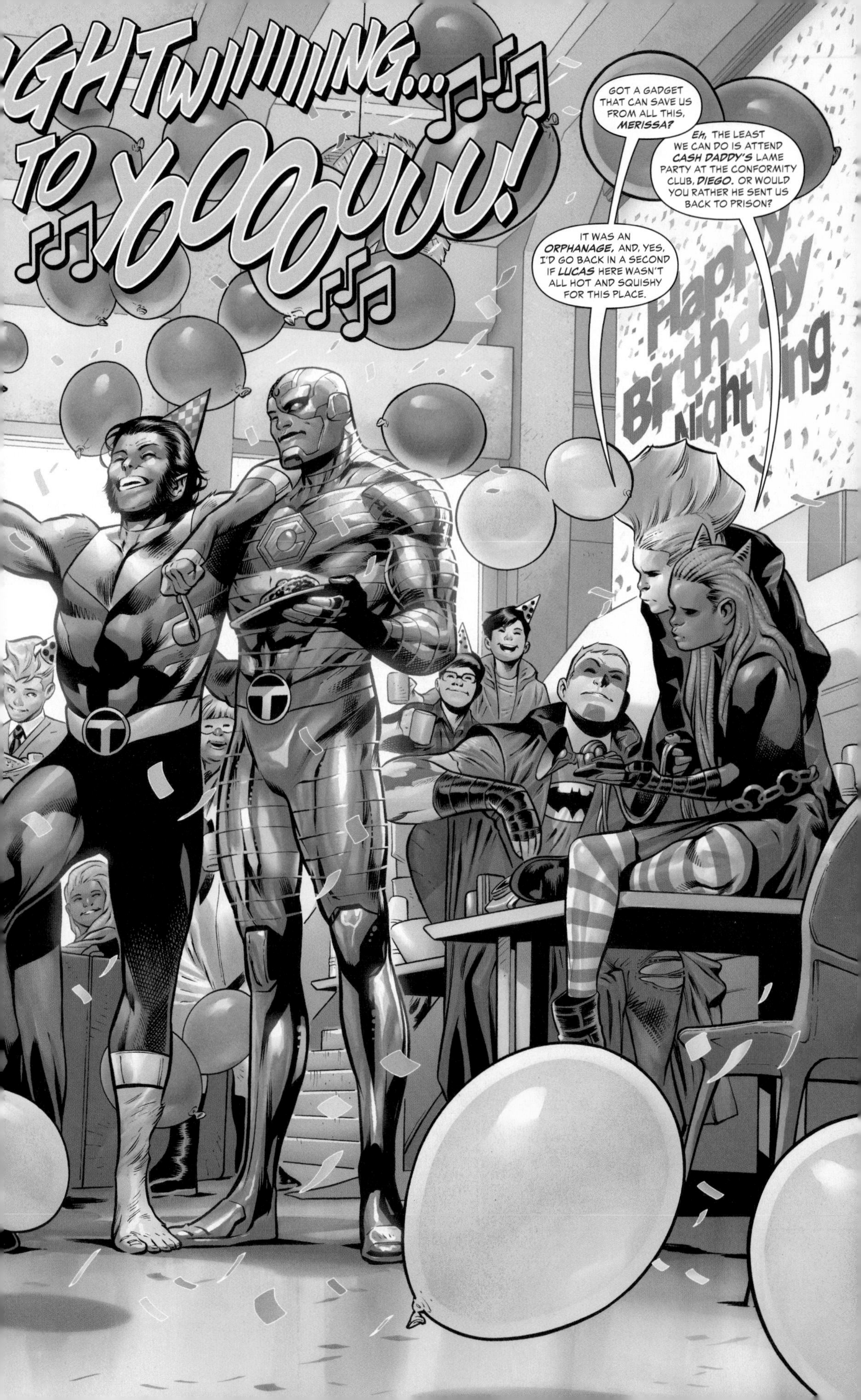

GHTWIIIIIIING... TO YOOOOUUU!
GOT A GADGET THAT CAN SAVE US FROM ALL THIS, MERISSA?
EH, THE LEAST WE CAN DO IS ATTEND CASH DADDY'S LAME PARTY AT THE CONFORMITY CLUB, DIEGO. OR WOULD YOU RATHER HE SENT US BACK TO PRISON?
IT WAS AN ORPHANAGE, AND, YES, I'D GO BACK IN A SECOND IF LUCAS HERE WASN'T ALL HOT AND SQUISHY FOR THIS PLACE.
Happy Birthday Nightwing

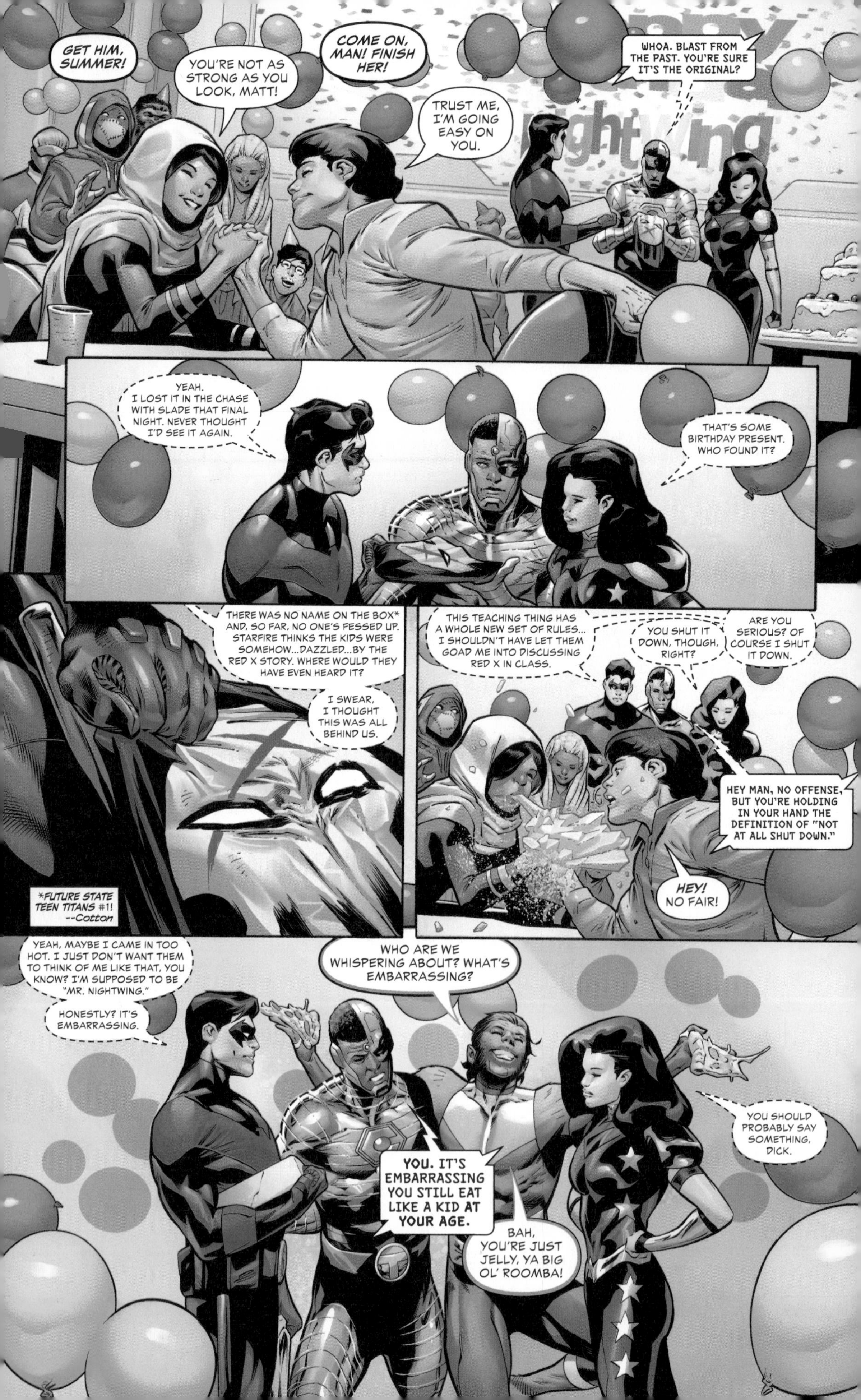

GET HIM, SUMMER!
YOU'RE NOT AS STRONG AS YOU LOOK, MATT!
COME ON, MAN! FINISH HER!
TRUST ME, I'M GOING EASY ON YOU.
WHOA. BLAST FROM THE PAST. YOU'RE SURE IT'S THE ORIGINAL?
YEAH. I LOST IT IN THE CHASE WITH SLADE THAT FINAL NIGHT. NEVER THOUGHT I'D SEE IT AGAIN.
THAT'S SOME BIRTHDAY PRESENT. WHO FOUND IT?
THERE WAS NO NAME ON THE BOX* AND, SO FAR, NO ONE'S FESSED UP. STARFIRE THINKS THE KIDS WERE SOMEHOW...DAZZLED...BY THE RED X STORY. WHERE WOULD THEY HAVE EVEN HEARD IT?
I SWEAR, I THOUGHT THIS WAS ALL BEHIND US.
*FUTURE STATE TEEN TITANS #1! --Cotton
THIS TEACHING THING HAS A WHOLE NEW SET OF RULES... I SHOULDN'T HAVE LET THEM GOAD ME INTO DISCUSSING RED X IN CLASS.
YOU SHUT IT DOWN, THOUGH, RIGHT?
ARE YOU SERIOUS? OF COURSE I SHUT IT DOWN.
HEY MAN, NO OFFENSE, BUT YOU'RE HOLDING IN YOUR HAND THE DEFINITION OF "NOT AT ALL SHUT DOWN."
HEY! NO FAIR!
YEAH, MAYBE I CAME IN TOO HOT. I JUST DON'T WANT THEM TO THINK OF ME LIKE THAT, YOU KNOW? I'M SUPPOSED TO BE "MR. NIGHTWING."
HONESTLY? IT'S EMBARRASSING.
WHO ARE WE WHISPERING ABOUT? WHAT'S EMBARRASSING?
YOU. IT'S EMBARRASSING YOU STILL EAT LIKE A KID AT YOUR AGE.
BAH, YOU'RE JUST JELLY, YA BIG OL' ROOMBA!
YOU SHOULD PROBABLY SAY SOMETHING, DICK.

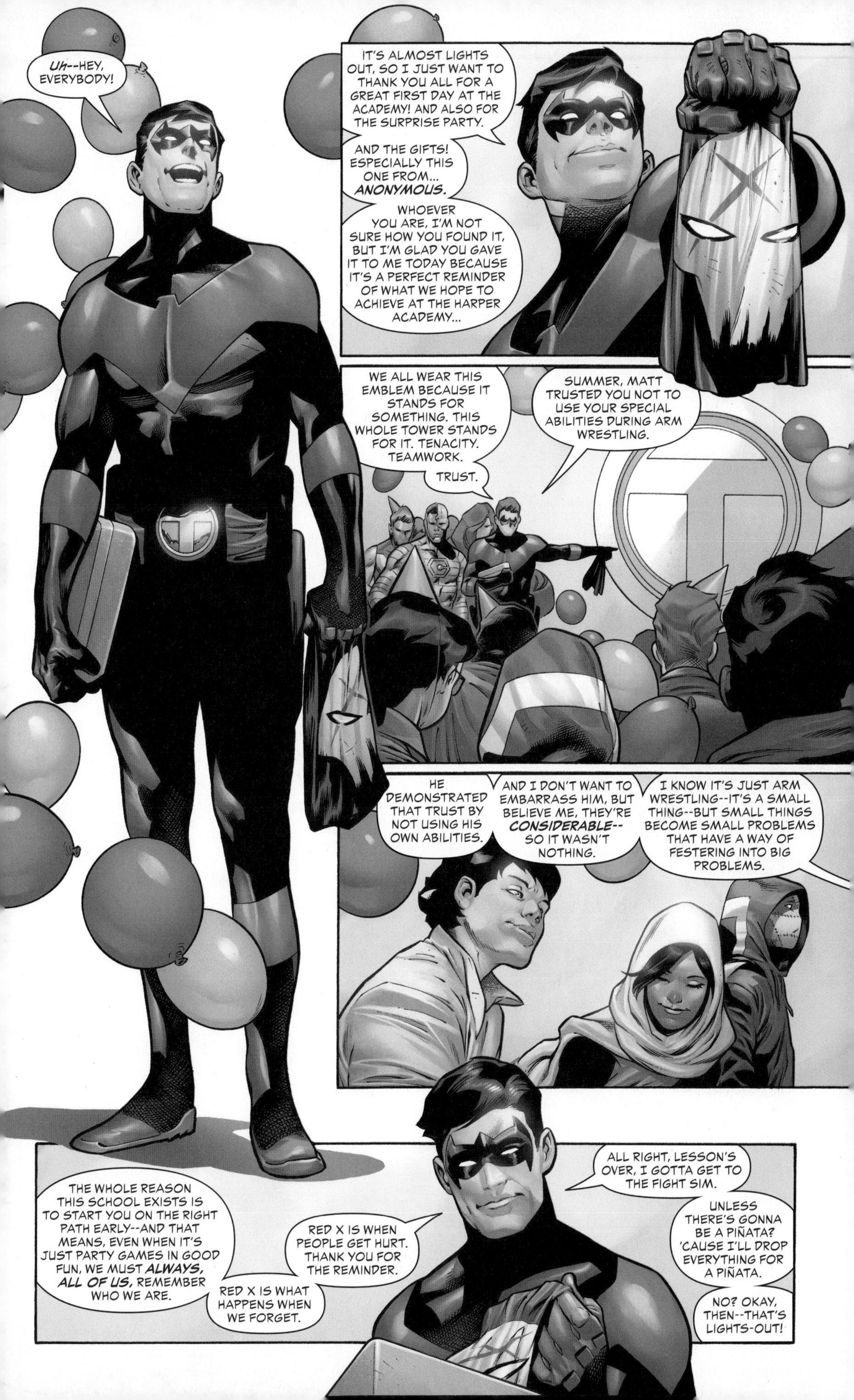

Uh--HEY, EVERYBODY!
IT'S ALMOST LIGHTS OUT, SO I JUST WANT TO THANK YOU ALL FOR A GREAT FIRST DAY AT THE ACADEMY! AND ALSO FOR THE SURPRISE PARTY.
AND THE GIFTS! ESPECIALLY THIS ONE FROM... ***ANONYMOUS.***
WHOEVER YOU ARE, I'M NOT SURE HOW YOU FOUND IT, BUT I'M GLAD YOU GAVE IT TO ME TODAY BECAUSE IT'S A PERFECT REMINDER OF WHAT WE HOPE TO ACHIEVE AT THE HARPER ACADEMY...
WE ALL WEAR THIS EMBLEM BECAUSE IT STANDS FOR SOMETHING. THIS WHOLE TOWER STANDS FOR IT. TENACITY. TEAMWORK.
TRUST.
SUMMER, MATT TRUSTED YOU NOT TO USE YOUR SPECIAL ABILITIES DURING ARM WRESTLING.
HE DEMONSTRATED THAT TRUST BY NOT USING HIS OWN ABILITIES.
AND I DON'T WANT TO EMBARRASS HIM, BUT BELIEVE ME, THEY'RE ***CONSIDERABLE***-- SO IT WASN'T NOTHING.
I KNOW IT'S JUST ARM WRESTLING--IT'S A SMALL THING--BUT SMALL THINGS BECOME SMALL PROBLEMS THAT HAVE A WAY OF FESTERING INTO BIG PROBLEMS.
THE WHOLE REASON THIS SCHOOL EXISTS IS TO START YOU ON THE RIGHT PATH EARLY--AND THAT MEANS, EVEN WHEN IT'S JUST PARTY GAMES IN GOOD FUN, WE MUST ***ALWAYS, ALL OF US,*** REMEMBER WHO WE ARE.
RED X IS WHAT HAPPENS WHEN WE FORGET.
RED X IS WHEN PEOPLE GET HURT. THANK YOU FOR THE REMINDER.
ALL RIGHT, LESSON'S OVER, I GOTTA GET TO THE FIGHT SIM.
UNLESS THERE'S GONNA BE A PIÑATA? 'CAUSE I'LL DROP EVERYTHING FOR A PIÑATA.
NO? OKAY, THEN--THAT'S LIGHTS-OUT!

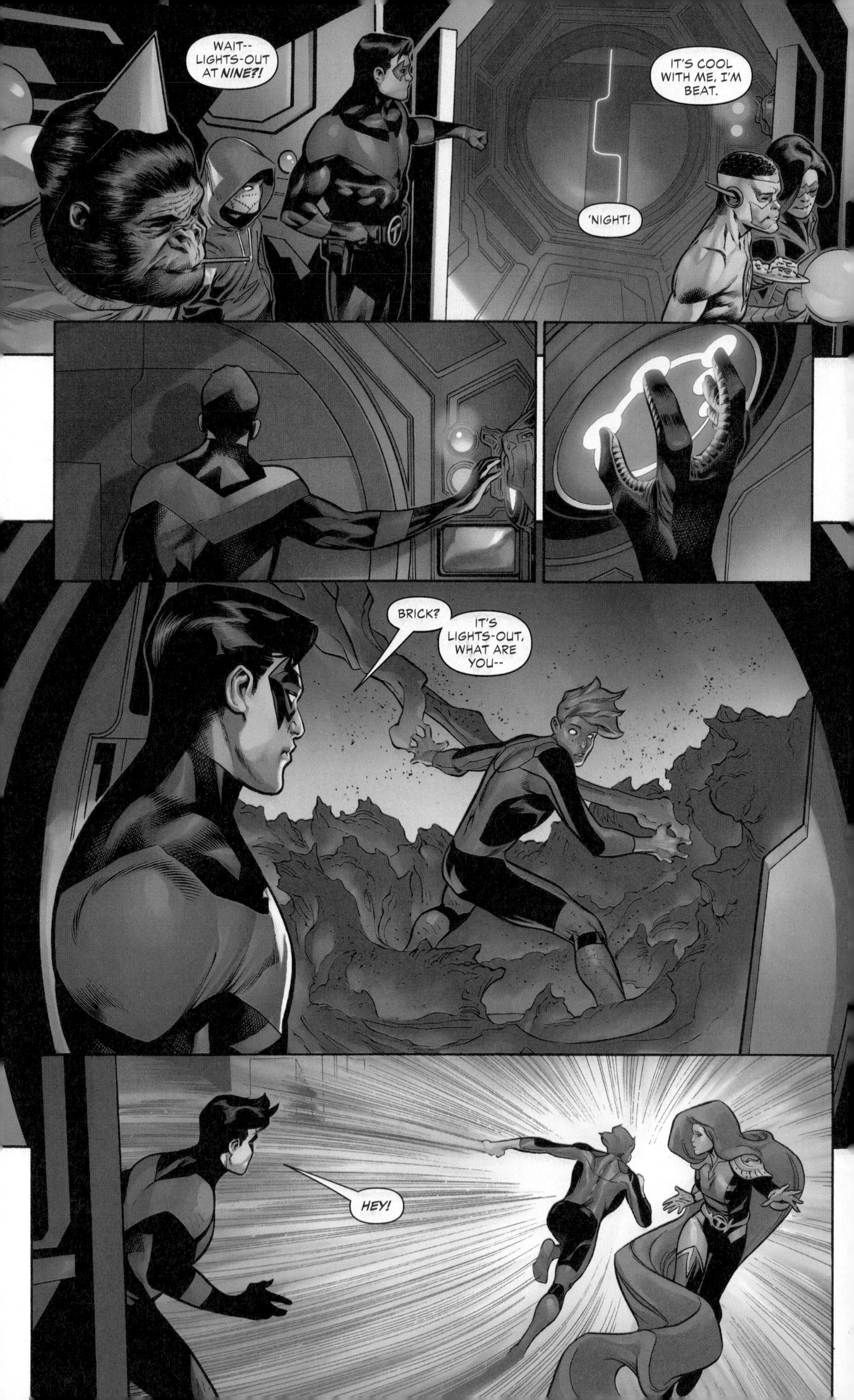
WAIT-- LIGHTS-OUT AT NINE?!
IT'S COOL WITH ME, I'M BEAT.
'NIGHT!
BRICK?
IT'S LIGHTS-OUT, WHAT ARE YOU--
HEY!

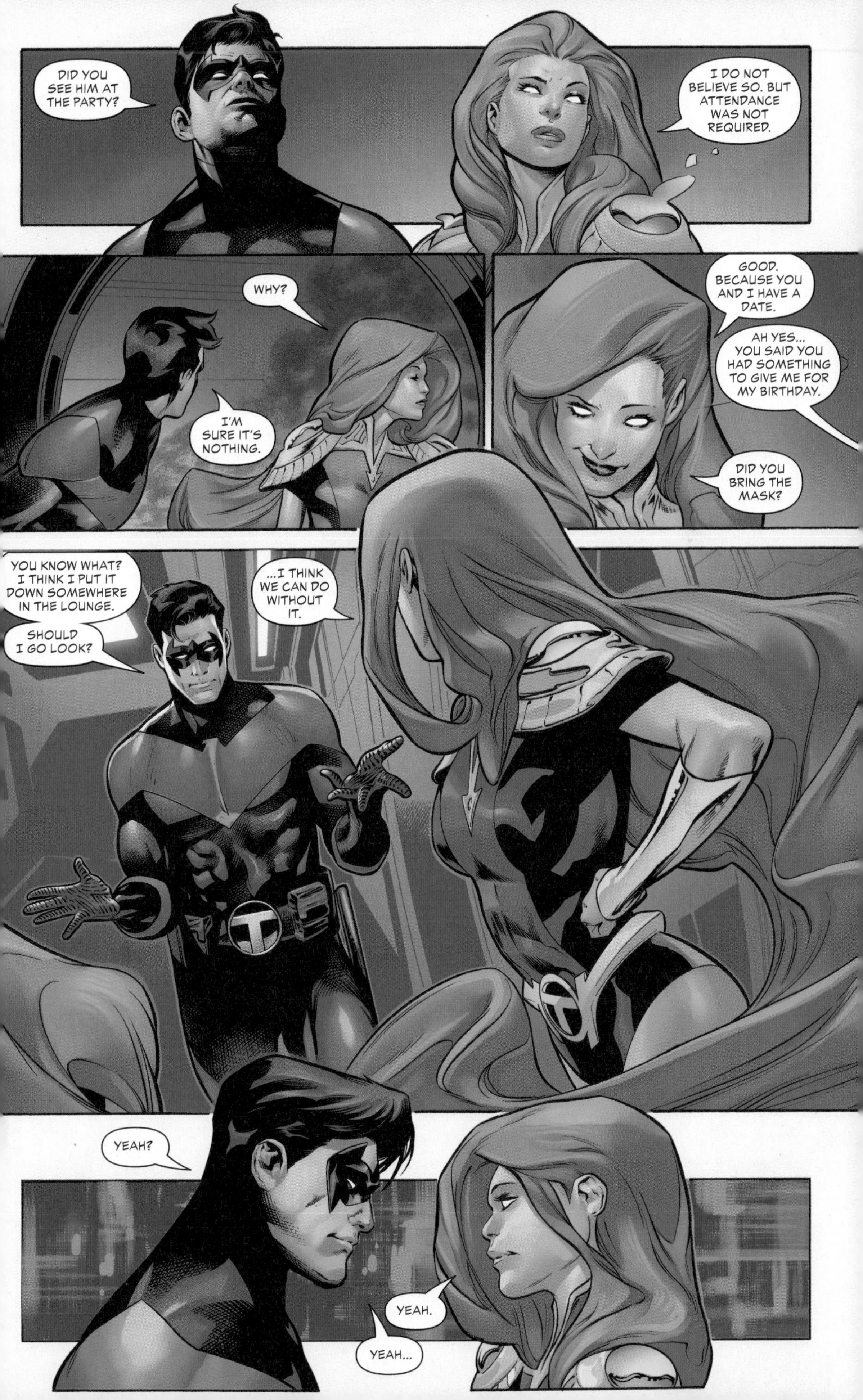
DID YOU SEE HIM AT THE PARTY?
I DO NOT BELIEVE SO. BUT ATTENDANCE WAS NOT REQUIRED.
WHY?
I'M SURE IT'S NOTHING.
GOOD. BECAUSE YOU AND I HAVE A DATE.
AH YES... YOU SAID YOU HAD SOMETHING TO GIVE ME FOR MY BIRTHDAY.
DID YOU BRING THE MASK?
YOU KNOW WHAT? I THINK I PUT IT DOWN SOMEWHERE IN THE LOUNGE.
SHOULD I GO LOOK?
...I THINK WE CAN DO WITHOUT IT.
YEAH?
YEAH.
YEAH...

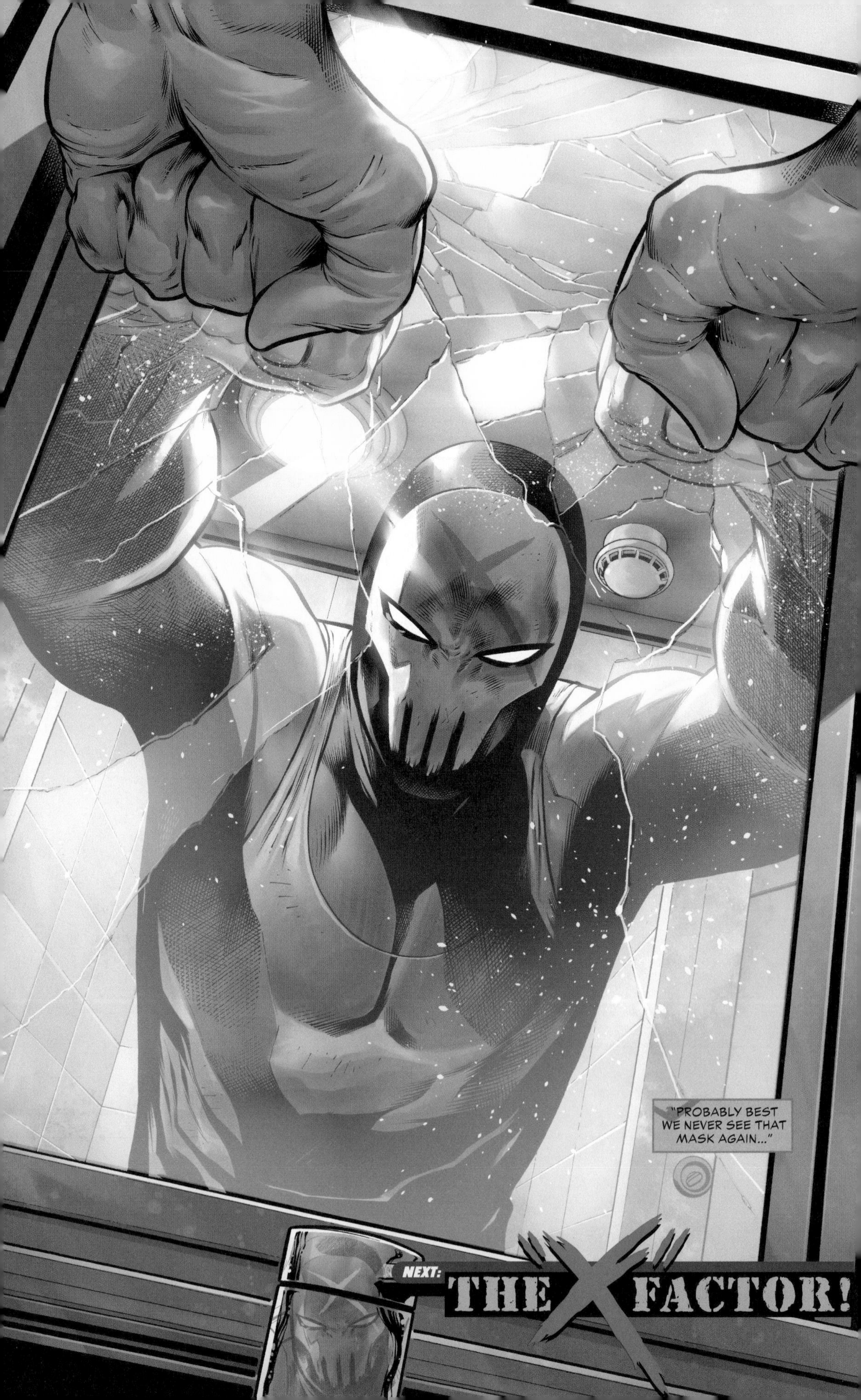
"PROBABLY BEST WE NEVER SEE THAT MASK AGAIN..."
NEXT: THE X FACTOR!

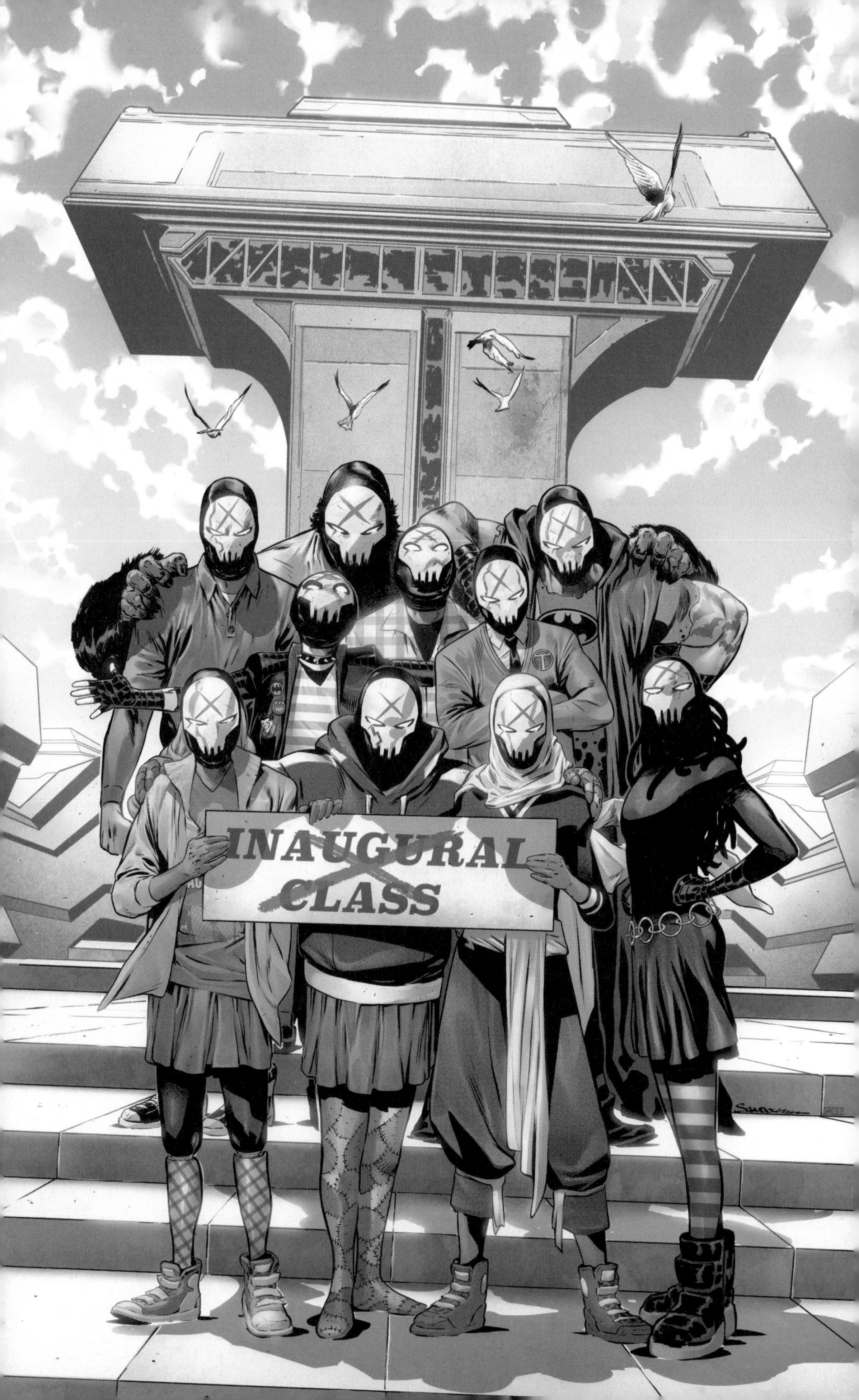
INAUGURAL
CLASS

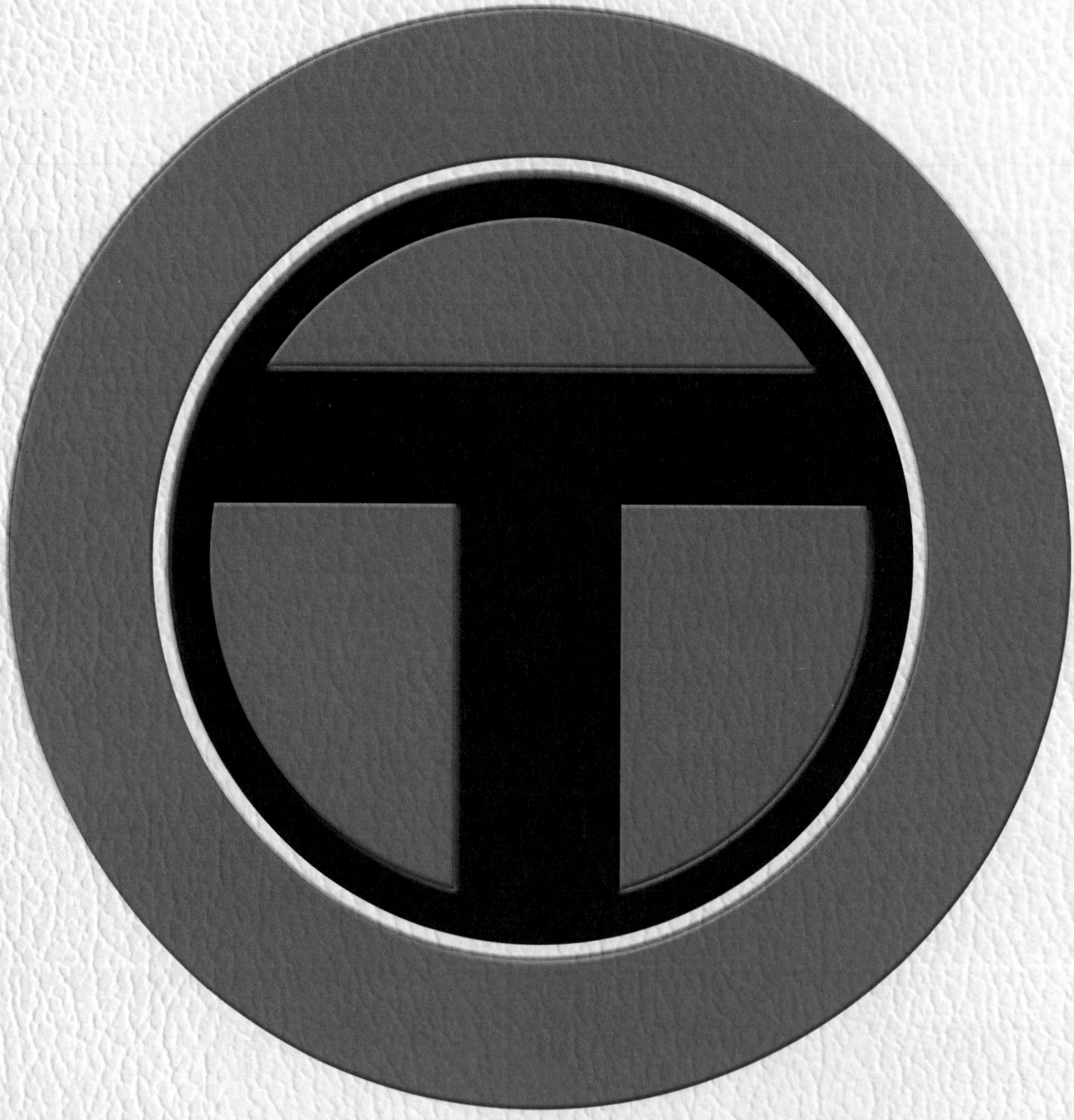

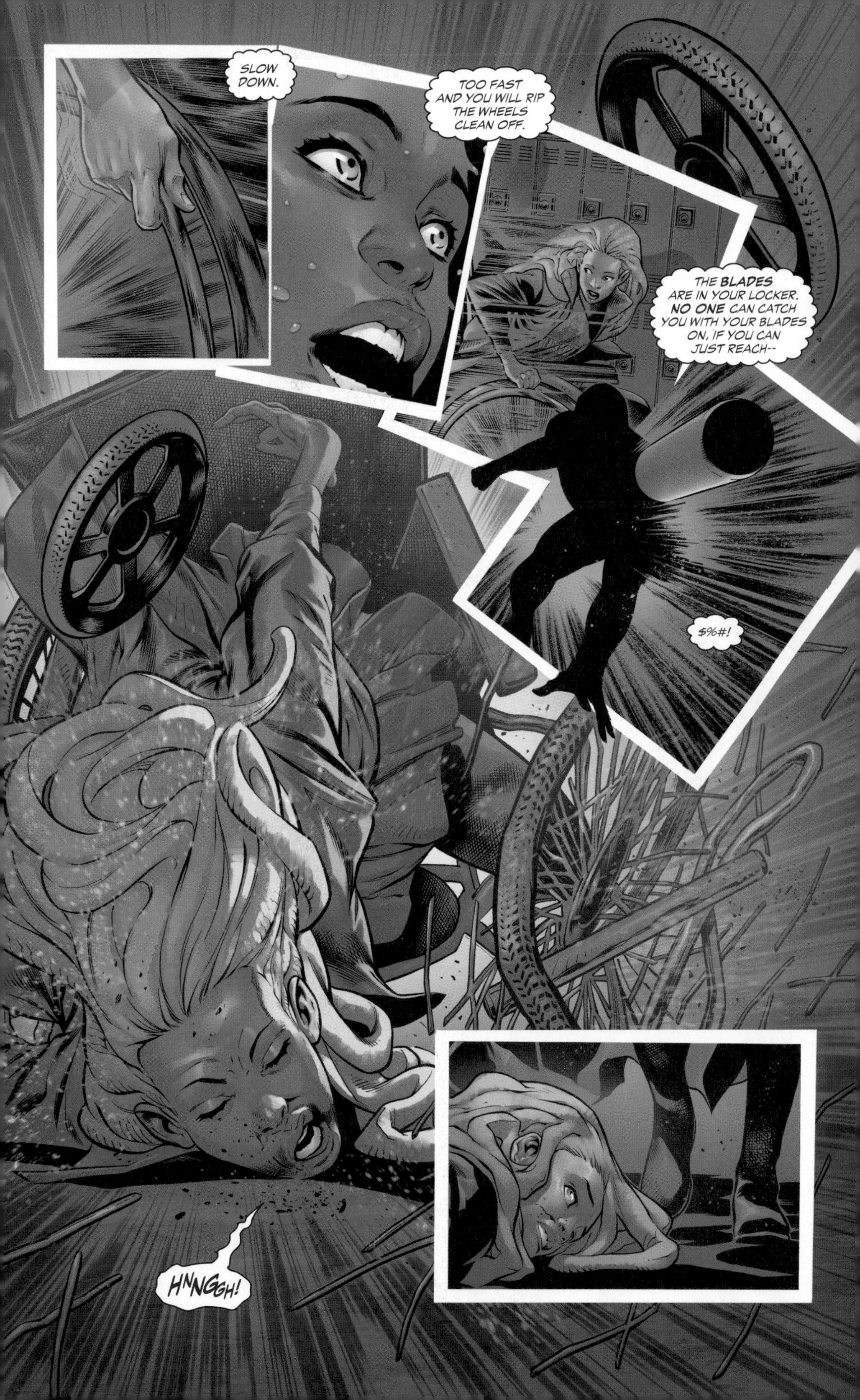
SLOW DOWN.
TOO FAST AND YOU WILL RIP THE WHEELS CLEAN OFF.
THE BLADES ARE IN YOUR LOCKER. NO ONE CAN CATCH YOU WITH YOUR BLADES ON, IF YOU CAN JUST REACH--
$%#!
HNNGGH!

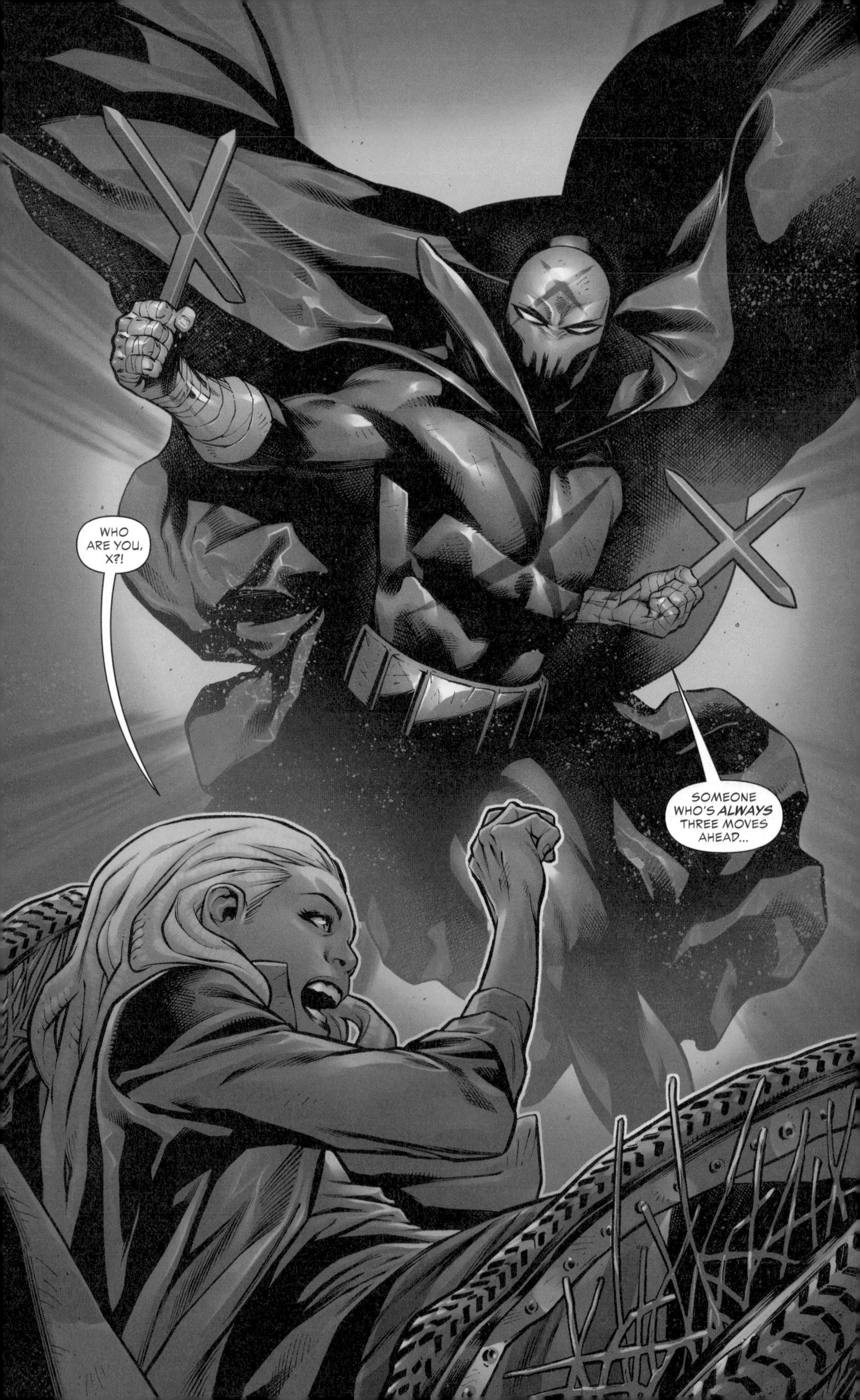
WHO ARE YOU, X?!
SOMEONE WHO'S *ALWAYS* THREE MOVES AHEAD...

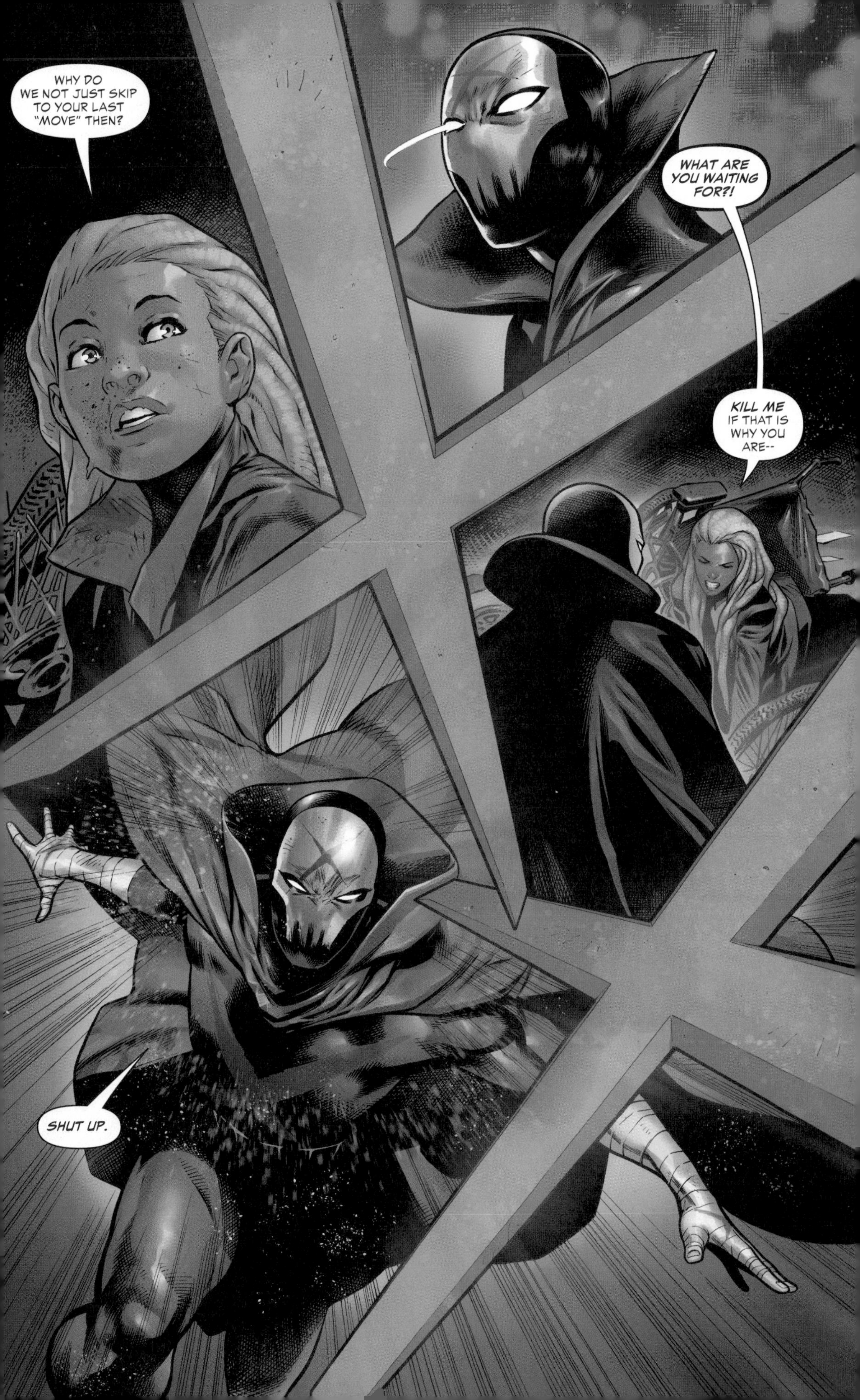
WHY DO WE NOT JUST SKIP TO YOUR LAST "MOVE" THEN?
WHAT ARE YOU WAITING FOR?!
KILL ME IF THAT IS WHY YOU ARE--
SHUT UP.

THE X FACTOR

TIM SHERIDAN
writer
RAFA SANDOVAL
penciller
JORDI TARRAGONA
inker
ALEJANDRO SANCHEZ
colorist
ROB LEIGH
letterer
SANDOVAL & SANCHEZ
cover
PHILIP TAN &
ELMER SANTOS
variant cover
DIEGO LOPEZ
associate editor
MIKE COTTON
editor
JAMIE S. RICH
group editor

Original Titans NIGHTWING, STARFIRE, RAVEN, DONNA TROY, CYBORG, and BEAST BOY reassemble to mentor the next generation of heroes! Now, TEEN TITANS ACADEMY opens its doors to a new crop of gifted youngsters eager to earn their place on the team's permanent roster, innocent of the many treacherous challenges they will face—in and out of school—over the months and years to come...

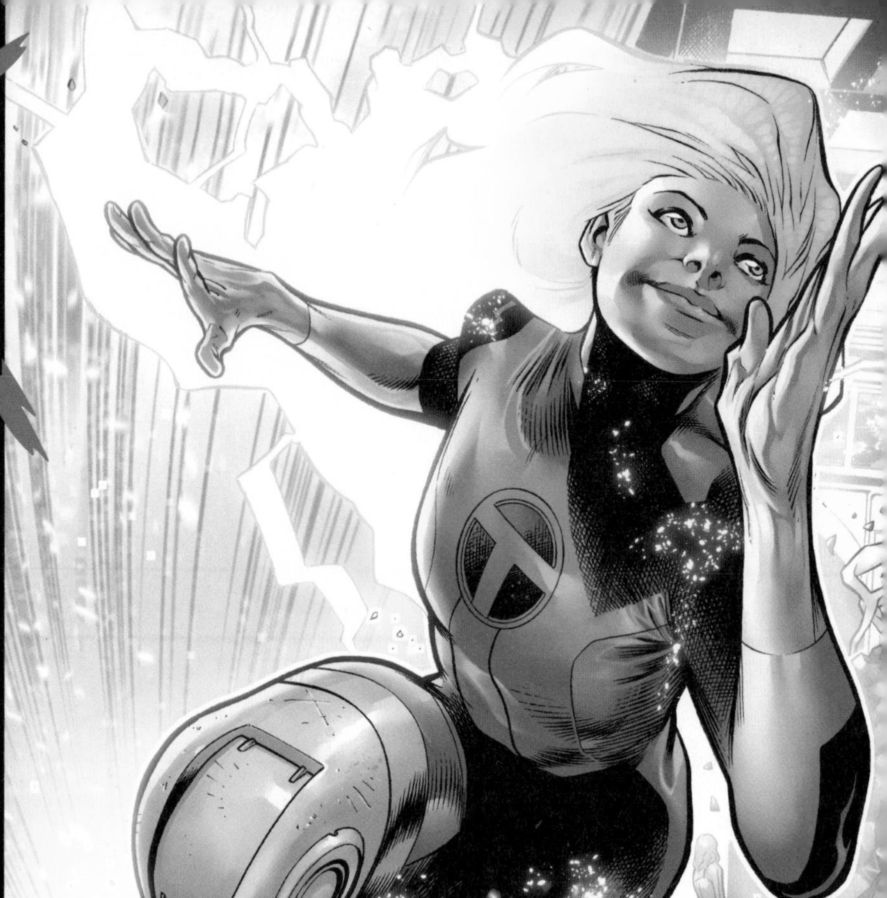

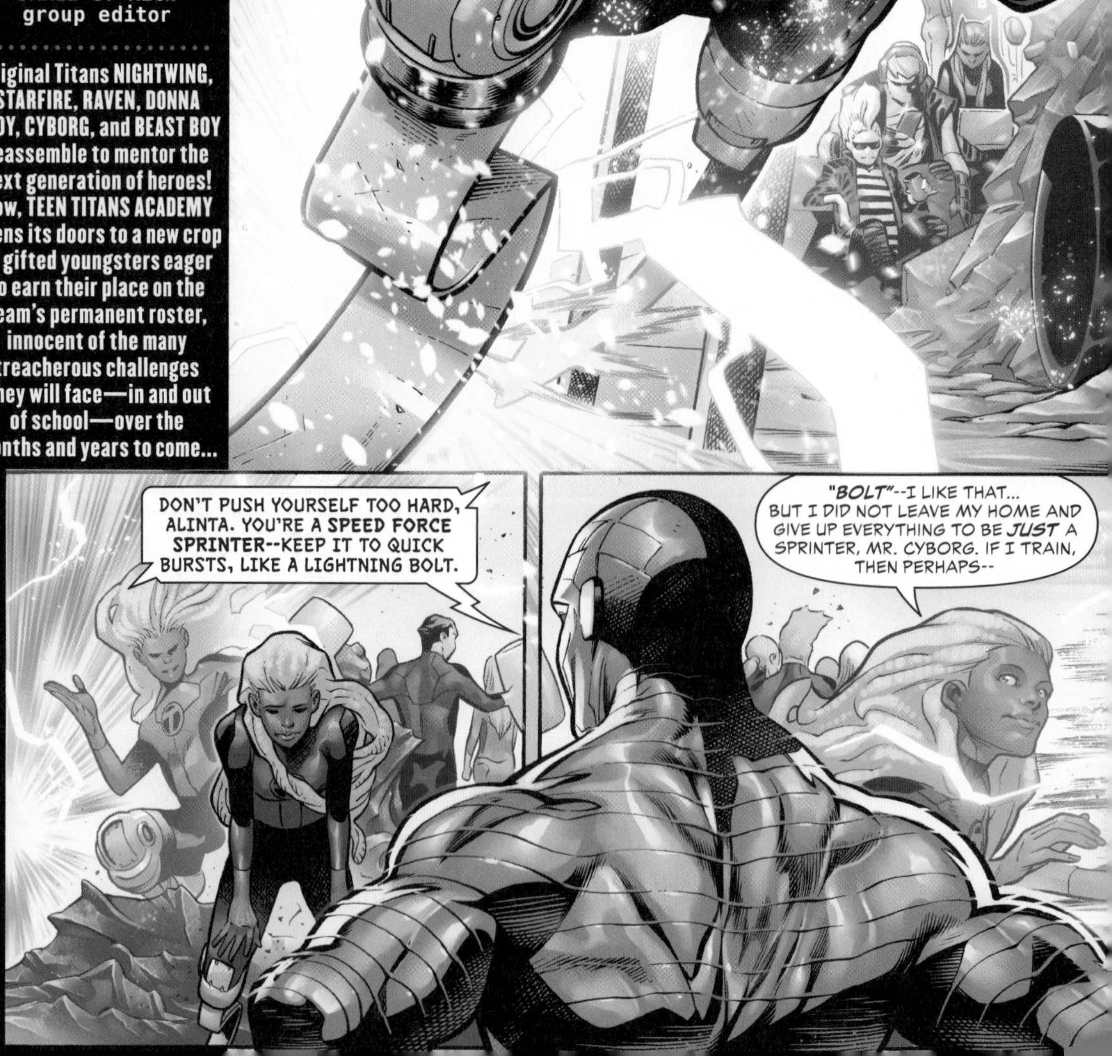
DON'T PUSH YOURSELF TOO HARD, ALINTA. YOU'RE A SPEED FORCE SPRINTER--KEEP IT TO QUICK BURSTS, LIKE A LIGHTNING BOLT.
"BOLT"--I LIKE THAT... BUT I DID NOT LEAVE MY HOME AND GIVE UP EVERYTHING TO BE JUST A SPRINTER, MR. CYBORG. IF I TRAIN, THEN PERHAPS--

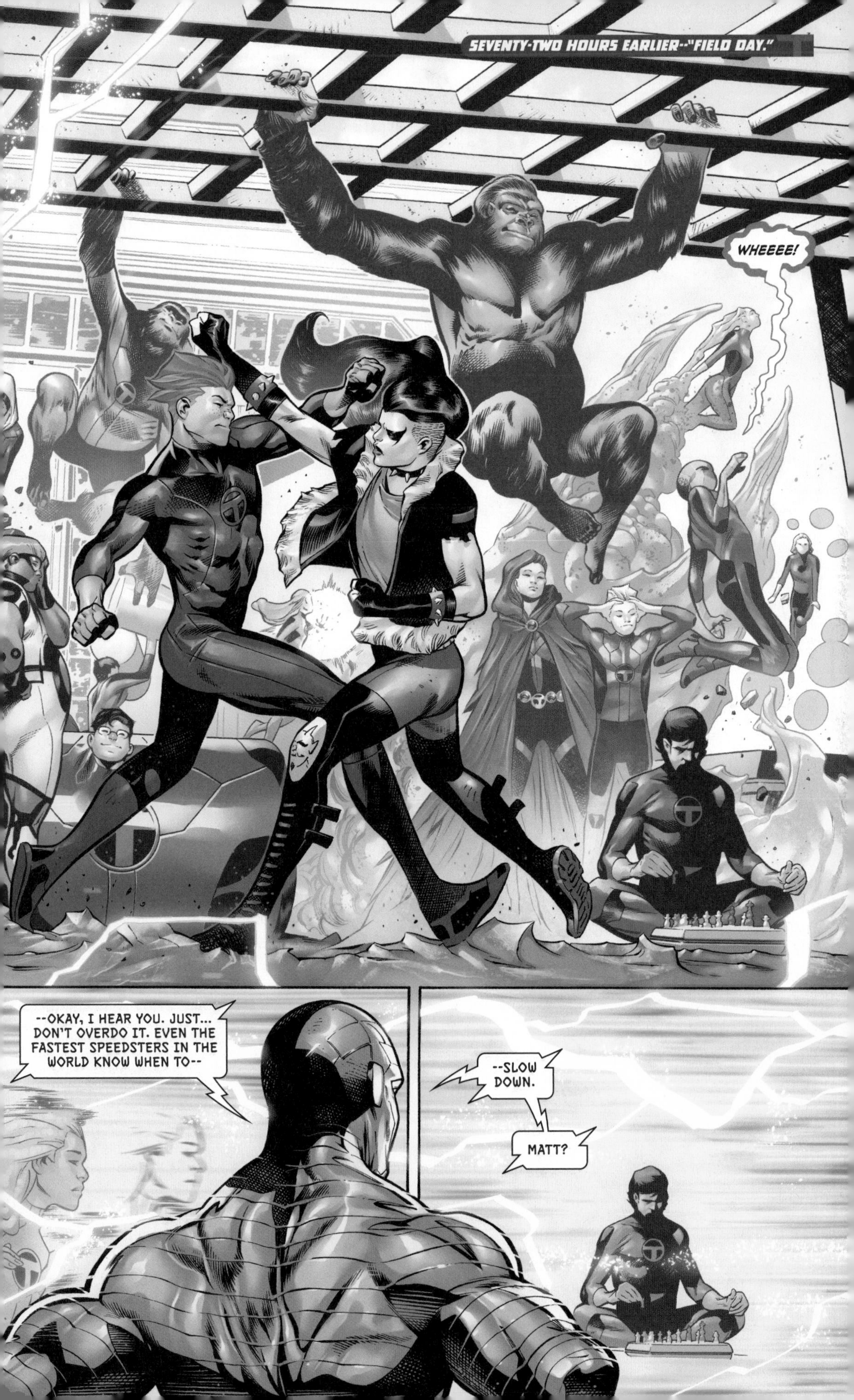
SEVENTY-TWO HOURS EARLIER--"FIELD DAY."
WHEEEE!
--OKAY, I HEAR YOU. JUST... DON'T OVERDO IT. EVEN THE FASTEST SPEEDSTERS IN THE WORLD KNOW WHEN TO--
--SLOW DOWN.
MATT?

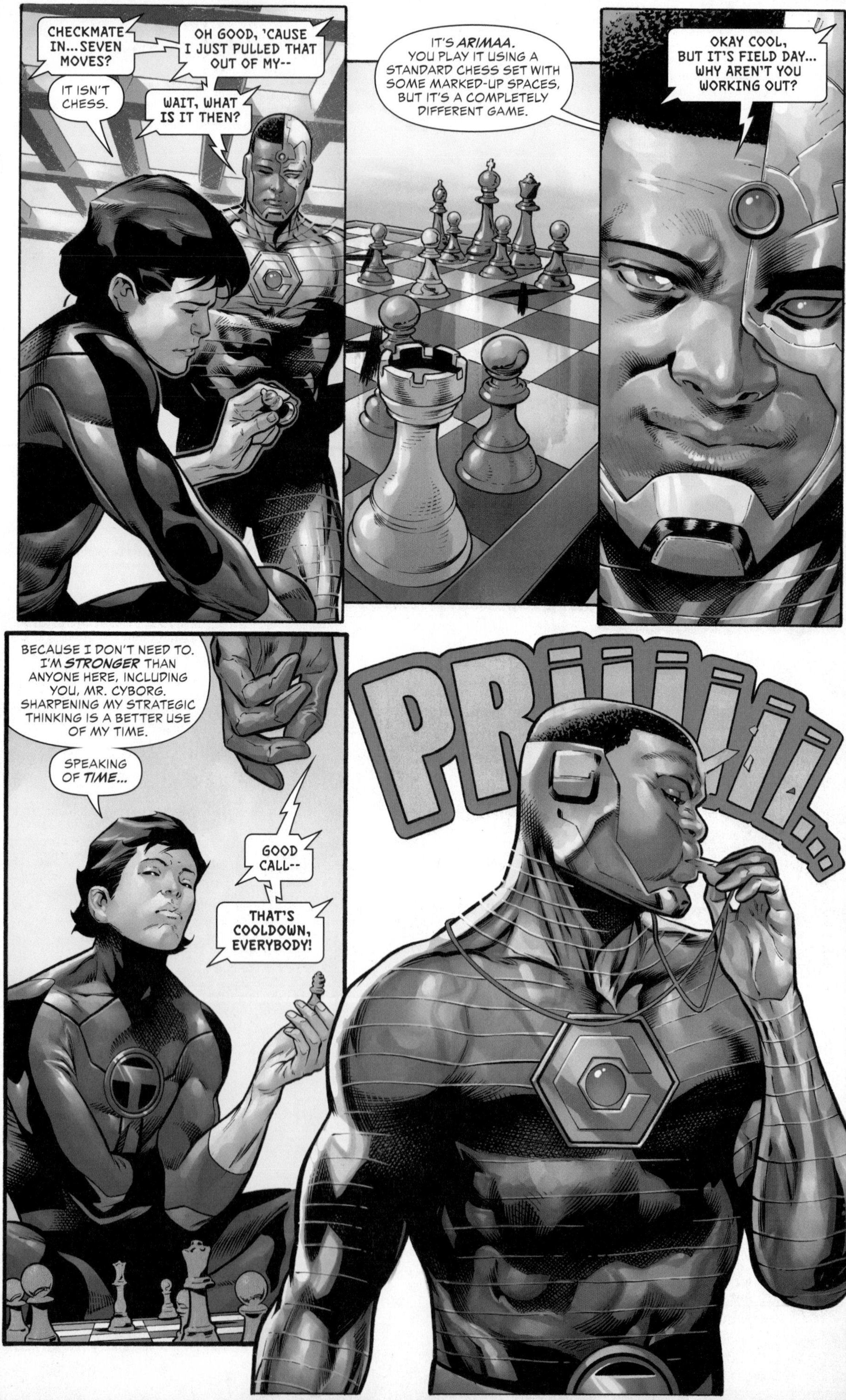
CHECKMATE IN...SEVEN MOVES?
OH GOOD, 'CAUSE I JUST PULLED THAT OUT OF MY--
IT ISN'T CHESS.
WAIT, WHAT IS IT THEN?
IT'S ARIMAA. YOU PLAY IT USING A STANDARD CHESS SET WITH SOME MARKED-UP SPACES, BUT IT'S A COMPLETELY DIFFERENT GAME.
OKAY COOL, BUT IT'S FIELD DAY... WHY AREN'T YOU WORKING OUT?
BECAUSE I DON'T NEED TO. I'M STRONGER THAN ANYONE HERE, INCLUDING YOU, MR. CYBORG. SHARPENING MY STRATEGIC THINKING IS A BETTER USE OF MY TIME.
SPEAKING OF TIME...
GOOD CALL--
THAT'S COOLDOWN, EVERYBODY!
PRiiiiii...

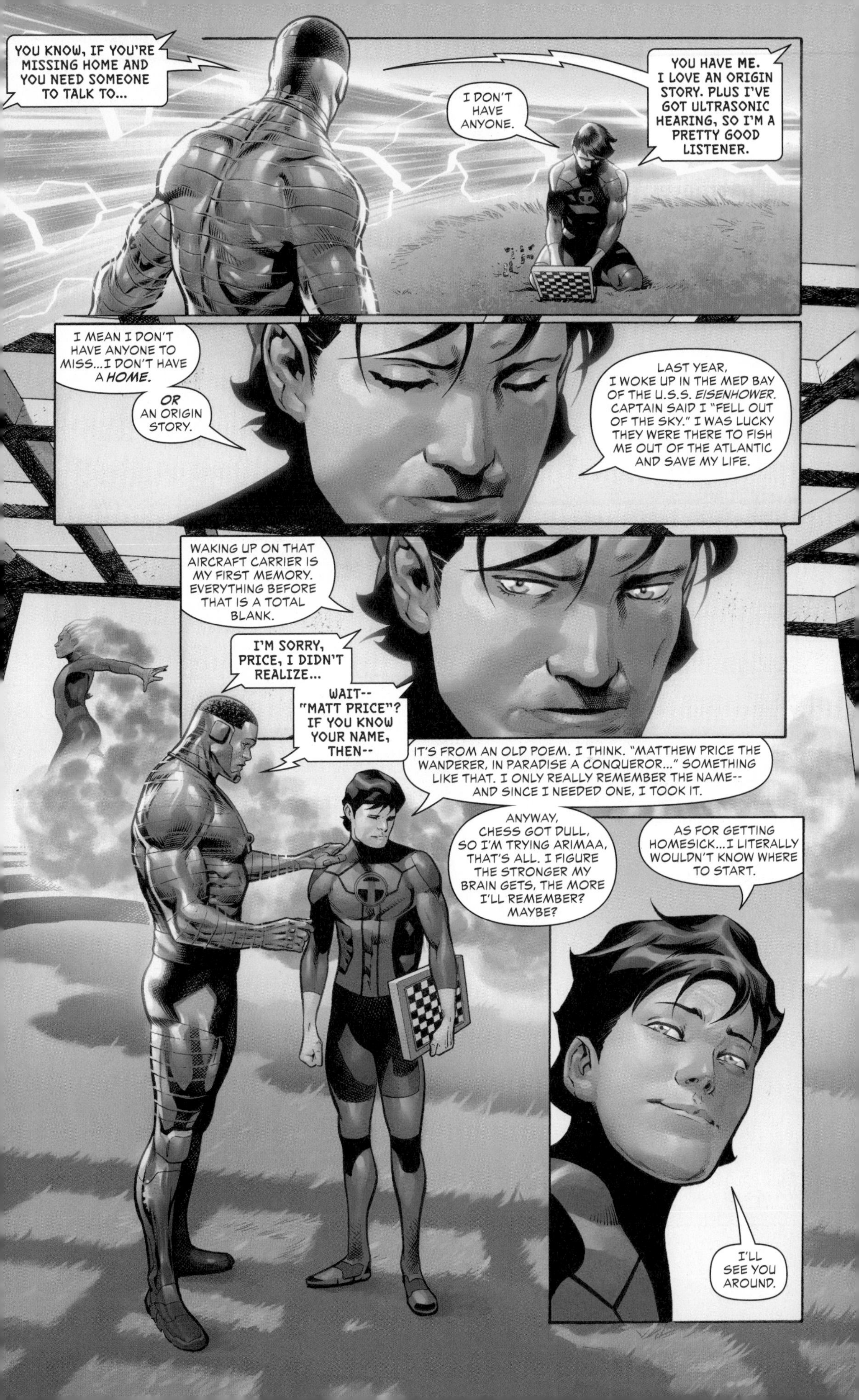

YOU KNOW, IF YOU'RE MISSING HOME AND YOU NEED SOMEONE TO TALK TO...
I DON'T HAVE ANYONE.
YOU HAVE ME. I LOVE AN ORIGIN STORY. PLUS I'VE GOT ULTRASONIC HEARING, SO I'M A PRETTY GOOD LISTENER.
I MEAN I DON'T HAVE ANYONE TO MISS...I DON'T HAVE A *HOME.*
OR AN ORIGIN STORY.
LAST YEAR, I WOKE UP IN THE MED BAY OF THE U.S.S. *EISENHOWER*. CAPTAIN SAID I "FELL OUT OF THE SKY." I WAS LUCKY THEY WERE THERE TO FISH ME OUT OF THE ATLANTIC AND SAVE MY LIFE.
WAKING UP ON THAT AIRCRAFT CARRIER IS MY FIRST MEMORY. EVERYTHING BEFORE THAT IS A TOTAL BLANK.
I'M SORRY, PRICE, I DIDN'T REALIZE...
WAIT-- "MATT PRICE"? IF YOU KNOW YOUR NAME, THEN--
IT'S FROM AN OLD POEM. I THINK. "MATTHEW PRICE THE WANDERER, IN PARADISE A CONQUEROR..." SOMETHING LIKE THAT. I ONLY REALLY REMEMBER THE NAME-- AND SINCE I NEEDED ONE, I TOOK IT.
ANYWAY, CHESS GOT DULL, SO I'M TRYING ARIMAA, THAT'S ALL. I FIGURE THE STRONGER MY BRAIN GETS, THE MORE I'LL REMEMBER? MAYBE?
AS FOR GETTING HOMESICK...I LITERALLY WOULDN'T KNOW WHERE TO START.
I'LL SEE YOU AROUND.

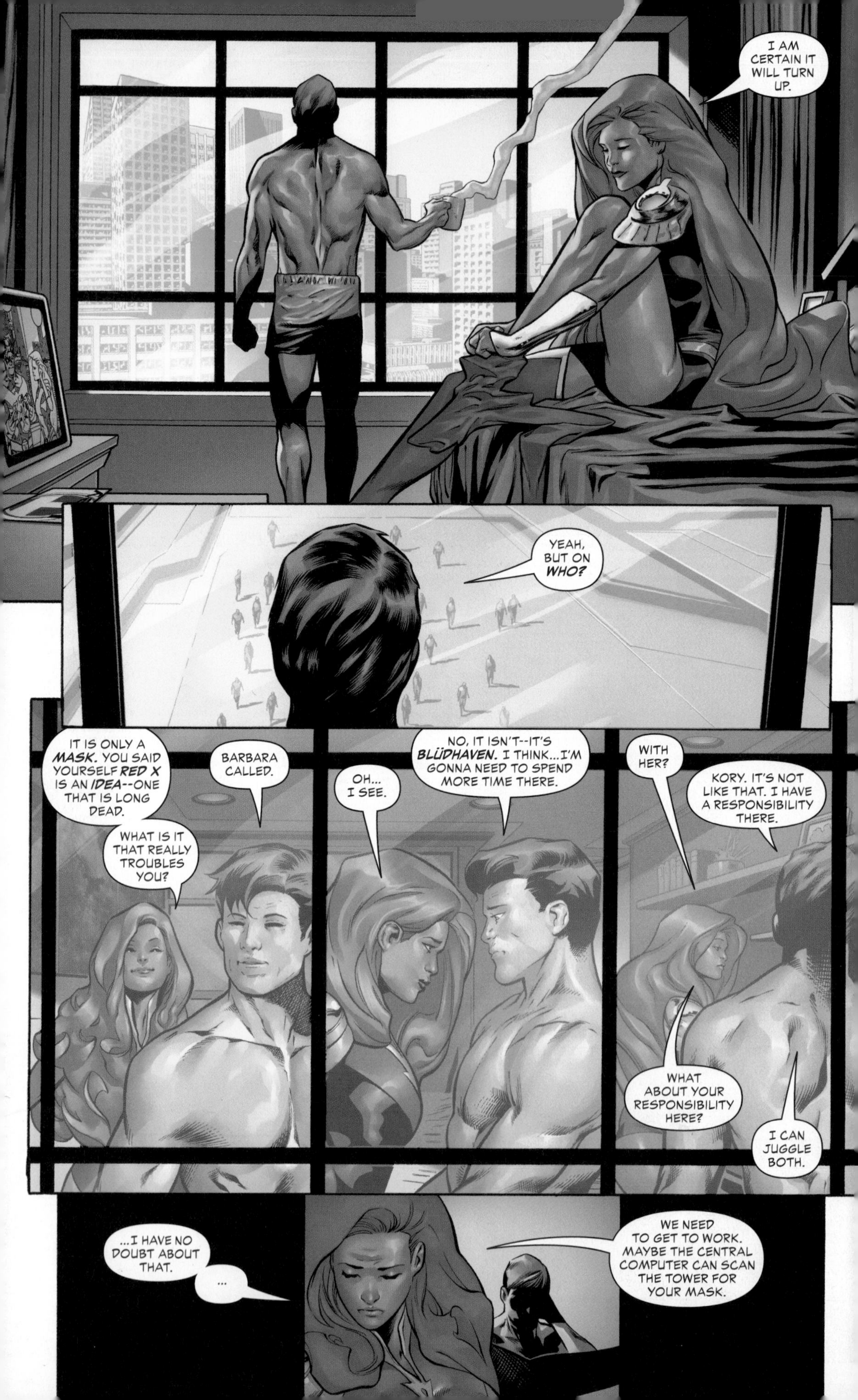
I AM CERTAIN IT WILL TURN UP.
YEAH, BUT ON *WHO?*
IT IS ONLY A *MASK.* YOU SAID YOURSELF *RED X* IS AN *IDEA*--ONE THAT IS LONG DEAD.
WHAT IS IT THAT REALLY TROUBLES YOU?
BARBARA CALLED.
OH... I SEE.
NO, IT ISN'T--IT'S *BLÜDHAVEN.* I THINK...I'M GONNA NEED TO SPEND MORE TIME THERE.
WITH HER?
KORY. IT'S NOT LIKE THAT. I HAVE A RESPONSIBILITY THERE.
WHAT ABOUT YOUR RESPONSIBILITY HERE?
I CAN JUGGLE BOTH.
...I HAVE NO DOUBT ABOUT THAT.
...
WE NEED TO GET TO WORK. MAYBE THE CENTRAL COMPUTER CAN SCAN THE TOWER FOR YOUR MASK.

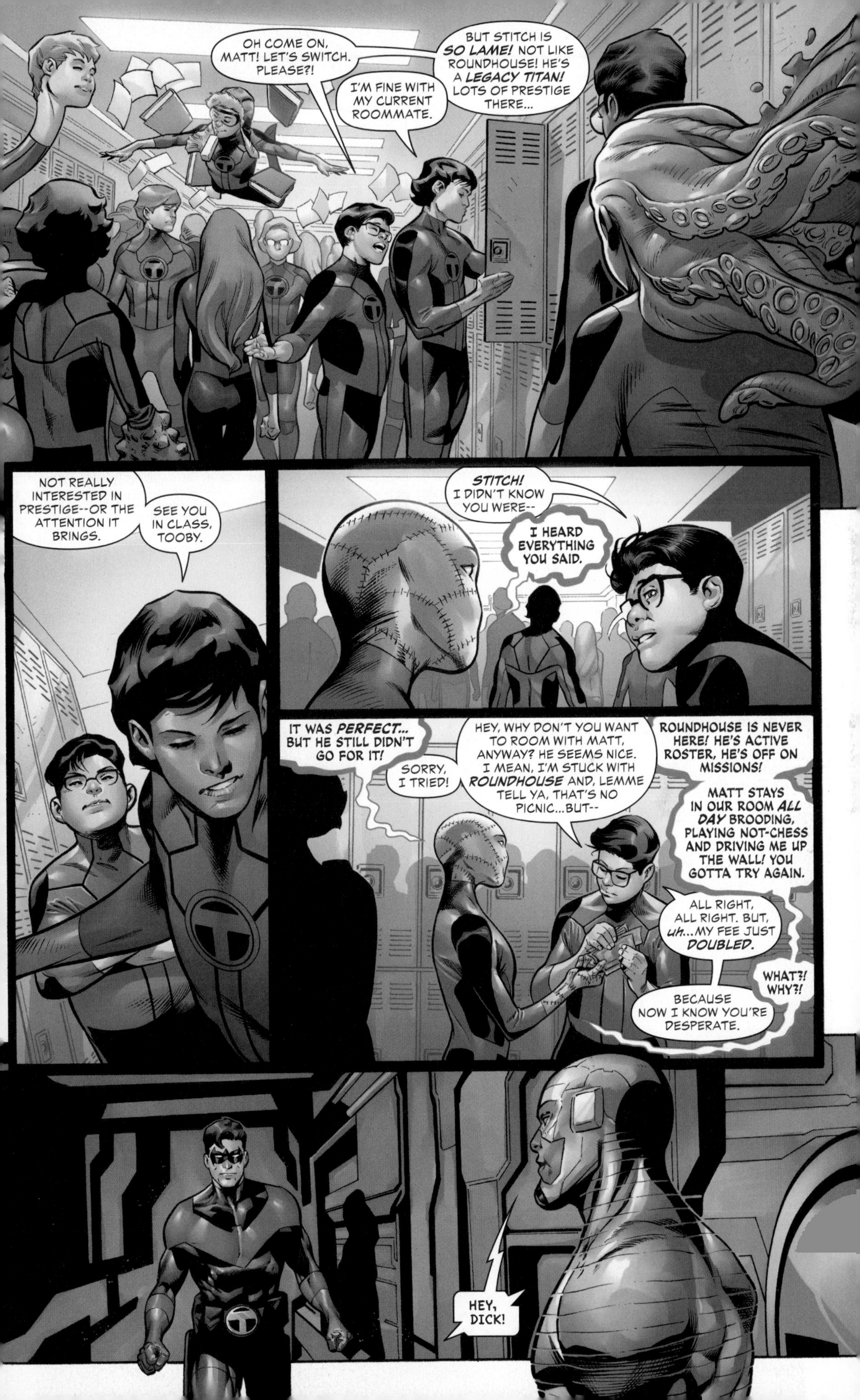
OH COME ON, MATT! LET'S SWITCH. PLEASE?!
I'M FINE WITH MY CURRENT ROOMMATE.
BUT STITCH IS SO LAME! NOT LIKE ROUNDHOUSE! HE'S A LEGACY TITAN! LOTS OF PRESTIGE THERE...
NOT REALLY INTERESTED IN PRESTIGE--OR THE ATTENTION IT BRINGS.
SEE YOU IN CLASS, TOOBY.
STITCH! I DIDN'T KNOW YOU WERE--
I HEARD EVERYTHING YOU SAID.
IT WAS PERFECT... BUT HE STILL DIDN'T GO FOR IT!
SORRY, I TRIED!
HEY, WHY DON'T YOU WANT TO ROOM WITH MATT, ANYWAY? HE SEEMS NICE. I MEAN, I'M STUCK WITH ROUNDHOUSE AND, LEMME TELL YA, THAT'S NO PICNIC...BUT--
ROUNDHOUSE IS NEVER HERE! HE'S ACTIVE ROSTER, HE'S OFF ON MISSIONS!
MATT STAYS IN OUR ROOM ALL DAY BROODING, PLAYING NOT-CHESS AND DRIVING ME UP THE WALL! YOU GOTTA TRY AGAIN.
ALL RIGHT, ALL RIGHT. BUT, uh...MY FEE JUST DOUBLED.
WHAT?! WHY?!
BECAUSE NOW I KNOW YOU'RE DESPERATE.
HEY, DICK!

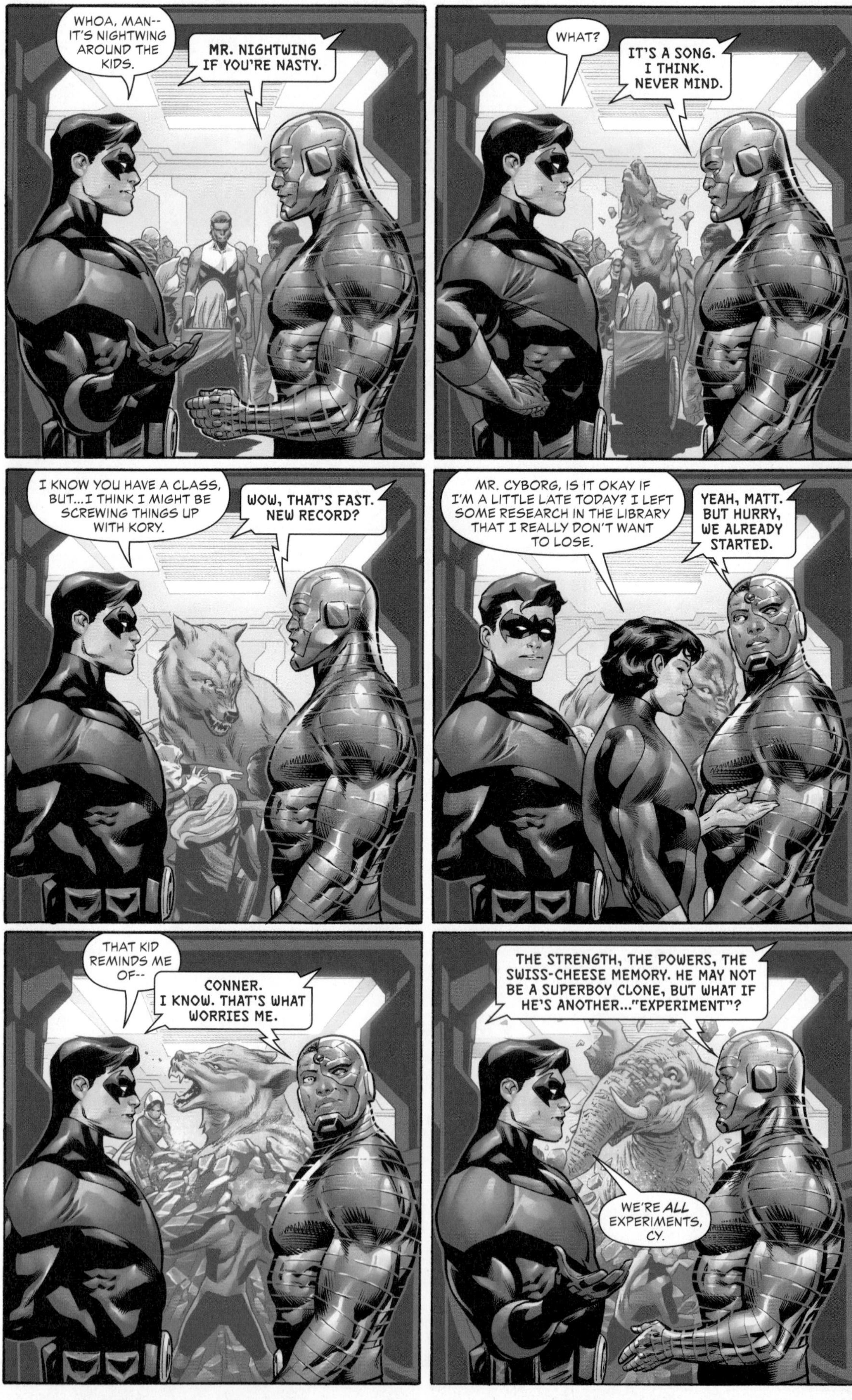
WHOA, MAN-- IT'S NIGHTWING AROUND THE KIDS.
MR. NIGHTWING IF YOU'RE NASTY.
WHAT?
IT'S A SONG. I THINK. NEVER MIND.
I KNOW YOU HAVE A CLASS, BUT...I THINK I MIGHT BE SCREWING THINGS UP WITH KORY.
WOW, THAT'S FAST. NEW RECORD?
MR. CYBORG, IS IT OKAY IF I'M A LITTLE LATE TODAY? I LEFT SOME RESEARCH IN THE LIBRARY THAT I REALLY DON'T WANT TO LOSE.
YEAH, MATT. BUT HURRY, WE ALREADY STARTED.
THAT KID REMINDS ME OF--
CONNER. I KNOW. THAT'S WHAT WORRIES ME.
THE STRENGTH, THE POWERS, THE SWISS-CHEESE MEMORY. HE MAY NOT BE A SUPERBOY CLONE, BUT WHAT IF HE'S ANOTHER..."EXPERIMENT"?
WE'RE *ALL* EXPERIMENTS, CY.

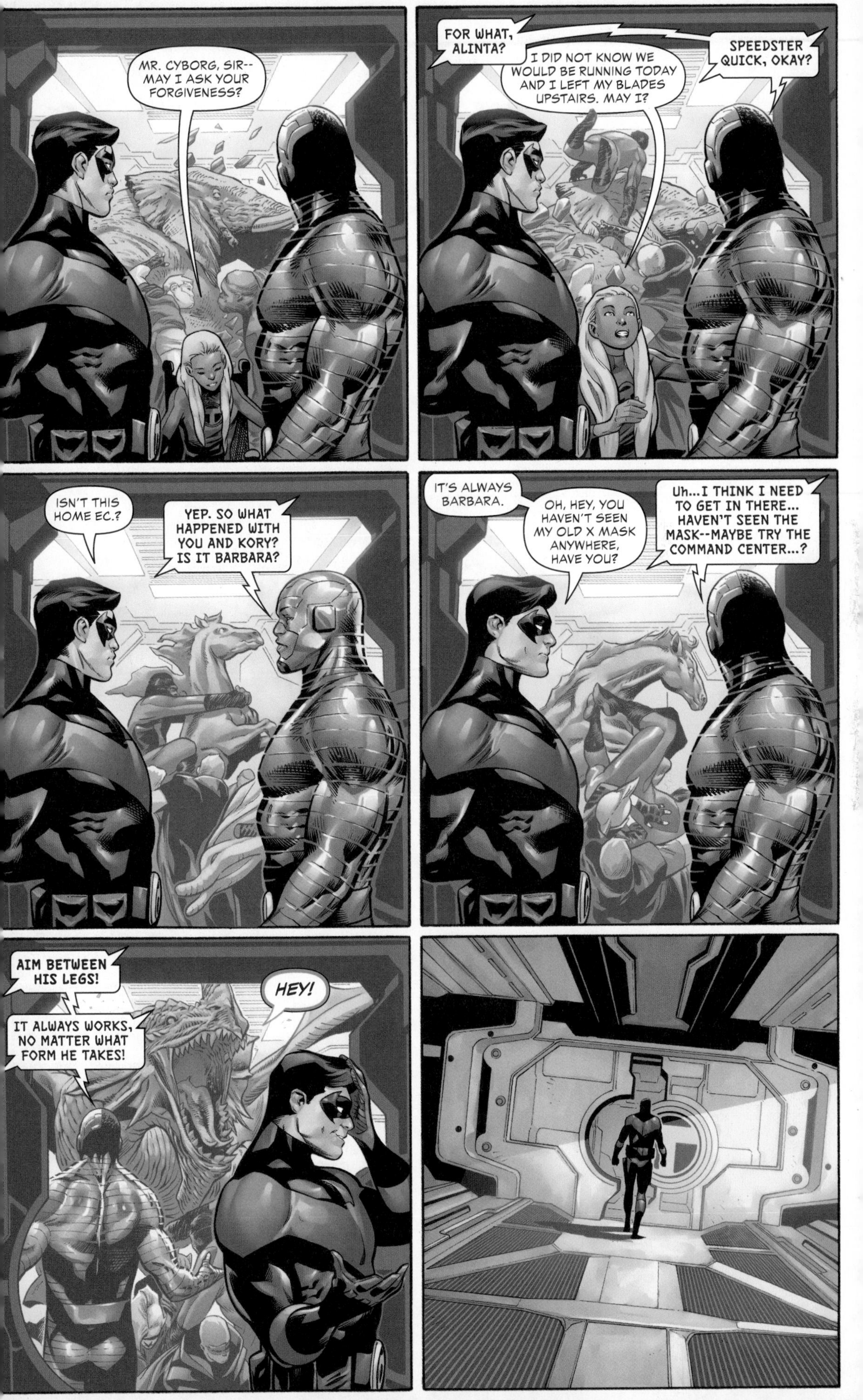
MR. CYBORG, SIR--
MAY I ASK YOUR
FORGIVENESS?
FOR WHAT,
ALINTA?
I DID NOT KNOW WE
WOULD BE RUNNING TODAY
AND I LEFT MY BLADES
UPSTAIRS. MAY I?
SPEEDSTER
QUICK, OKAY?
ISN'T THIS
HOME EC.?
YEP. SO WHAT
HAPPENED WITH
YOU AND KORY?
IS IT BARBARA?
IT'S ALWAYS
BARBARA.
OH, HEY, YOU
HAVEN'T SEEN
MY OLD X MASK
ANYWHERE,
HAVE YOU?
Uh...I THINK I NEED
TO GET IN THERE...
HAVEN'T SEEN THE
MASK--MAYBE TRY THE
COMMAND CENTER...?
AIM BETWEEN
HIS LEGS!
IT ALWAYS WORKS,
NO MATTER WHAT
FORM HE TAKES!
HEY!

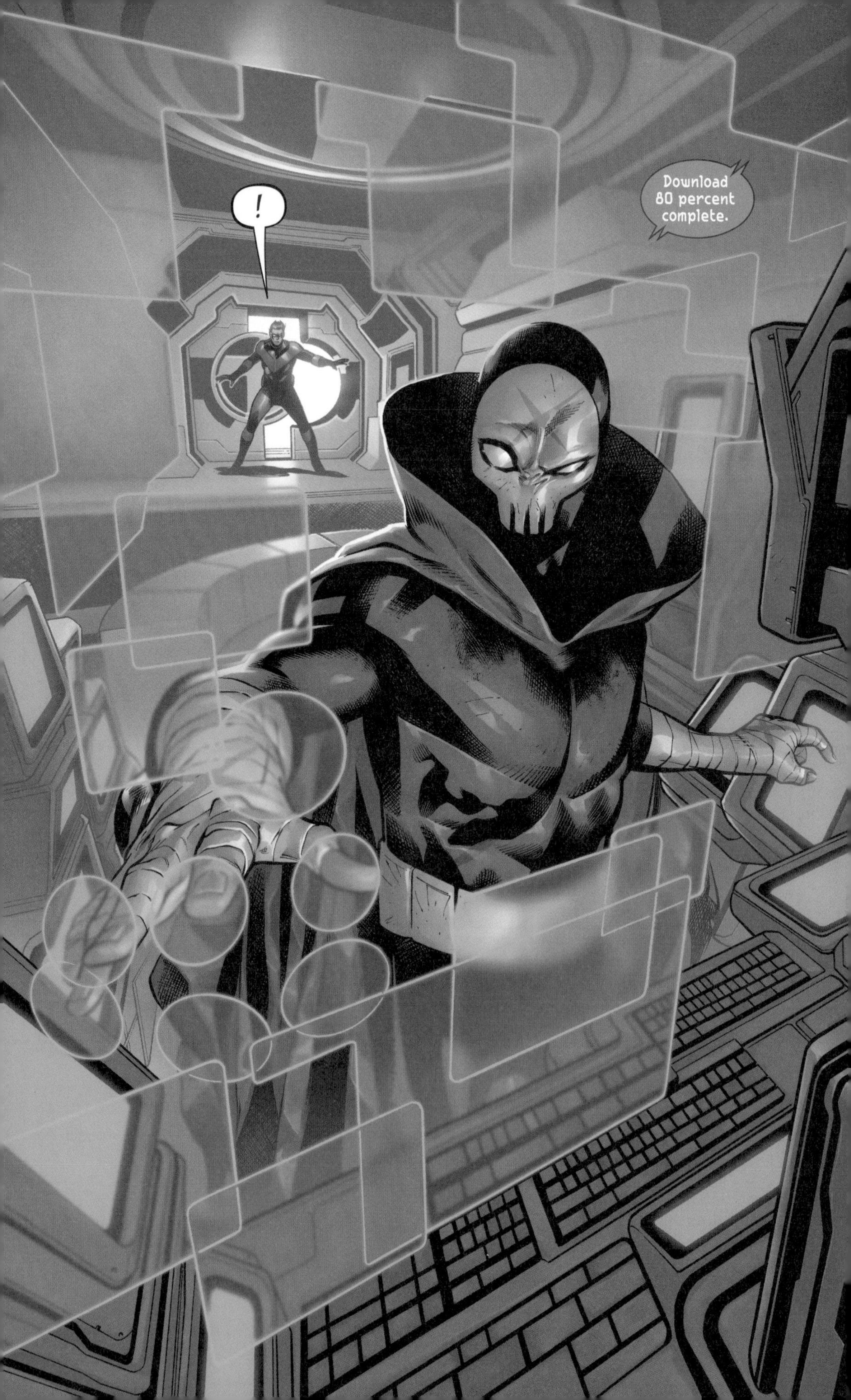
!
Download 80 percent complete.

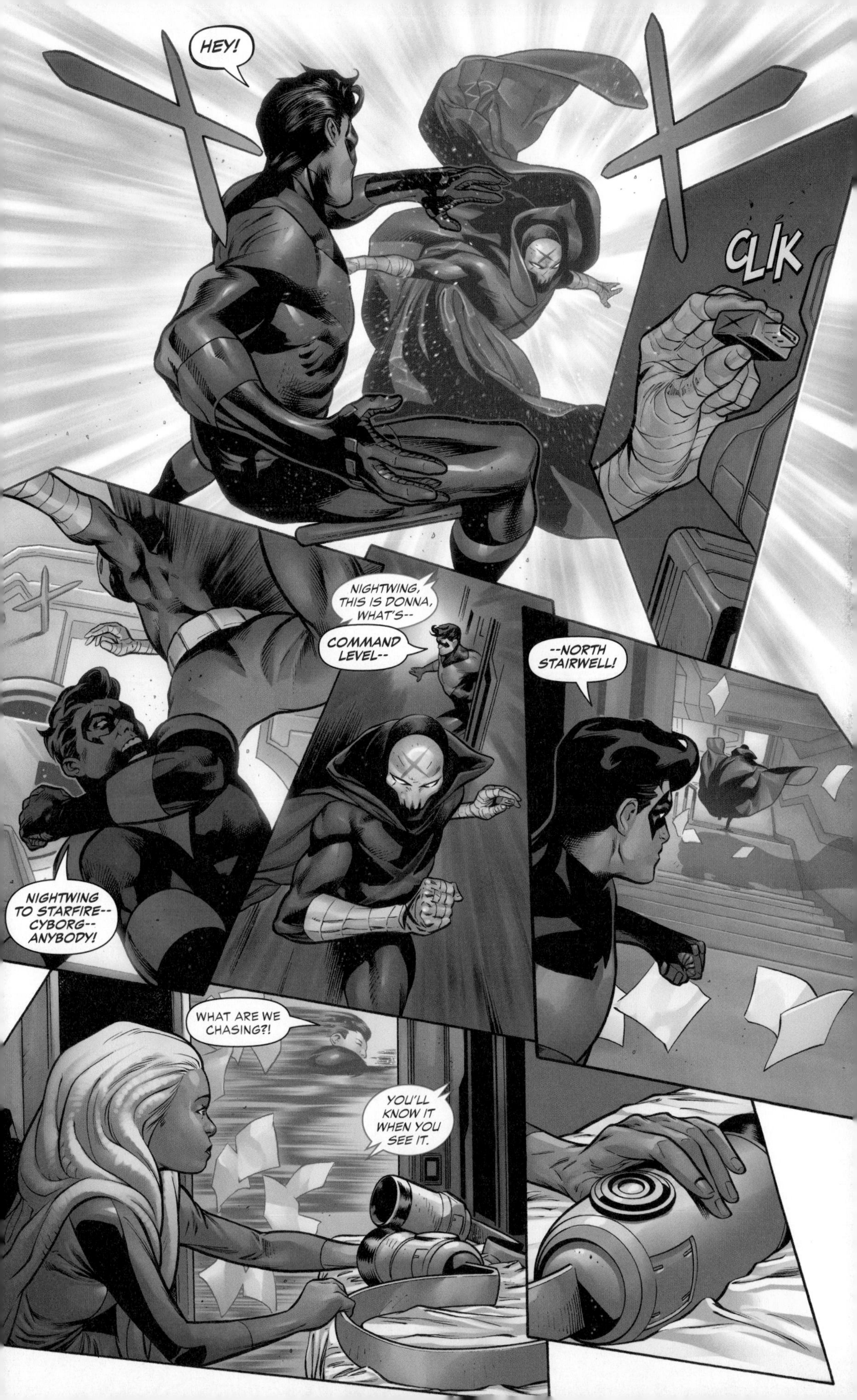
HEY!
CLIK
NIGHTWING, THIS IS DONNA, WHAT'S--
COMMAND LEVEL--
--NORTH STAIRWELL!
NIGHTWING TO STARFIRE-- CYBORG-- ANYBODY!
WHAT ARE WE CHASING?!
YOU'LL KNOW IT WHEN YOU SEE IT.

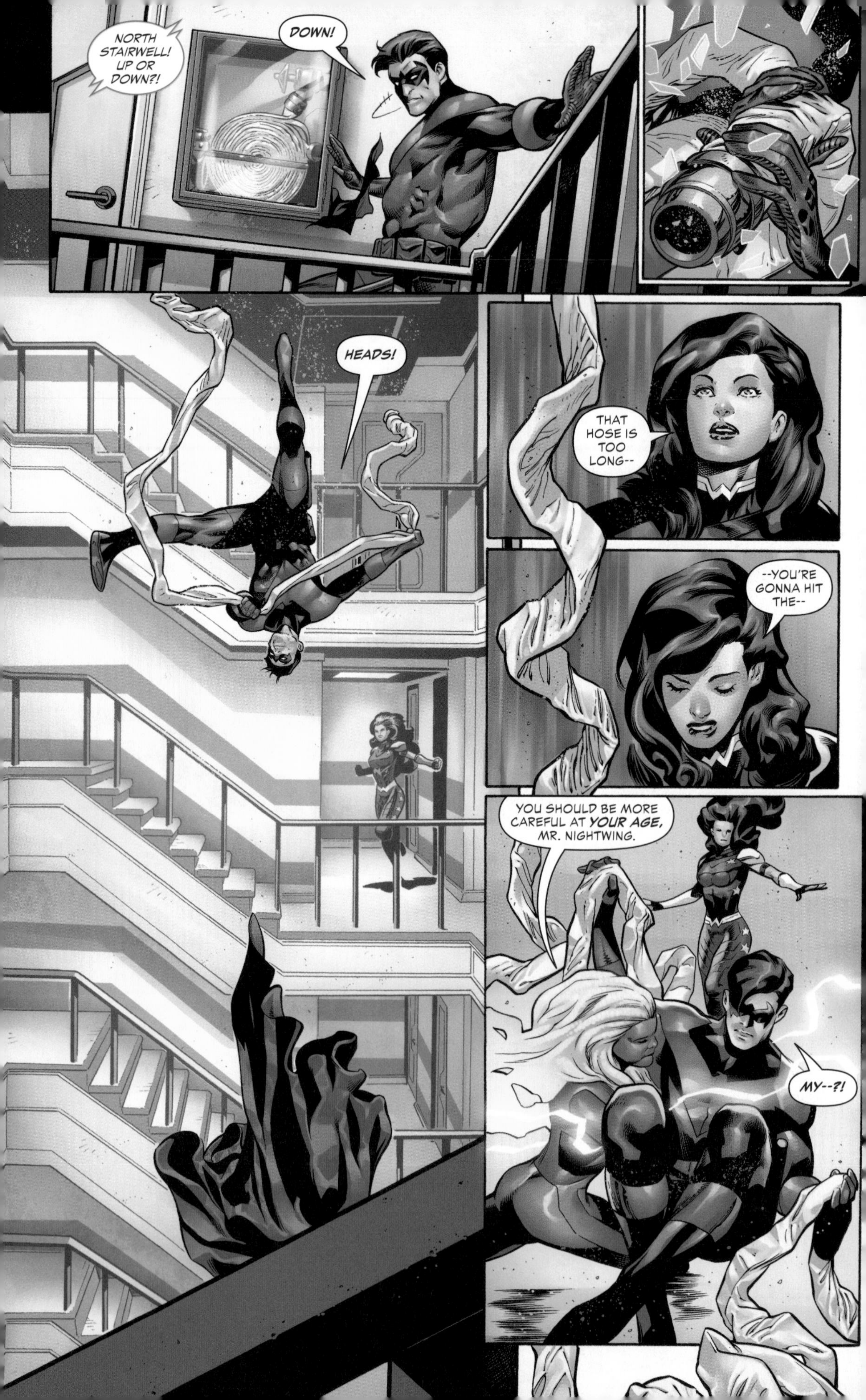
NORTH STAIRWELL! UP OR DOWN?!
DOWN!
HEADS!
THAT HOSE IS TOO LONG--
--YOU'RE GONNA HIT THE--
YOU SHOULD BE MORE CAREFUL AT YOUR AGE, MR. NIGHTWING.
MY--?!

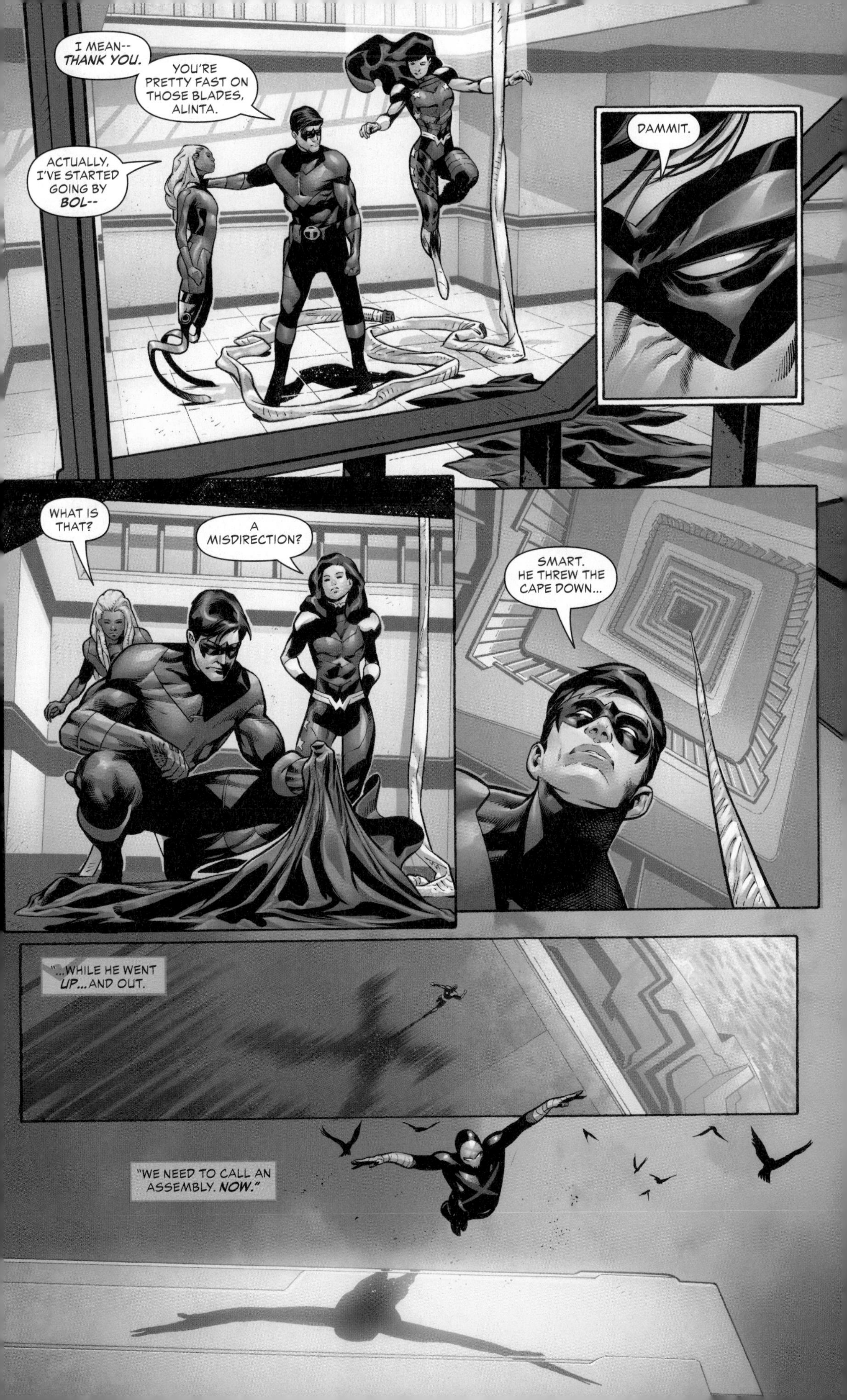
I MEAN-- THANK YOU.
YOU'RE PRETTY FAST ON THOSE BLADES, ALINTA.
ACTUALLY, I'VE STARTED GOING BY BOL--
DAMMIT.
WHAT IS THAT?
A MISDIRECTION?
SMART. HE THREW THE CAPE DOWN...
"...WHILE HE WENT UP...AND OUT.
"WE NEED TO CALL AN ASSEMBLY. NOW."

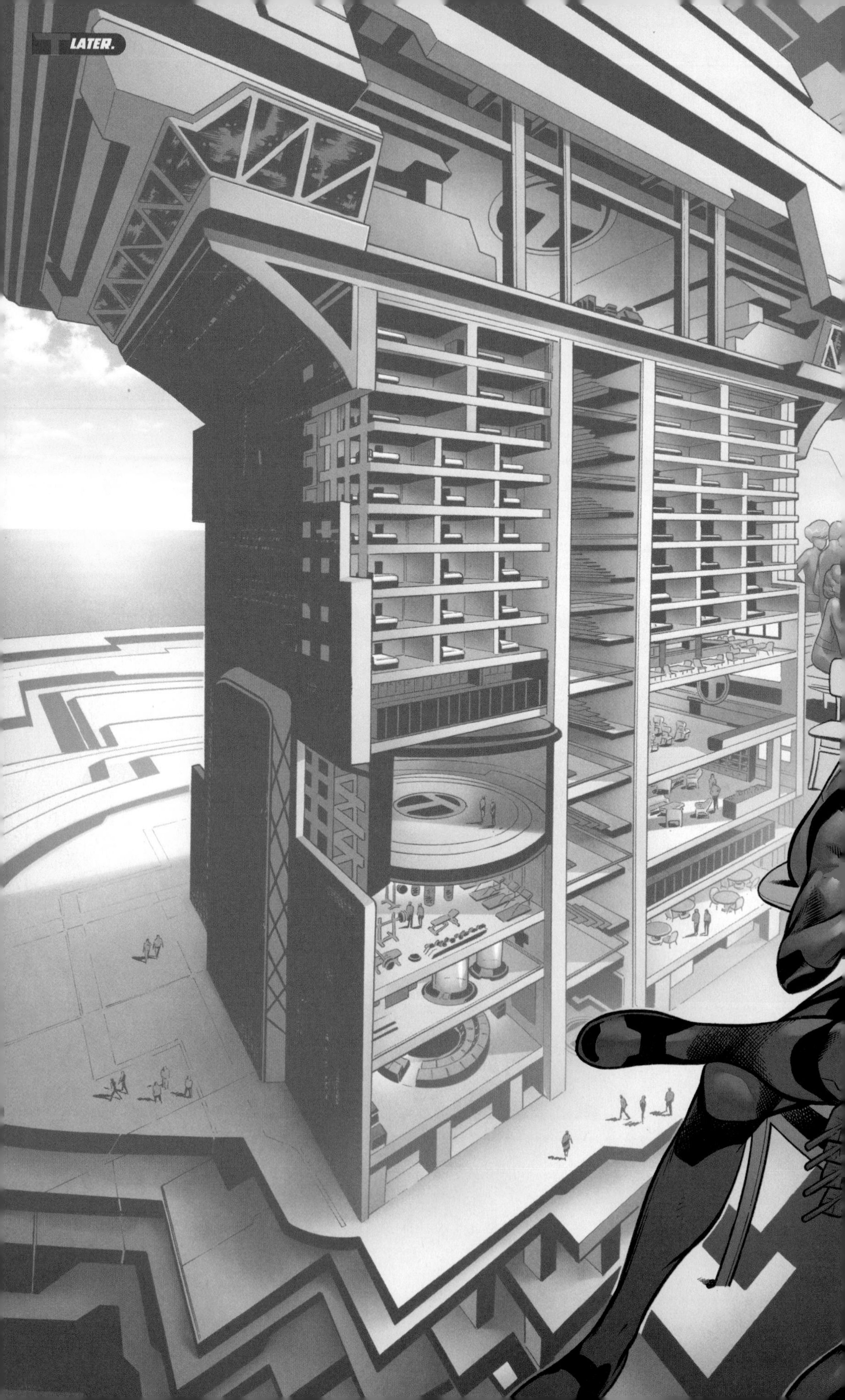
LATER.

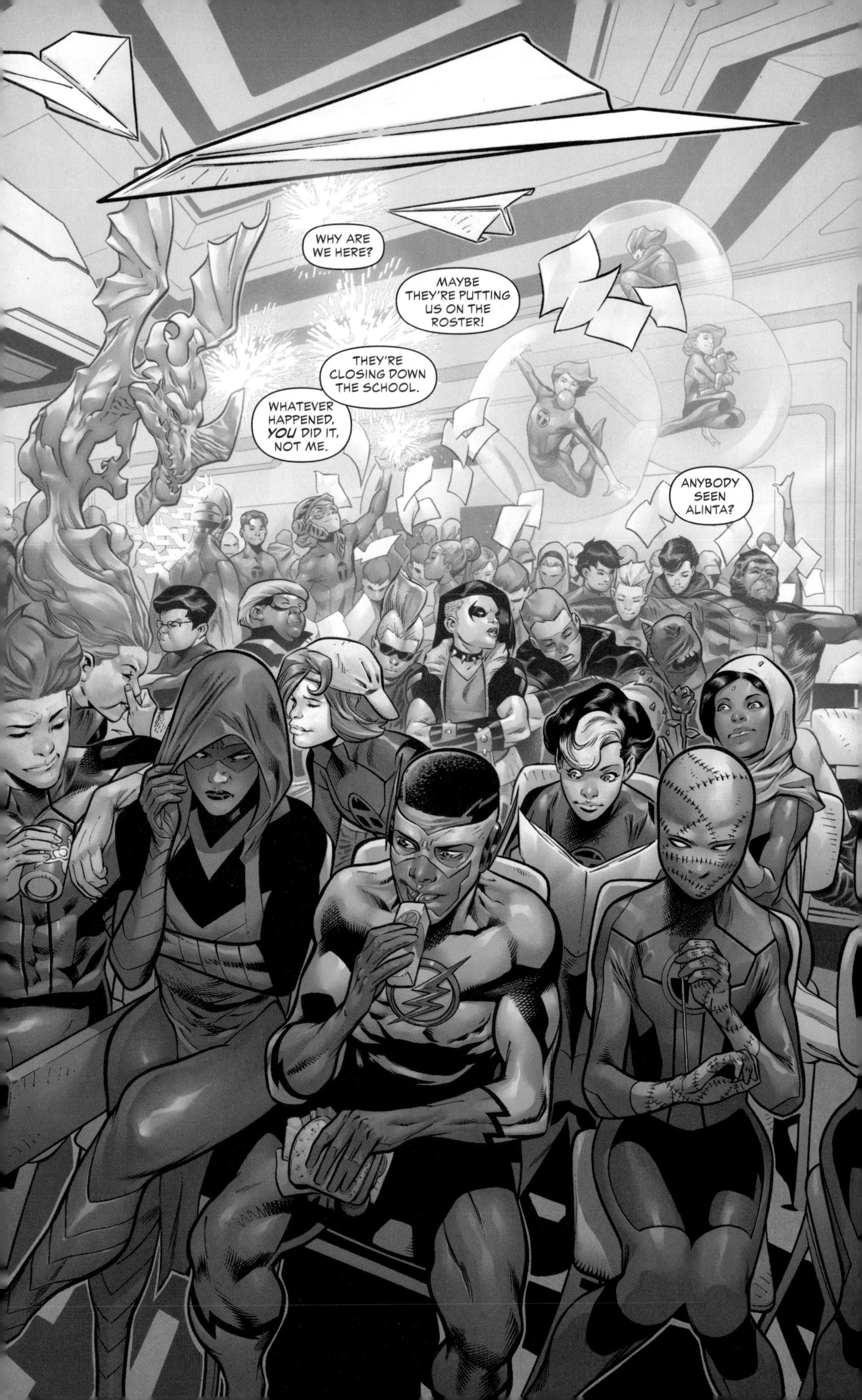
WHY ARE WE HERE?
MAYBE THEY'RE PUTTING US ON THE ROSTER!
THEY'RE CLOSING DOWN THE SCHOOL.
WHATEVER HAPPENED, ***YOU*** DID IT, NOT ME.
ANYBODY SEEN ALINTA?

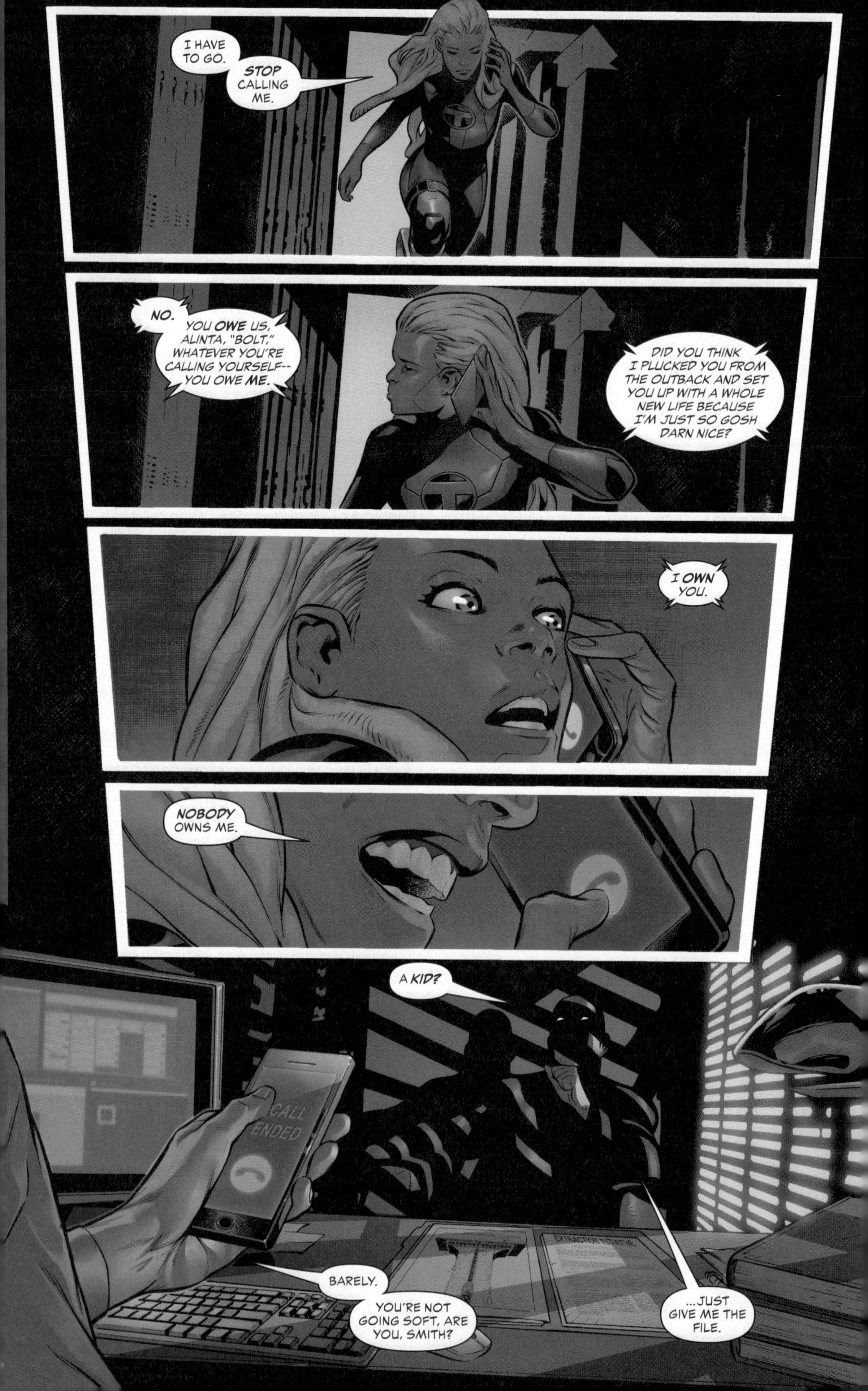

I HAVE TO GO.
STOP CALLING ME.
NO.
YOU OWE US, ALINTA, "BOLT," WHATEVER YOU'RE CALLING YOURSELF-- YOU OWE ME.
DID YOU THINK I PLUCKED YOU FROM THE OUTBACK AND SET YOU UP WITH A WHOLE NEW LIFE BECAUSE I'M JUST SO GOSH DARN NICE?
I OWN YOU.
NOBODY OWNS ME.
A KID?
CALL ENDED
BARELY.
YOU'RE NOT GOING SOFT, ARE YOU, SMITH?
...JUST GIVE ME THE FILE.

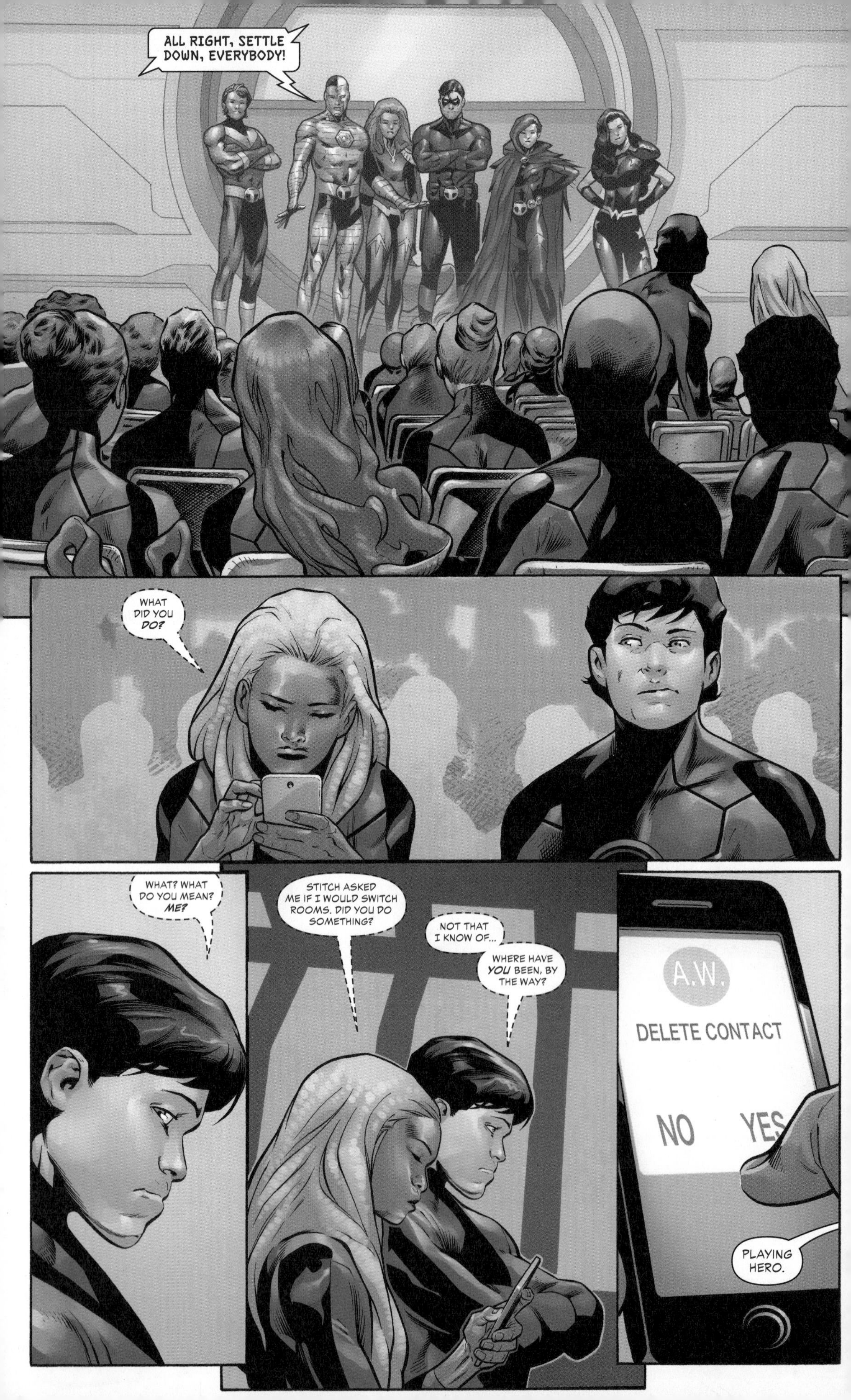
ALL RIGHT, SETTLE DOWN, EVERYBODY!
WHAT DID YOU DO?
WHAT? WHAT DO YOU MEAN? ME?
STITCH ASKED ME IF I WOULD SWITCH ROOMS. DID YOU DO SOMETHING?
NOT THAT I KNOW OF...
WHERE HAVE YOU BEEN, BY THE WAY?
A.W.
DELETE CONTACT
NO
YES
PLAYING HERO.

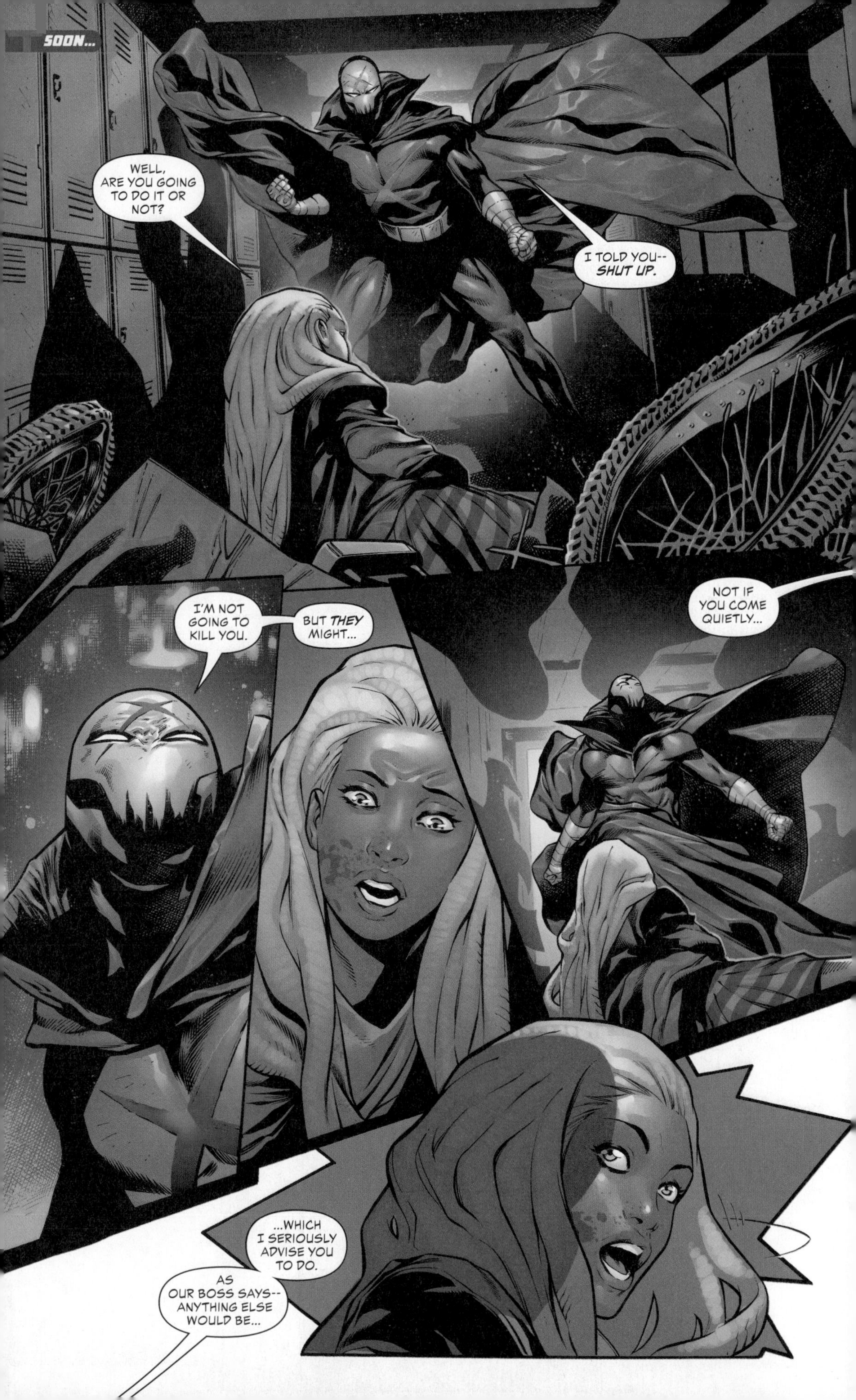
SOON...
WELL, ARE YOU GOING TO DO IT OR NOT?
I TOLD YOU-- SHUT UP.
I'M NOT GOING TO KILL YOU.
BUT THEY MIGHT...
NOT IF YOU COME QUIETLY...
...WHICH I SERIOUSLY ADVISE YOU TO DO.
AS OUR BOSS SAYS-- ANYTHING ELSE WOULD BE...

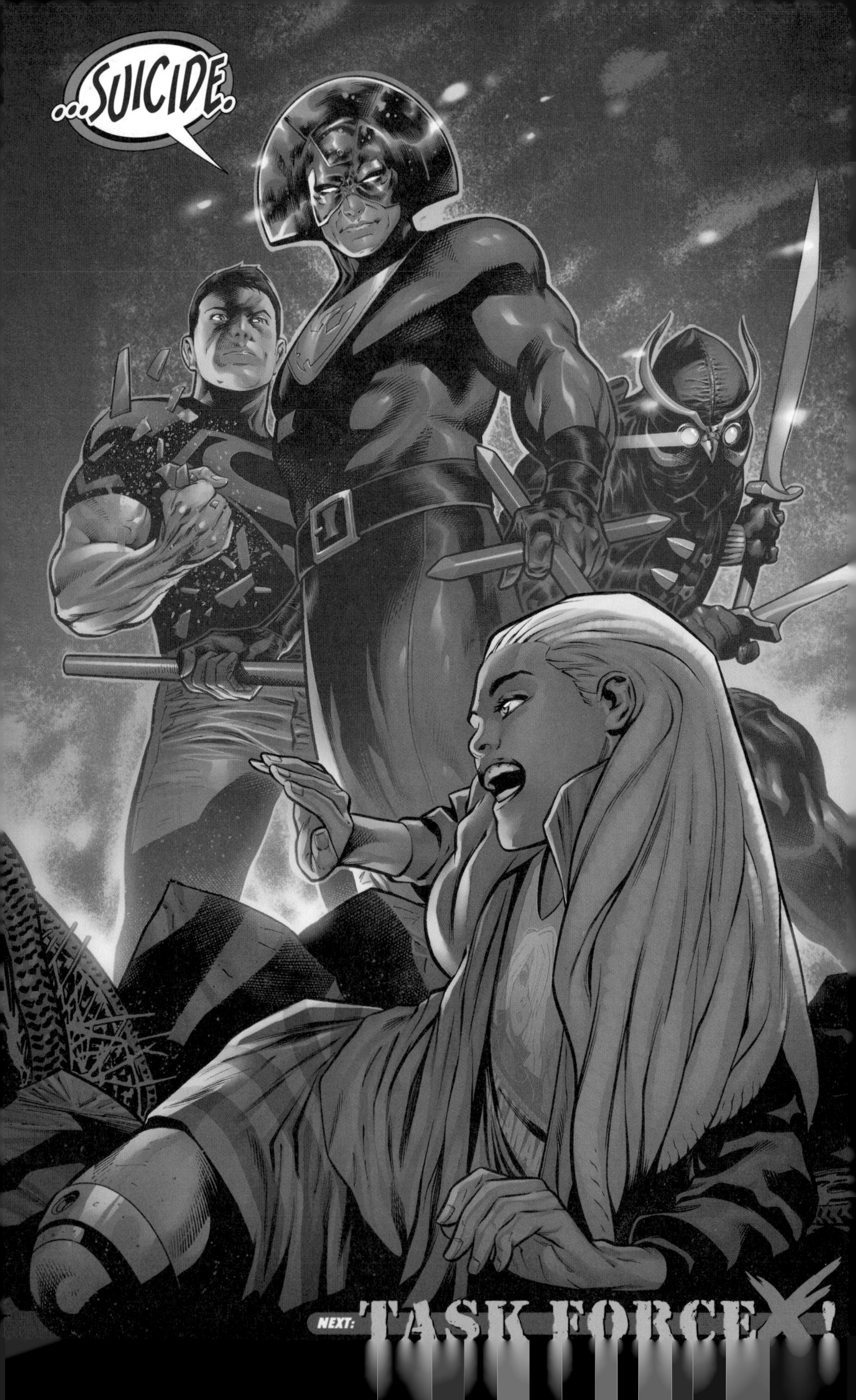
...SUICIDE...
NEXT: TASK FORCE X!

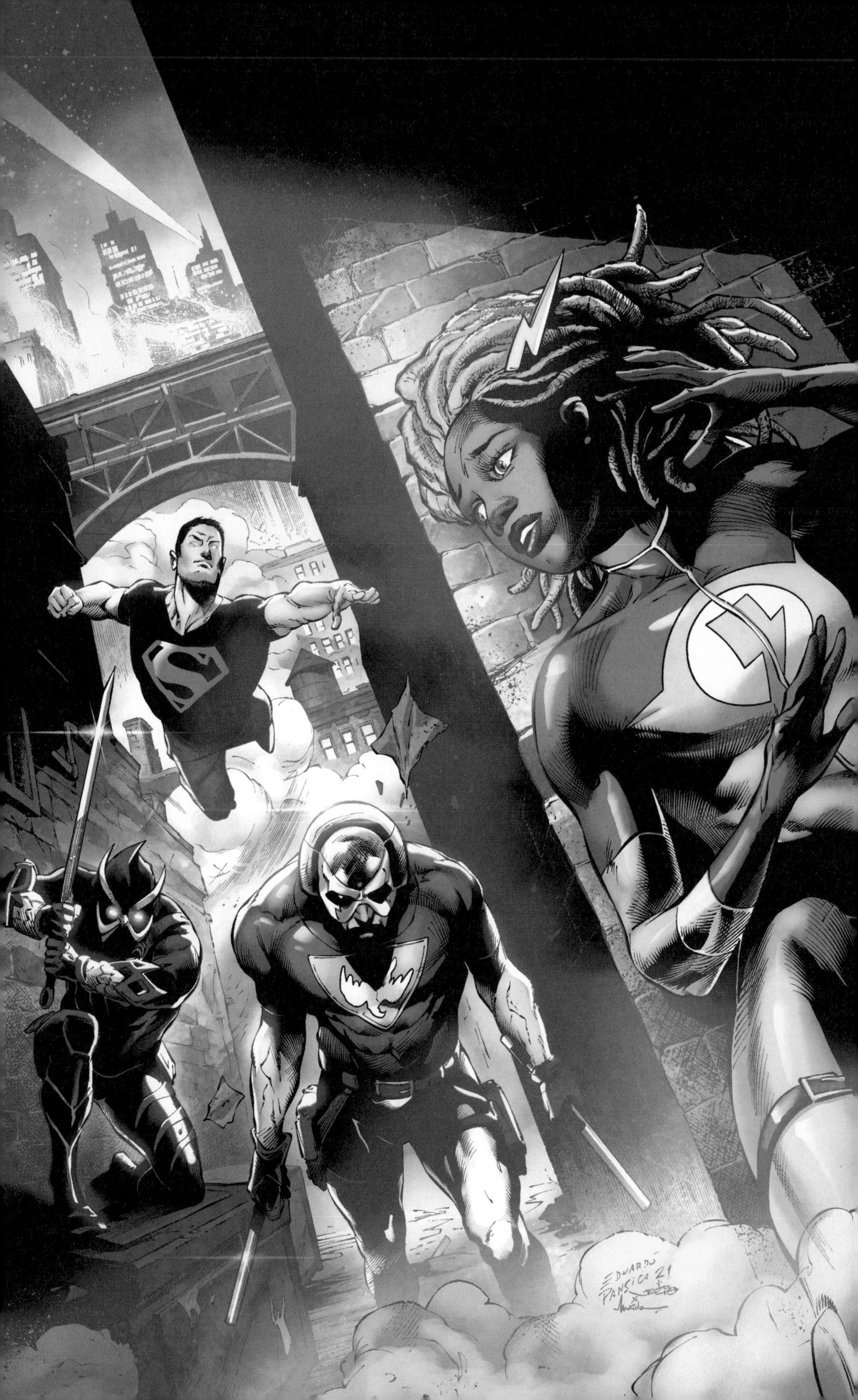
EDUARDO
PANSICA 21

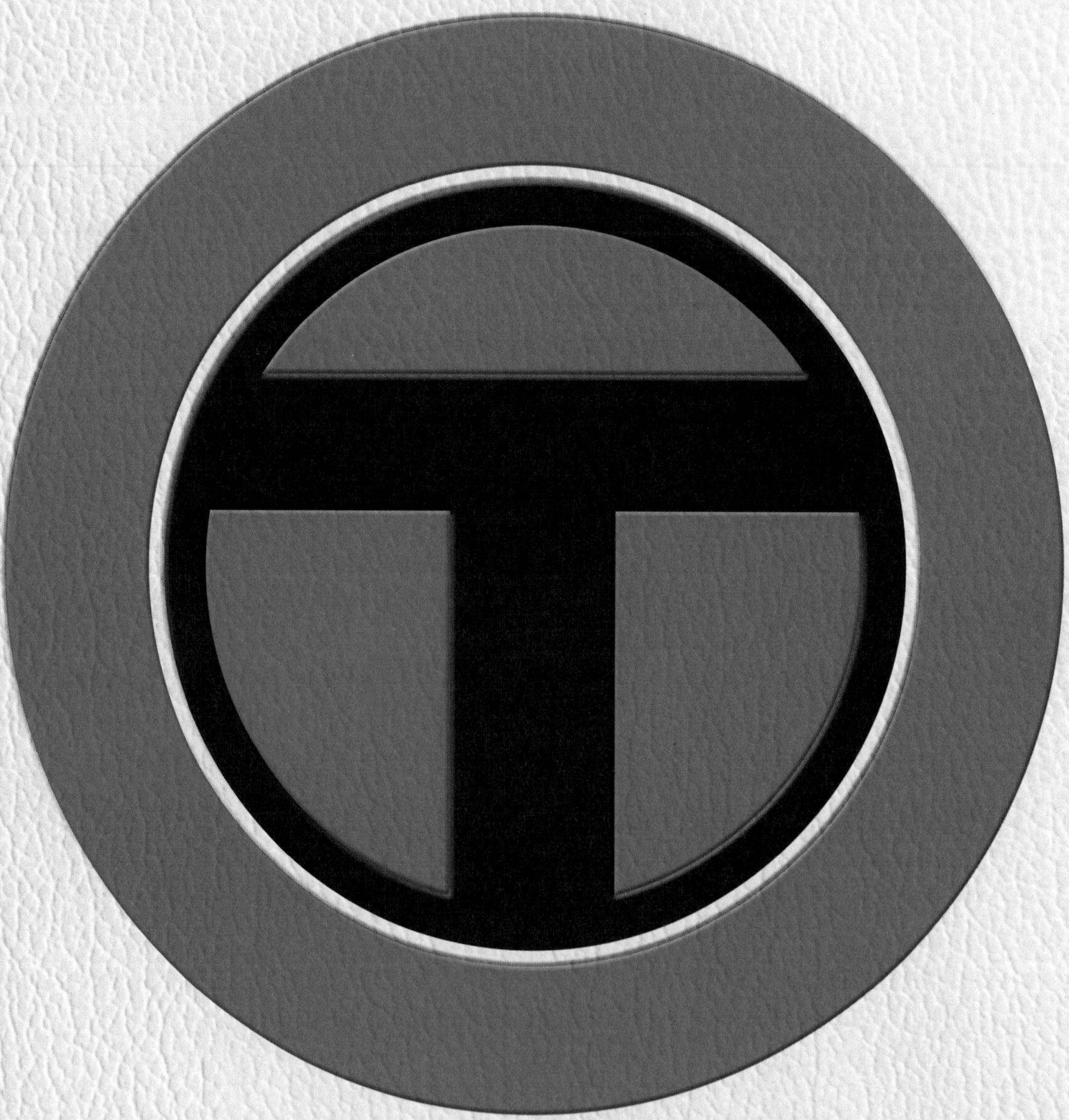

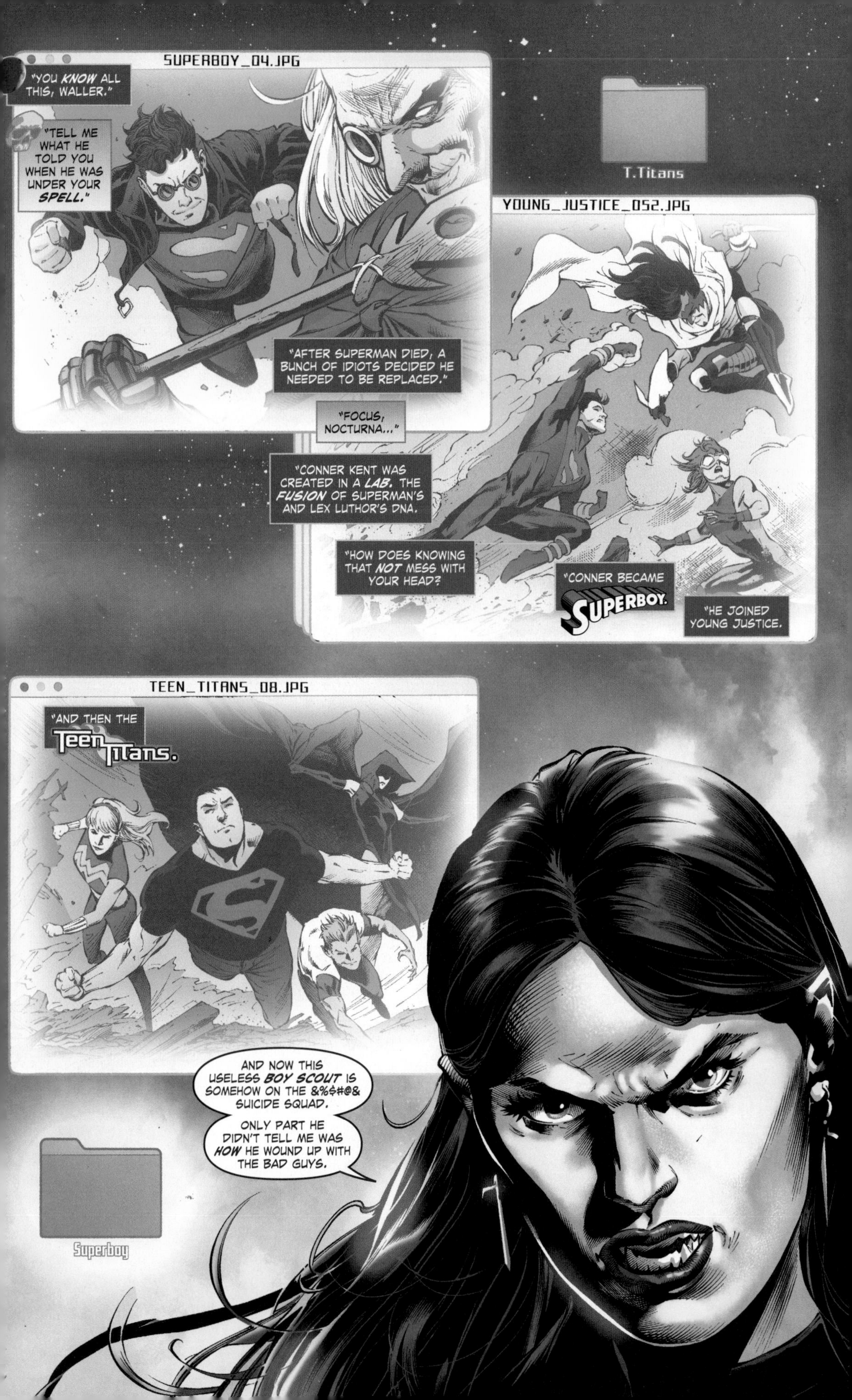
SUPERBOY_04.JPG
"YOU KNOW ALL THIS, WALLER."
"TELL ME WHAT HE TOLD YOU WHEN HE WAS UNDER YOUR SPELL."
"AFTER SUPERMAN DIED, A BUNCH OF IDIOTS DECIDED HE NEEDED TO BE REPLACED."
T.Titans
YOUNG_JUSTICE_052.JPG
"FOCUS, NOCTURNA..."
"CONNER KENT WAS CREATED IN A LAB. THE FUSION OF SUPERMAN'S AND LEX LUTHOR'S DNA.
"HOW DOES KNOWING THAT NOT MESS WITH YOUR HEAD?
"CONNER BECAME SUPERBOY.
"HE JOINED YOUNG JUSTICE.
TEEN_TITANS_08.JPG
"AND THEN THE TEEN TITANS.
AND NOW THIS USELESS BOY SCOUT IS SOMEHOW ON THE &%$#@& SUICIDE SQUAD.
ONLY PART HE DIDN'T TELL ME WAS HOW HE WOUND UP WITH THE BAD GUYS.
Superboy

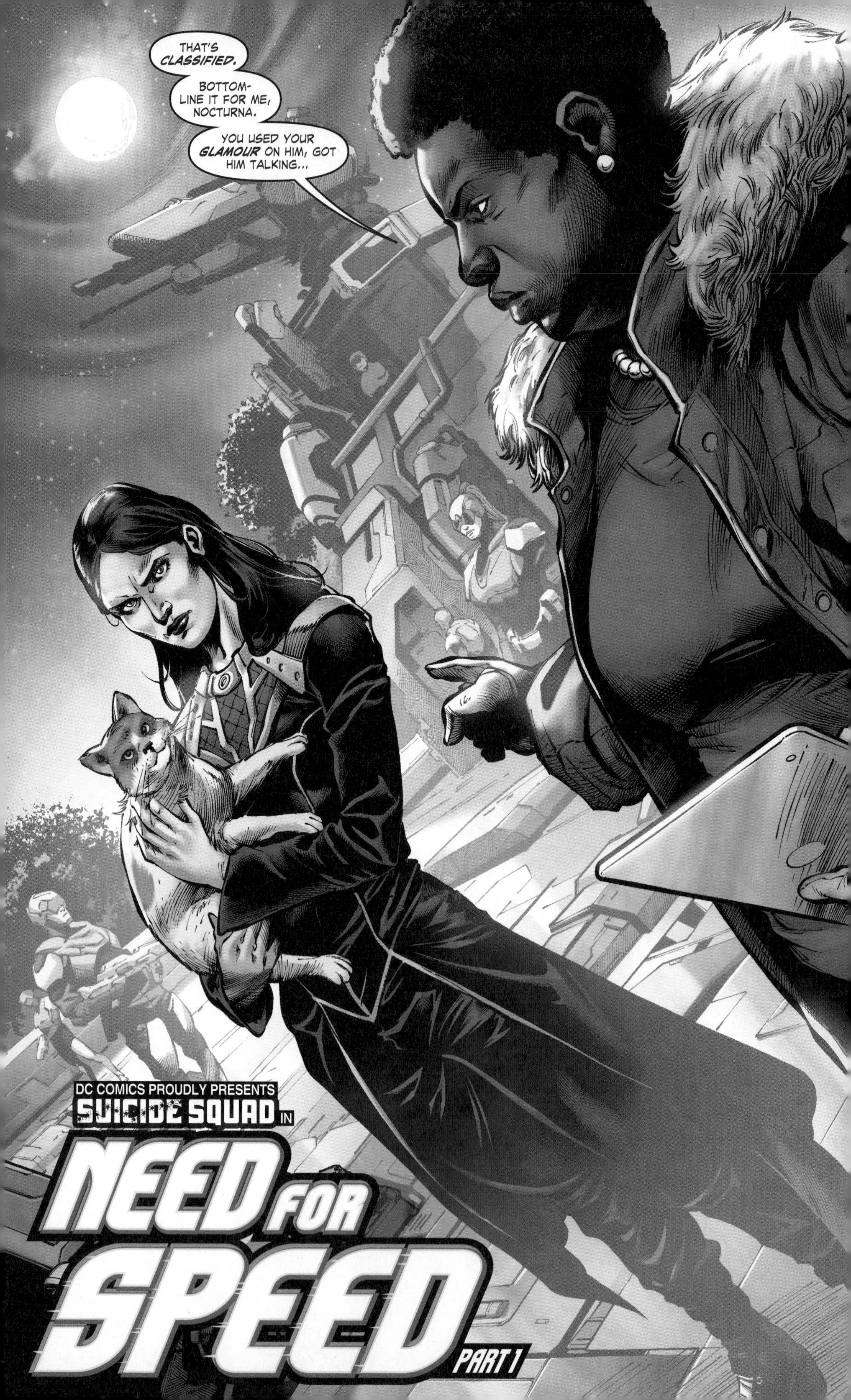
THAT'S *CLASSIFIED.*
BOTTOM-LINE IT FOR ME, NOCTURNA.
YOU USED YOUR *GLAMOUR* ON HIM, GOT HIM TALKING...
DC COMICS PROUDLY PRESENTS
SUICIDE SQUAD IN
NEED FOR SPEED
PART 1

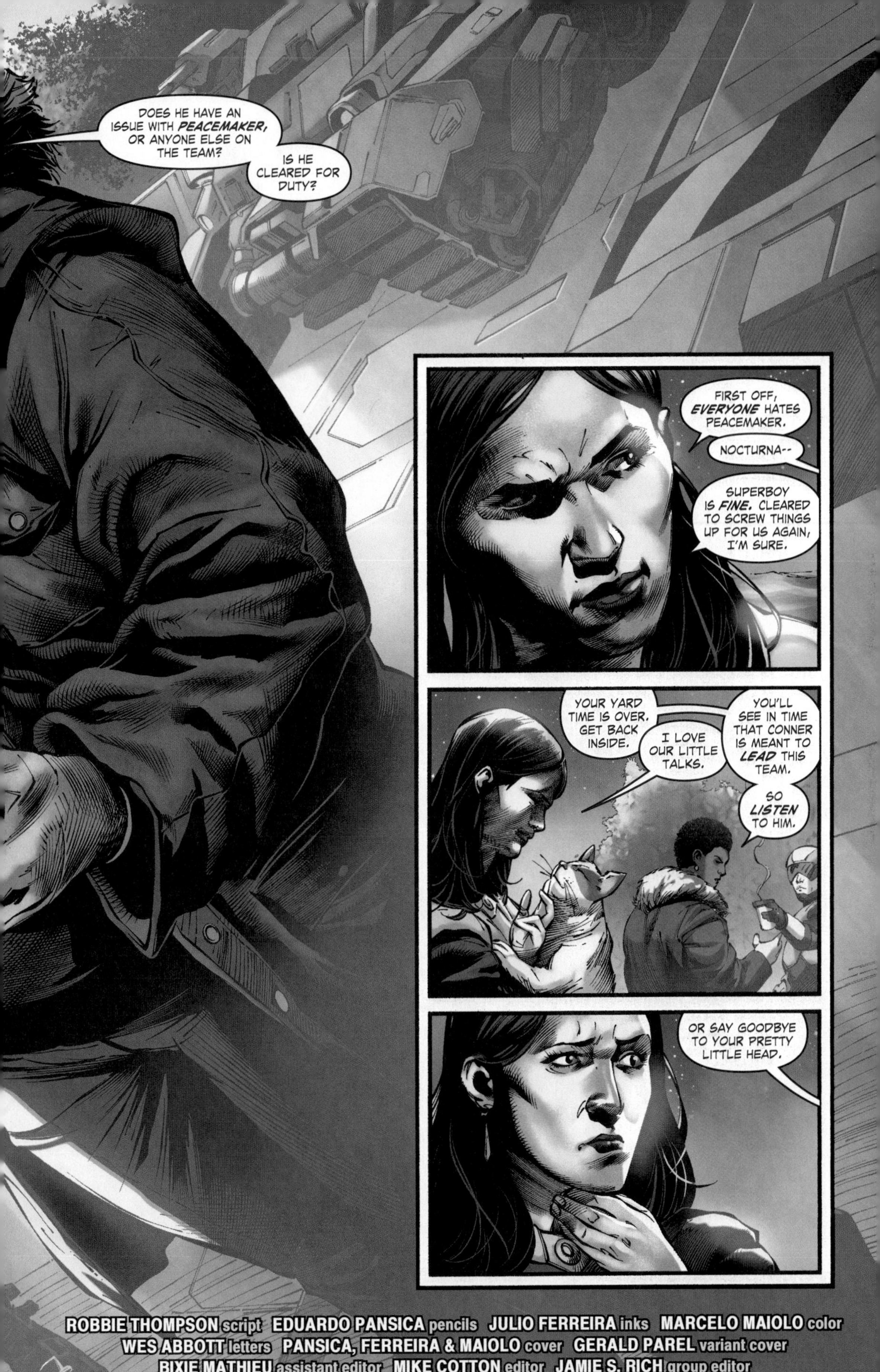
DOES HE HAVE AN ISSUE WITH PEACEMAKER, OR ANYONE ELSE ON THE TEAM?
IS HE CLEARED FOR DUTY?
FIRST OFF, EVERYONE HATES PEACEMAKER.
NOCTURNA--
SUPERBOY IS FINE. CLEARED TO SCREW THINGS UP FOR US AGAIN, I'M SURE.
YOUR YARD TIME IS OVER. GET BACK INSIDE.
I LOVE OUR LITTLE TALKS.
YOU'LL SEE IN TIME THAT CONNER IS MEANT TO LEAD THIS TEAM.
SO LISTEN TO HIM.
OR SAY GOODBYE TO YOUR PRETTY LITTLE HEAD.

ROBBIE THOMPSON script EDUARDO PANSICA pencils JULIO FERREIRA inks MARCELO MAIOLO color
WES ABBOTT letters PANSICA, FERREIRA & MAIOLO cover GERALD PAREL variant cover
BIXIE MATHIEU assistant editor MIKE COTTON editor JAMIE S. RICH group editor
Superboy created by JERRY SIEGEL. By special arrangement with the Jerry Siegel family.

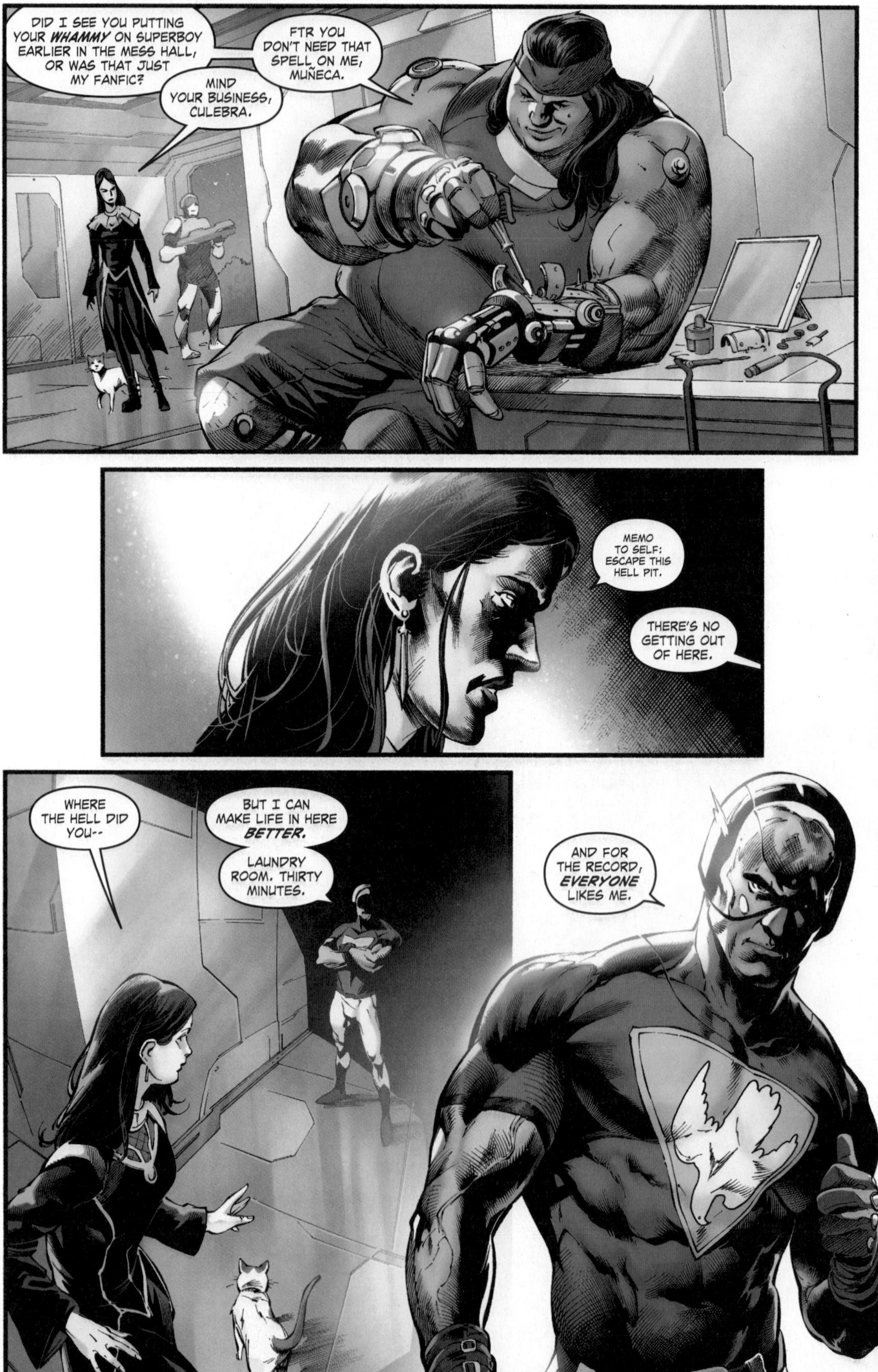
DID I SEE YOU PUTTING YOUR *WHAMMY* ON SUPERBOY EARLIER IN THE MESS HALL, OR WAS THAT JUST MY FANFIC?
FTR YOU DON'T NEED THAT SPELL ON ME, MUÑECA.
MIND YOUR BUSINESS, CULEBRA.
MEMO TO SELF: ESCAPE THIS HELL PIT.
THERE'S NO GETTING OUT OF HERE.
WHERE THE HELL DID YOU--
BUT I CAN MAKE LIFE IN HERE *BETTER.*
LAUNDRY ROOM. THIRTY MINUTES.
AND FOR THE RECORD, *EVERYONE* LIKES ME.

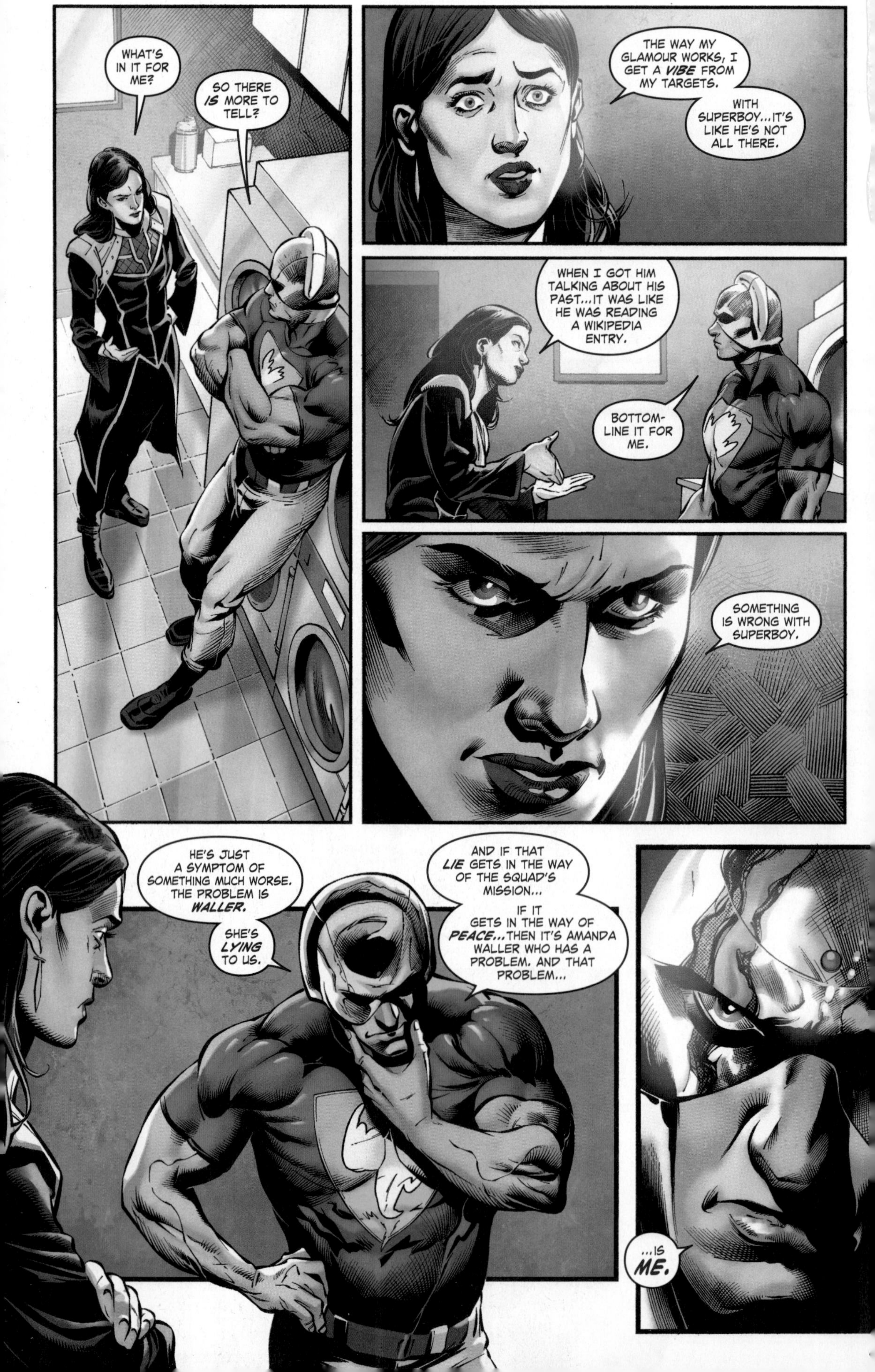
WHAT'S IN IT FOR ME?
SO THERE *IS* MORE TO TELL?
THE WAY MY GLAMOUR WORKS, I GET A *VIBE* FROM MY TARGETS.
WITH SUPERBOY...IT'S LIKE HE'S NOT ALL THERE.
WHEN I GOT HIM TALKING ABOUT HIS PAST...IT WAS LIKE HE WAS READING A WIKIPEDIA ENTRY.
BOTTOM-LINE IT FOR ME.
SOMETHING IS WRONG WITH SUPERBOY.
HE'S JUST A SYMPTOM OF SOMETHING MUCH WORSE. THE PROBLEM IS *WALLER.*
SHE'S *LYING* TO US.
AND IF THAT *LIE* GETS IN THE WAY OF THE SQUAD'S MISSION...
IF IT GETS IN THE WAY OF *PEACE...*THEN IT'S AMANDA WALLER WHO HAS A PROBLEM. AND THAT PROBLEM...
...IS *ME.*

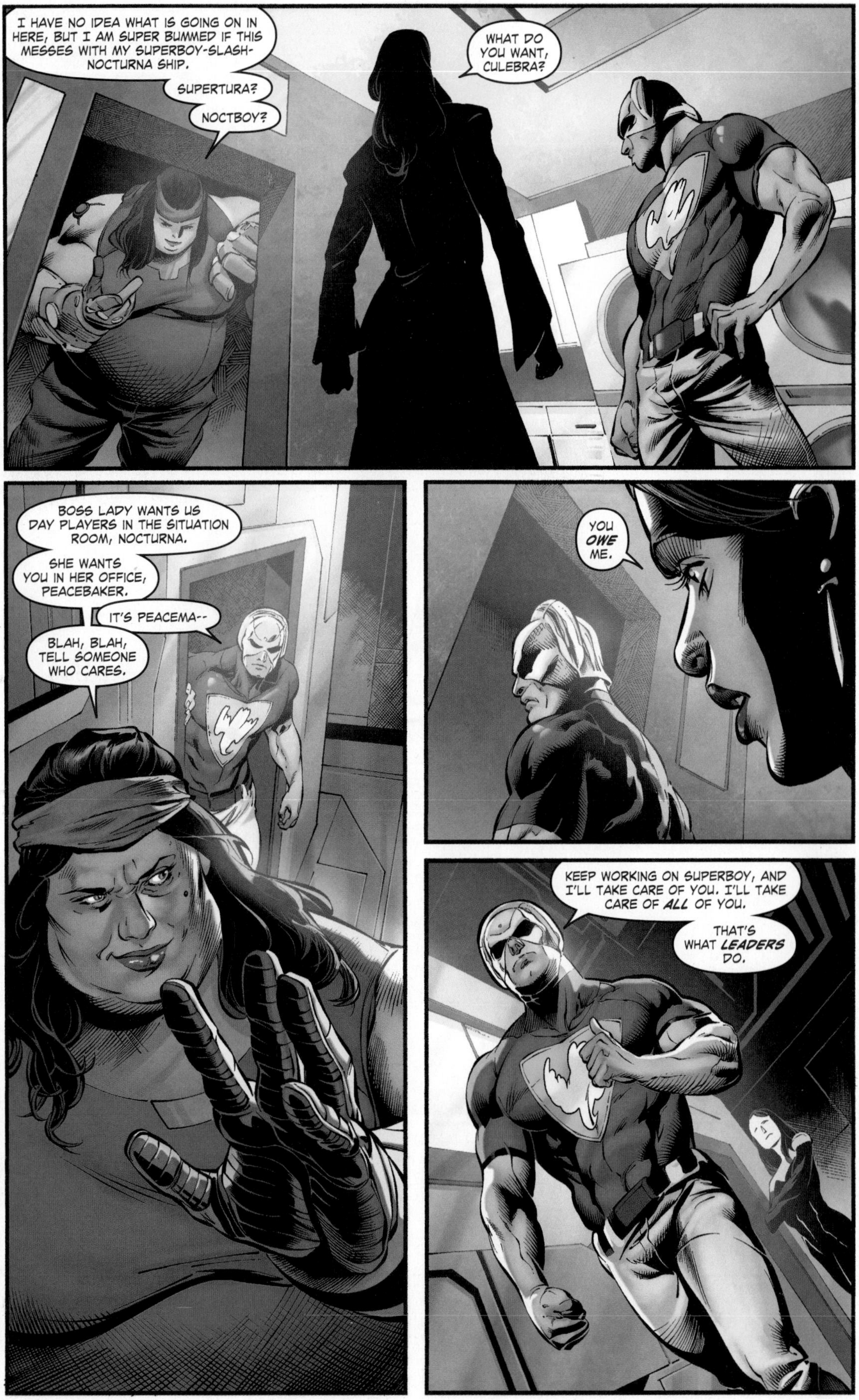
I HAVE NO IDEA WHAT IS GOING ON IN HERE, BUT I AM SUPER BUMMED IF THIS MESSES WITH MY SUPERBOY-SLASH-NOCTURNA SHIP.
SUPERTURA?
NOCTBOY?
WHAT DO YOU WANT, CULEBRA?
BOSS LADY WANTS US DAY PLAYERS IN THE SITUATION ROOM, NOCTURNA.
SHE WANTS YOU IN HER OFFICE, PEACEBAKER.
IT'S PEACEMA--
BLAH, BLAH, TELL SOMEONE WHO CARES.
YOU *OWE* ME.
KEEP WORKING ON SUPERBOY, AND I'LL TAKE CARE OF YOU. I'LL TAKE CARE OF *ALL* OF YOU.
THAT'S WHAT *LEADERS* DO.

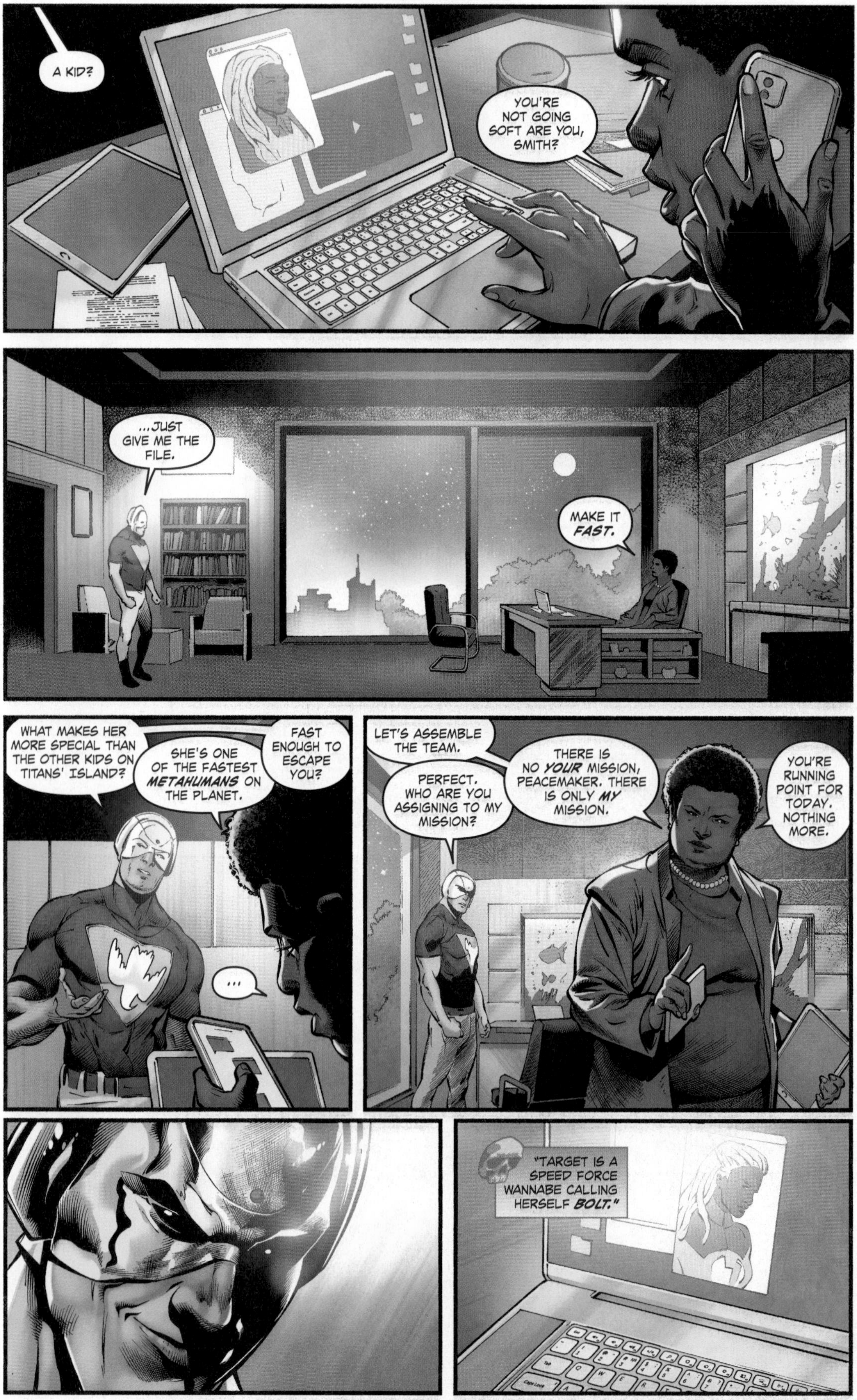
A KID?
YOU'RE NOT GOING SOFT ARE YOU, SMITH?
...JUST GIVE ME THE FILE.
MAKE IT *FAST.*
WHAT MAKES HER MORE SPECIAL THAN THE OTHER KIDS ON TITANS' ISLAND?
SHE'S ONE OF THE FASTEST *METAHUMANS* ON THE PLANET.
FAST ENOUGH TO ESCAPE YOU?
...
LET'S ASSEMBLE THE TEAM.
PERFECT. WHO ARE YOU ASSIGNING TO MY MISSION?
THERE IS NO *YOUR* MISSION, PEACEMAKER. THERE IS ONLY *MY* MISSION.
YOU'RE RUNNING POINT FOR TODAY. NOTHING MORE.
"TARGET IS A SPEED FORCE WANNABE CALLING HERSELF *BOLT.*"

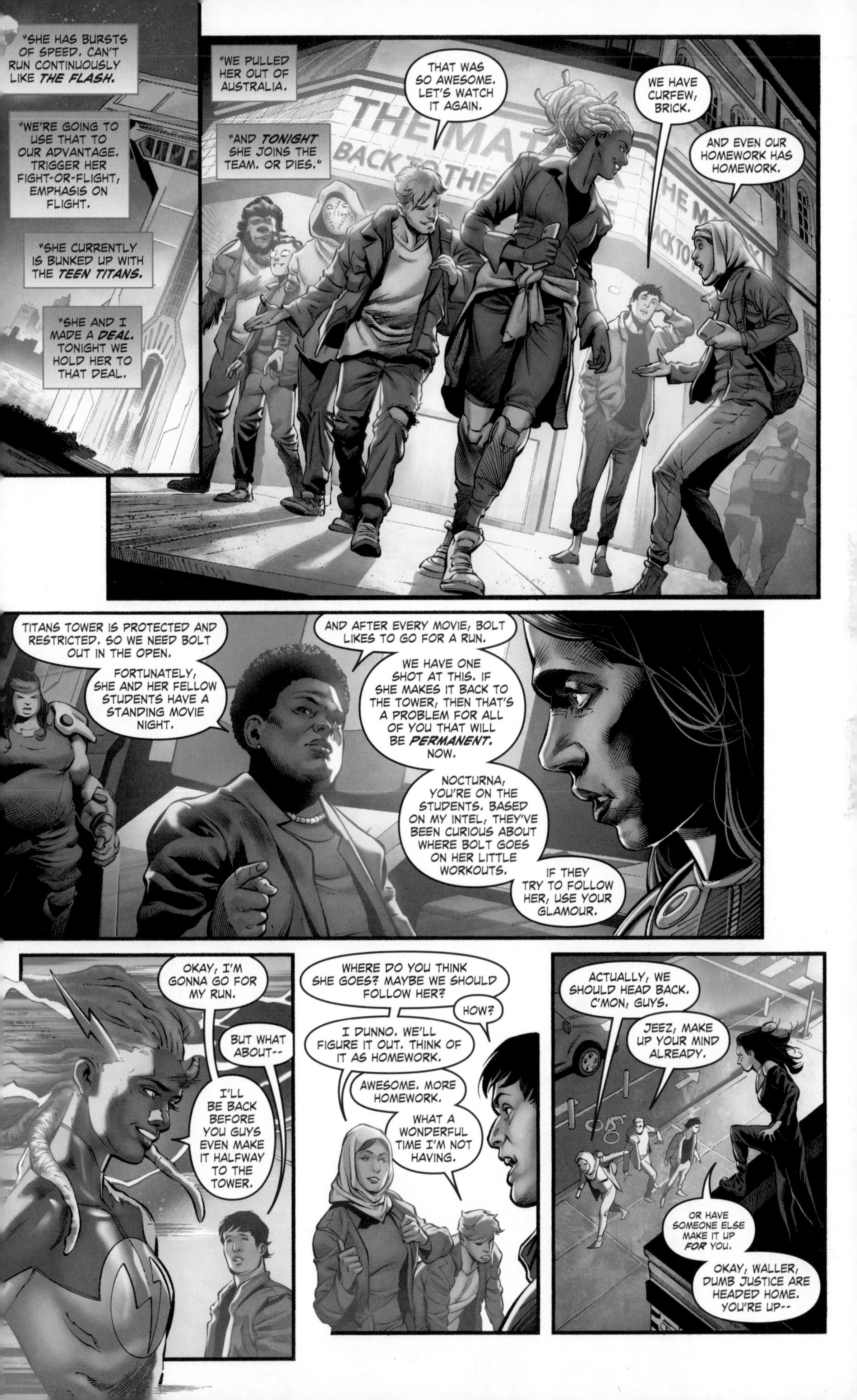

"SHE HAS BURSTS OF SPEED. CAN'T RUN CONTINUOUSLY LIKE THE FLASH.
"WE'RE GOING TO USE THAT TO OUR ADVANTAGE. TRIGGER HER FIGHT-OR-FLIGHT, EMPHASIS ON FLIGHT.
"SHE CURRENTLY IS BUNKED UP WITH THE TEEN TITANS.
"SHE AND I MADE A DEAL. TONIGHT WE HOLD HER TO THAT DEAL.
"WE PULLED HER OUT OF AUSTRALIA.
"AND TONIGHT SHE JOINS THE TEAM. OR DIES."
THAT WAS SO AWESOME. LET'S WATCH IT AGAIN.
WE HAVE CURFEW, BRICK.
AND EVEN OUR HOMEWORK HAS HOMEWORK.
TITANS TOWER IS PROTECTED AND RESTRICTED. SO WE NEED BOLT OUT IN THE OPEN.
FORTUNATELY, SHE AND HER FELLOW STUDENTS HAVE A STANDING MOVIE NIGHT.
AND AFTER EVERY MOVIE, BOLT LIKES TO GO FOR A RUN.
WE HAVE ONE SHOT AT THIS. IF SHE MAKES IT BACK TO THE TOWER, THEN THAT'S A PROBLEM FOR ALL OF YOU THAT WILL BE PERMANENT. NOW.
NOCTURNA, YOU'RE ON THE STUDENTS. BASED ON MY INTEL, THEY'VE BEEN CURIOUS ABOUT WHERE BOLT GOES ON HER LITTLE WORKOUTS.
IF THEY TRY TO FOLLOW HER, USE YOUR GLAMOUR.
OKAY, I'M GONNA GO FOR MY RUN.
BUT WHAT ABOUT--
I'LL BE BACK BEFORE YOU GUYS EVEN MAKE IT HALFWAY TO THE TOWER.
WHERE DO YOU THINK SHE GOES? MAYBE WE SHOULD FOLLOW HER?
HOW?
I DUNNO. WE'LL FIGURE IT OUT. THINK OF IT AS HOMEWORK.
AWESOME. MORE HOMEWORK.
WHAT A WONDERFUL TIME I'M NOT HAVING.
ACTUALLY, WE SHOULD HEAD BACK. C'MON, GUYS.
JEEZ, MAKE UP YOUR MIND ALREADY.
OR HAVE SOMEONE ELSE MAKE IT UP FOR YOU.
OKAY, WALLER, DUMB JUSTICE ARE HEADED HOME. YOU'RE UP--

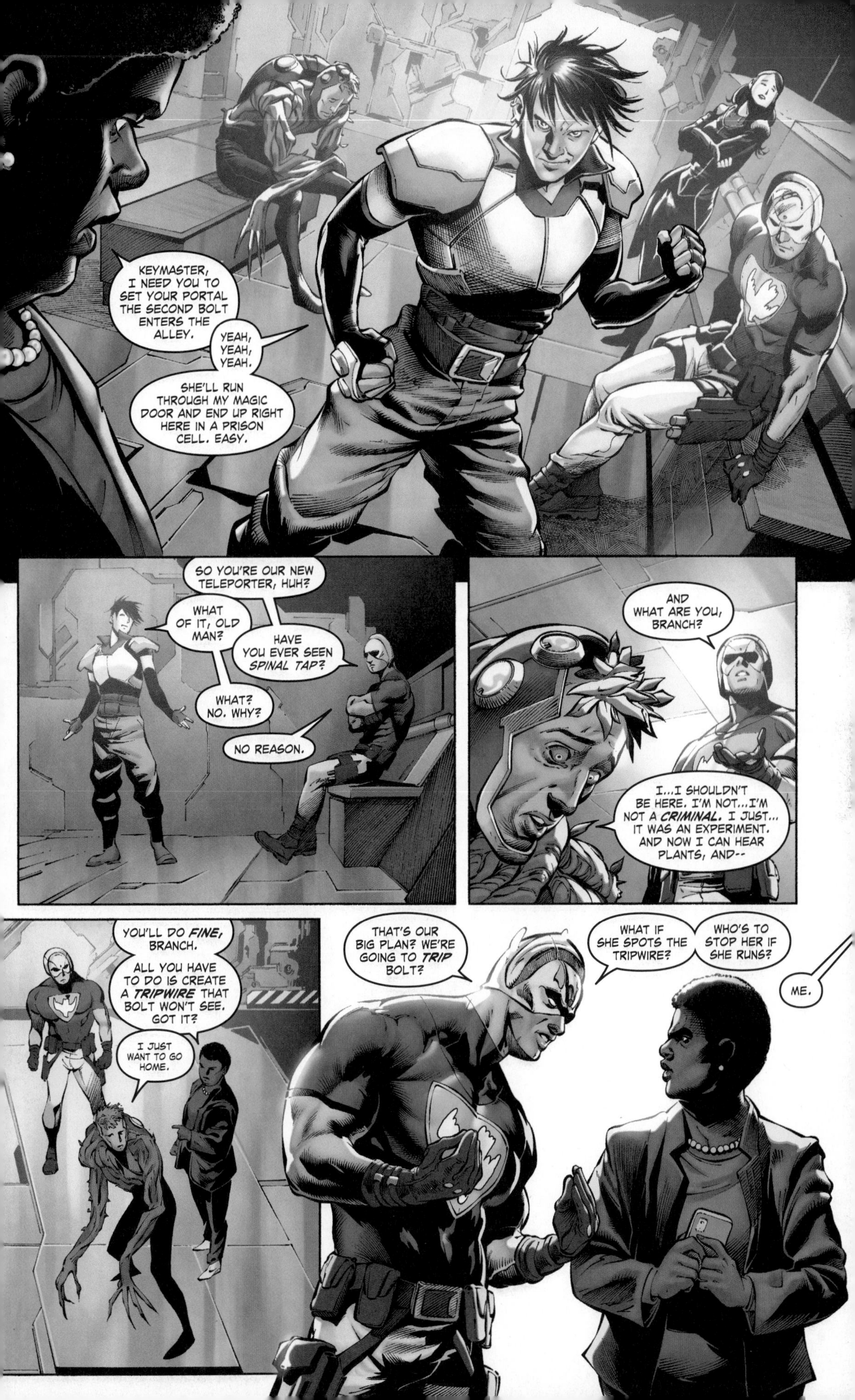
KEYMASTER, I NEED YOU TO SET YOUR PORTAL THE SECOND BOLT ENTERS THE ALLEY.
YEAH, YEAH, YEAH.
SHE'LL RUN THROUGH MY MAGIC DOOR AND END UP RIGHT HERE IN A PRISON CELL. EASY.
SO YOU'RE OUR NEW TELEPORTER, HUH?
WHAT OF IT, OLD MAN?
HAVE YOU EVER SEEN *SPINAL TAP*?
WHAT? NO. WHY?
NO REASON.
AND WHAT ARE YOU, BRANCH?
I...I SHOULDN'T BE HERE. I'M NOT...I'M NOT A ***CRIMINAL.*** I JUST... IT WAS AN EXPERIMENT. AND NOW I CAN HEAR PLANTS, AND--
YOU'LL DO ***FINE,*** BRANCH.
ALL YOU HAVE TO DO IS CREATE A ***TRIPWIRE*** THAT BOLT WON'T SEE. GOT IT?
I JUST WANT TO GO HOME.
THAT'S OUR BIG PLAN? WE'RE GOING TO ***TRIP*** BOLT?
WHAT IF SHE SPOTS THE TRIPWIRE?
WHO'S TO STOP HER IF SHE RUNS?
ME.

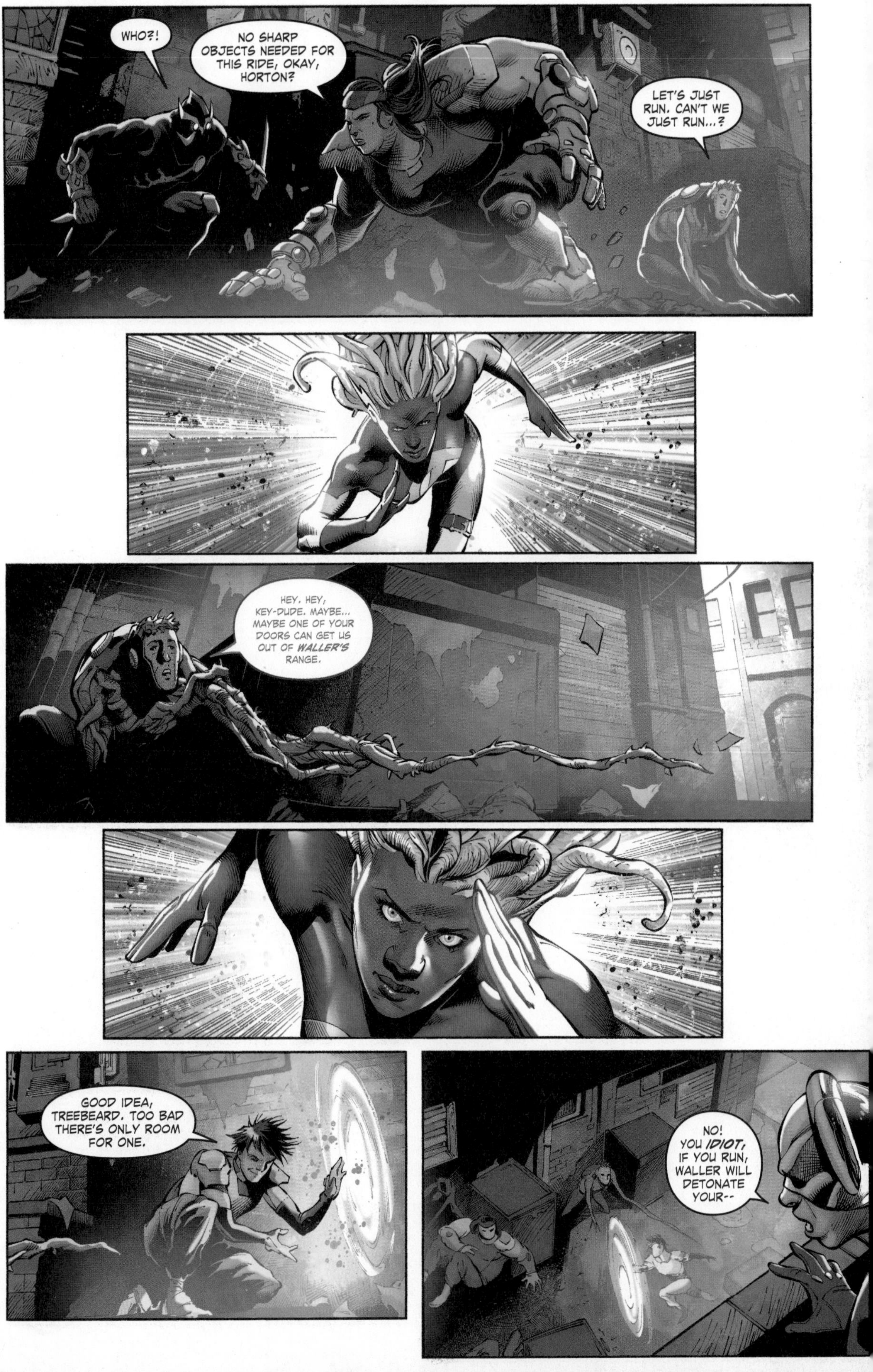
WHO?!
NO SHARP OBJECTS NEEDED FOR THIS RIDE, OKAY, HORTON?
LET'S JUST RUN. CAN'T WE JUST RUN...?
HEY. HEY, KEY-DUDE. MAYBE... MAYBE ONE OF YOUR DOORS CAN GET US OUT OF WALLER'S RANGE.
GOOD IDEA, TREEBEARD. TOO BAD THERE'S ONLY ROOM FOR ONE.
NO! YOU IDIOT, IF YOU RUN, WALLER WILL DETONATE YOUR--

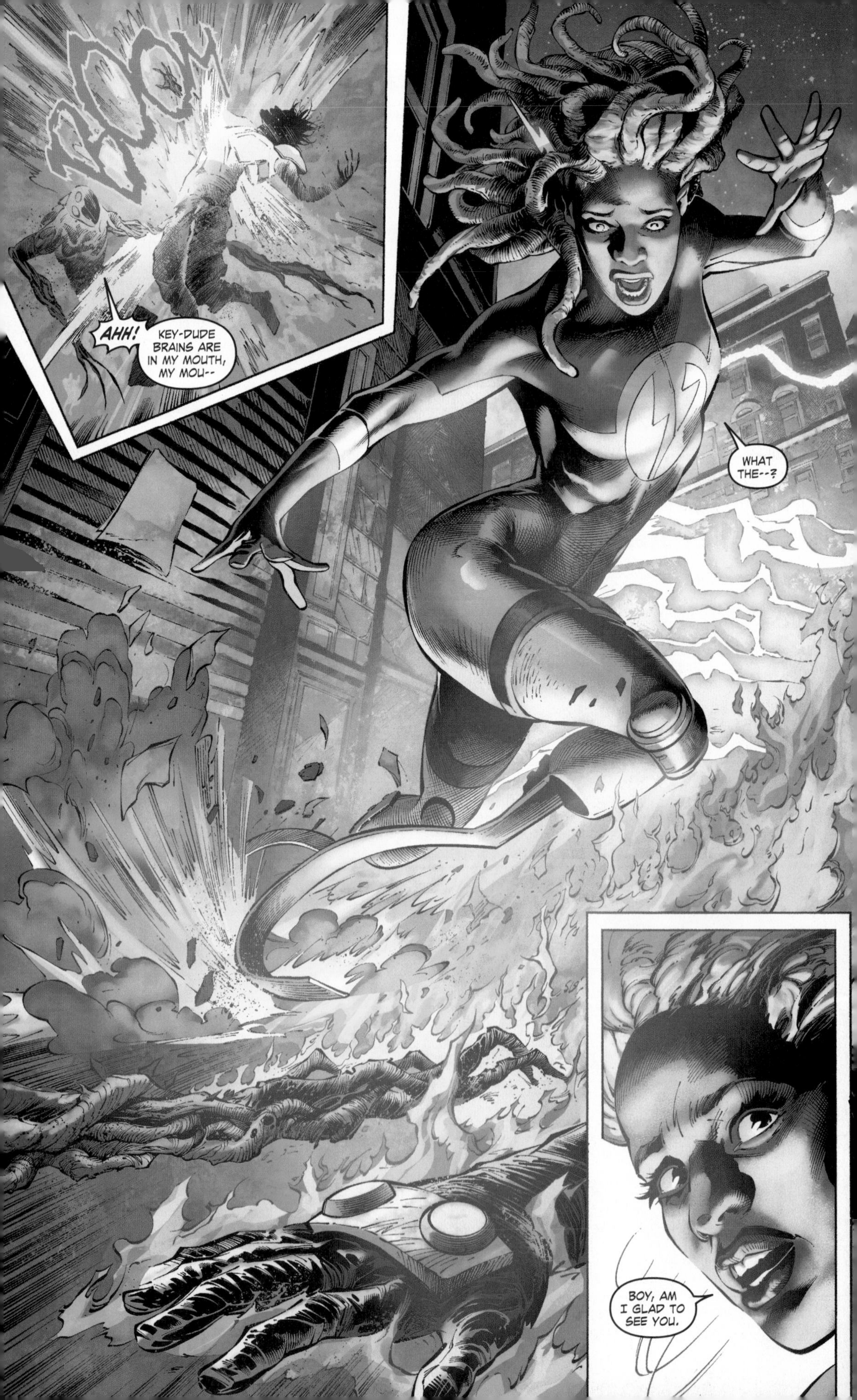
BOOM
AHH!
KEY-DUDE BRAINS ARE IN MY MOUTH, MY MOU--
WHAT THE--?
BOY, AM I GLAD TO SEE YOU.

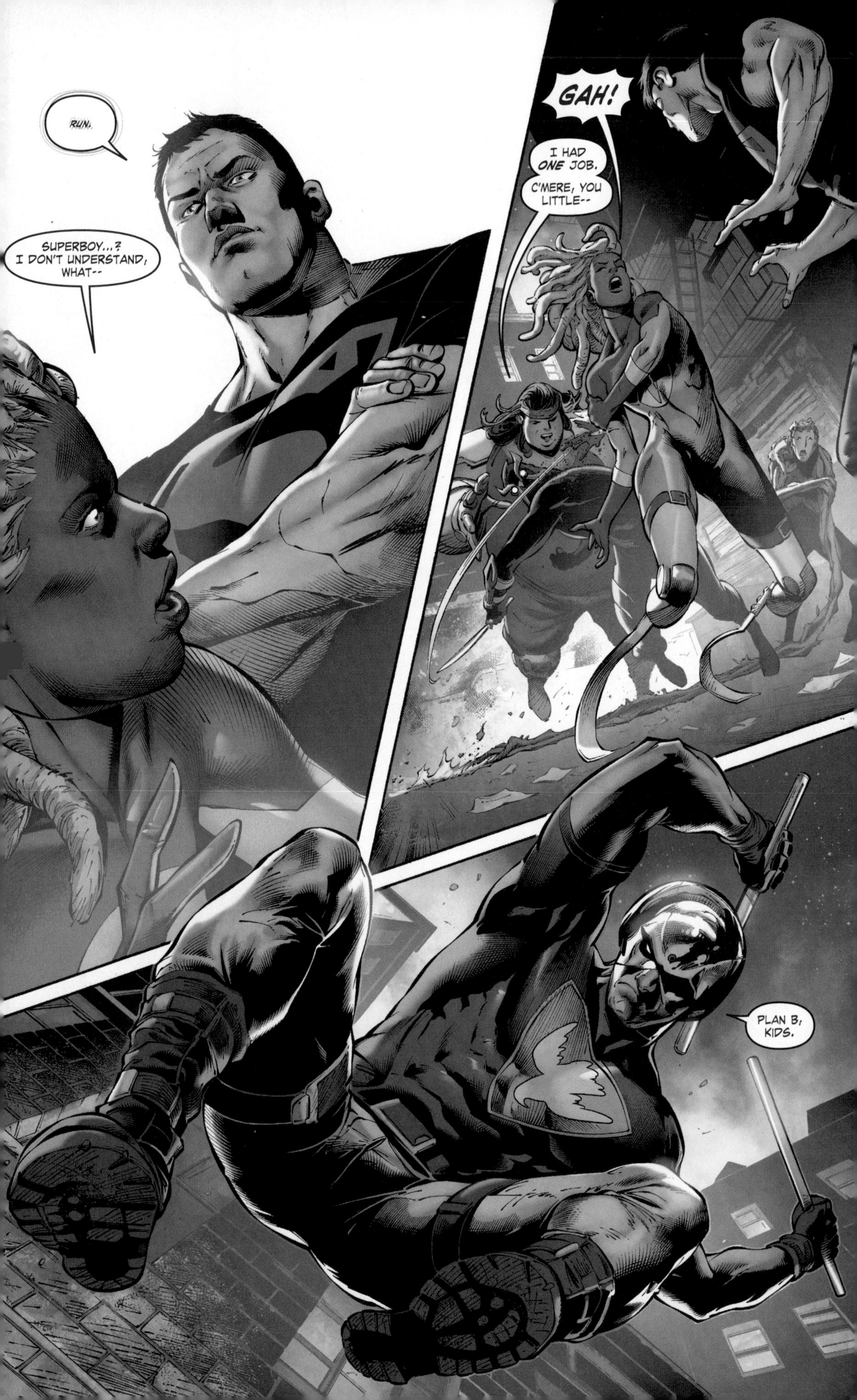
RUN.
SUPERBOY...? I DON'T UNDERSTAND, WHAT--
GAH!
I HAD ONE JOB.
C'MERE, YOU LITTLE--
PLAN B, KIDS.

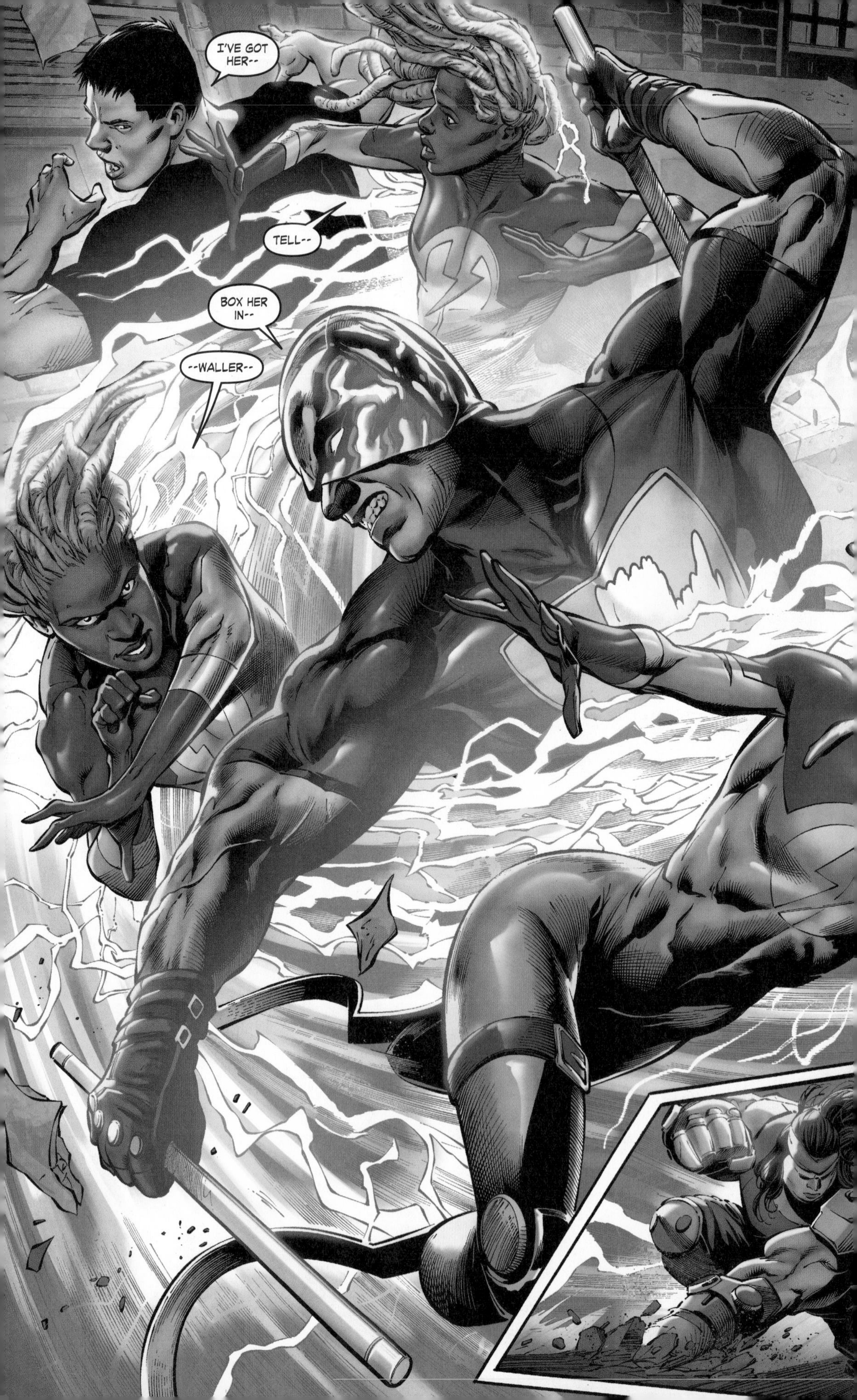
I'VE GOT HER--
TELL--
BOX HER IN--
--WALLER--

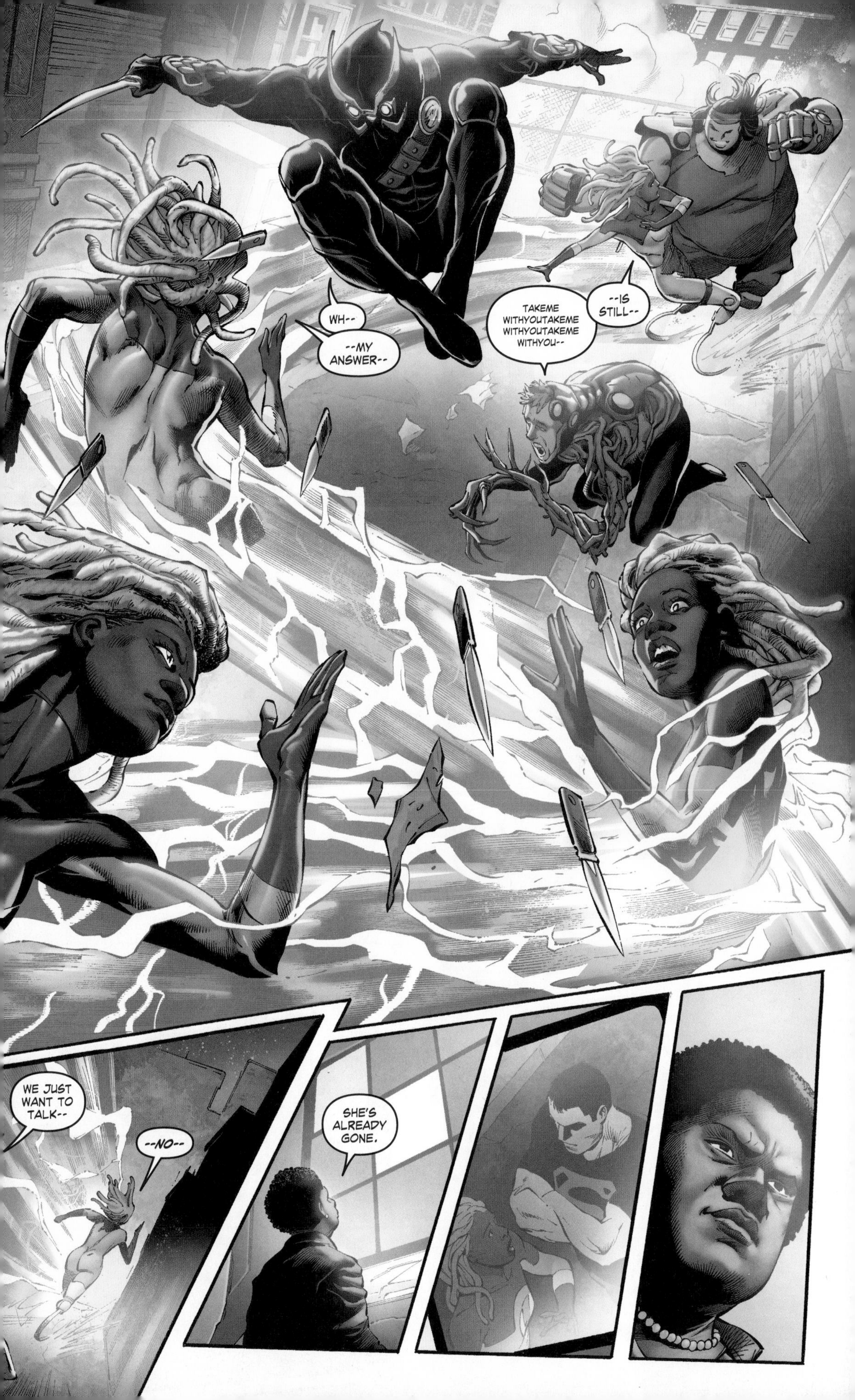
WH--
--MY ANSWER--
--IS STILL--
TAKEME WITHYOUTAKEME WITHYOUTAKEME WITHYOU--
WE JUST WANT TO TALK--
--NO--
SHE'S ALREADY GONE.

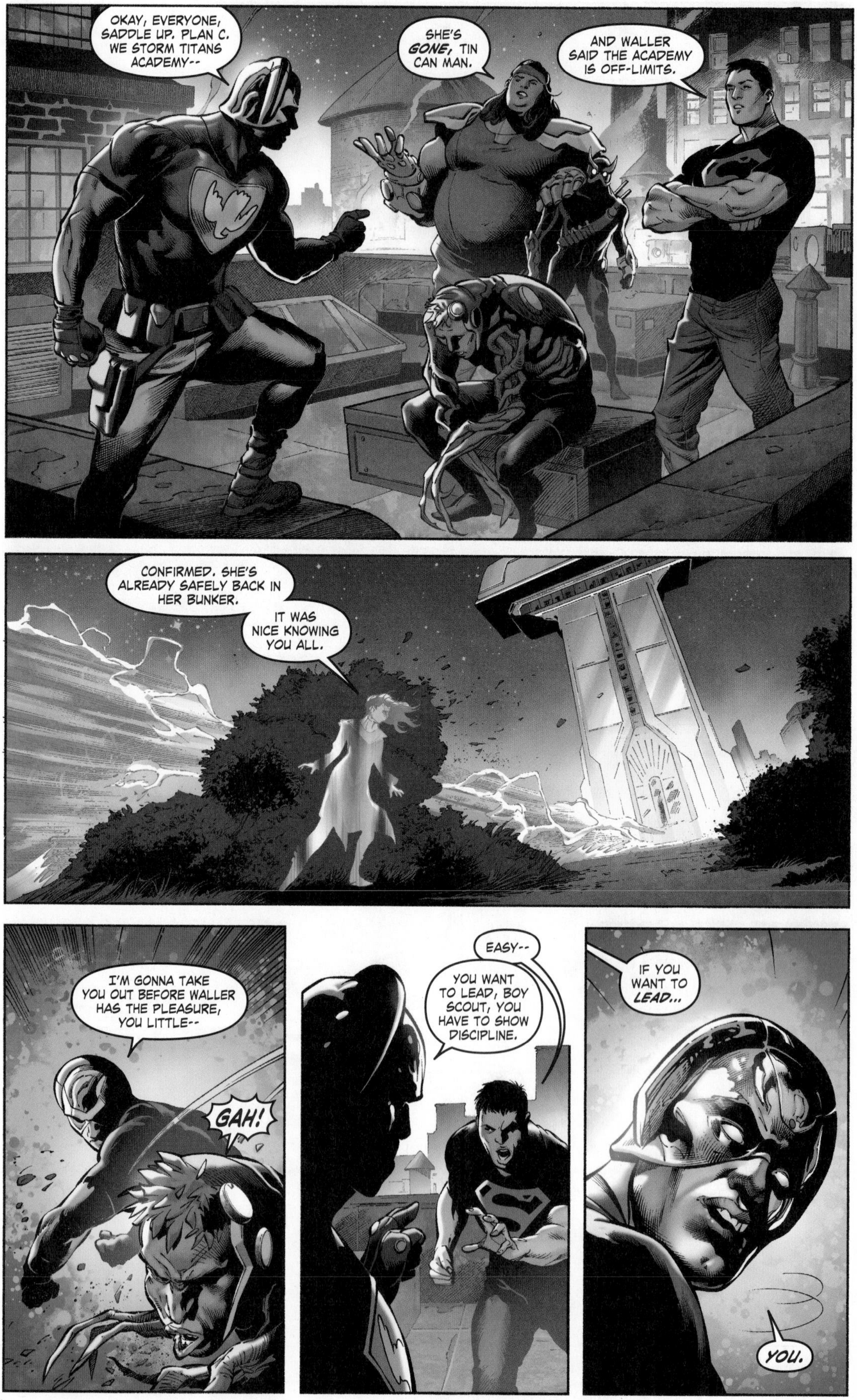
OKAY, EVERYONE, SADDLE UP. PLAN C. WE STORM TITANS ACADEMY--
SHE'S *GONE,* TIN CAN MAN.
AND WALLER SAID THE ACADEMY IS OFF-LIMITS.
CONFIRMED. SHE'S ALREADY SAFELY BACK IN HER BUNKER.
IT WAS NICE KNOWING YOU ALL.
I'M GONNA TAKE YOU OUT BEFORE WALLER HAS THE PLEASURE, YOU LITTLE--
GAH!
EASY--
YOU WANT TO LEAD, BOY SCOUT, YOU HAVE TO SHOW DISCIPLINE.
IF YOU WANT TO *LEAD...*
YOU.

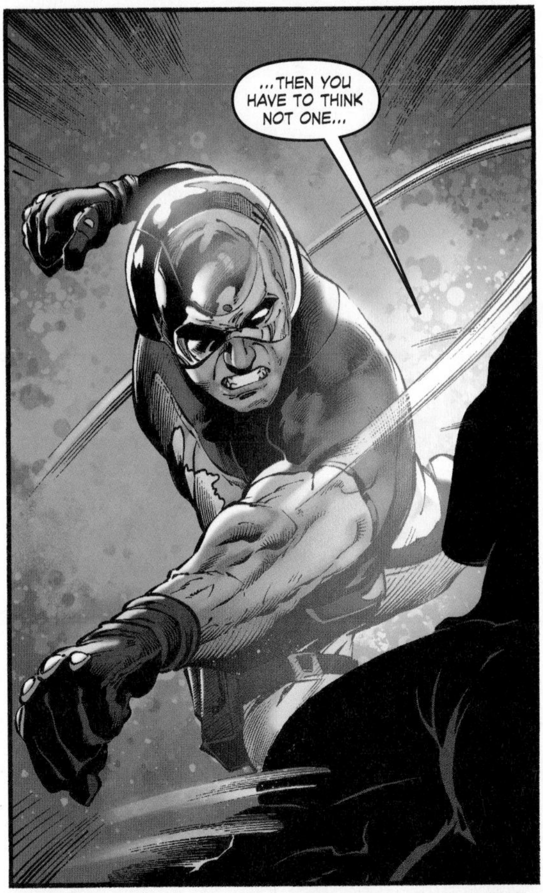
...THEN YOU HAVE TO THINK NOT ONE...

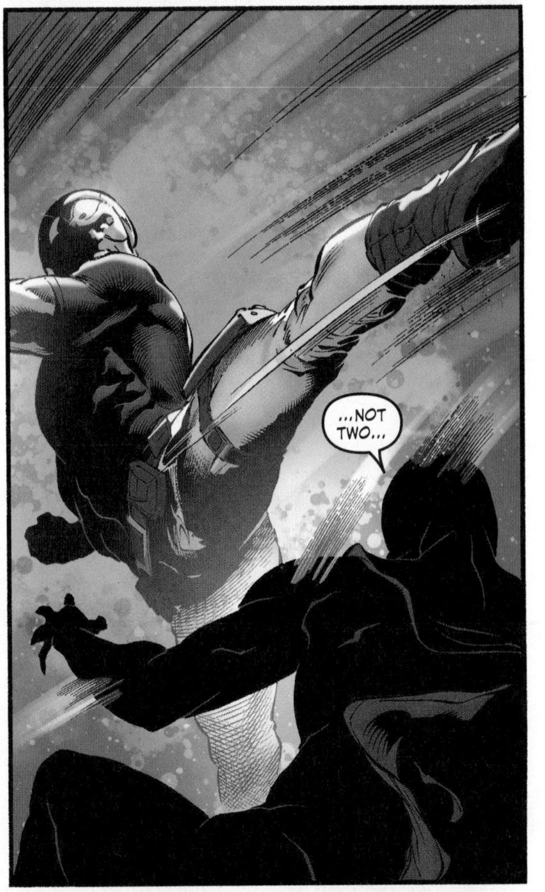
...NOT TWO...

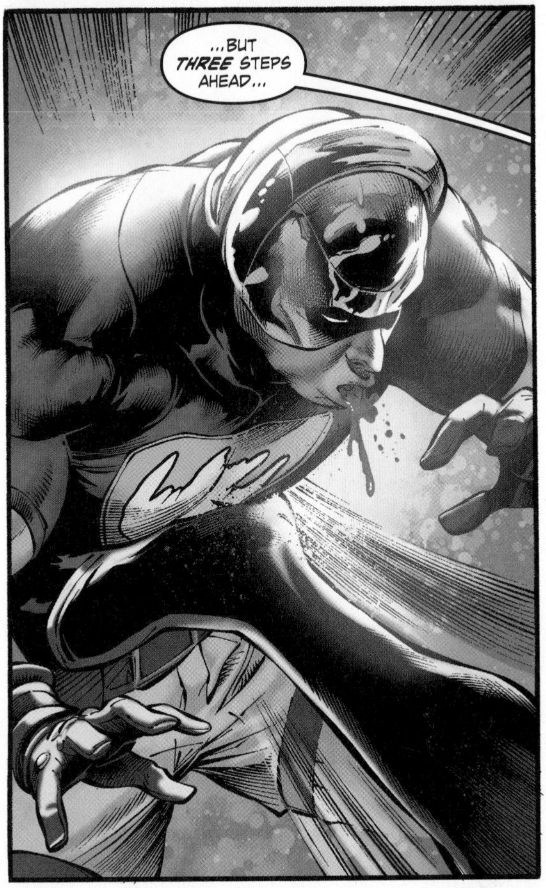
...BUT THREE STEPS AHEAD...

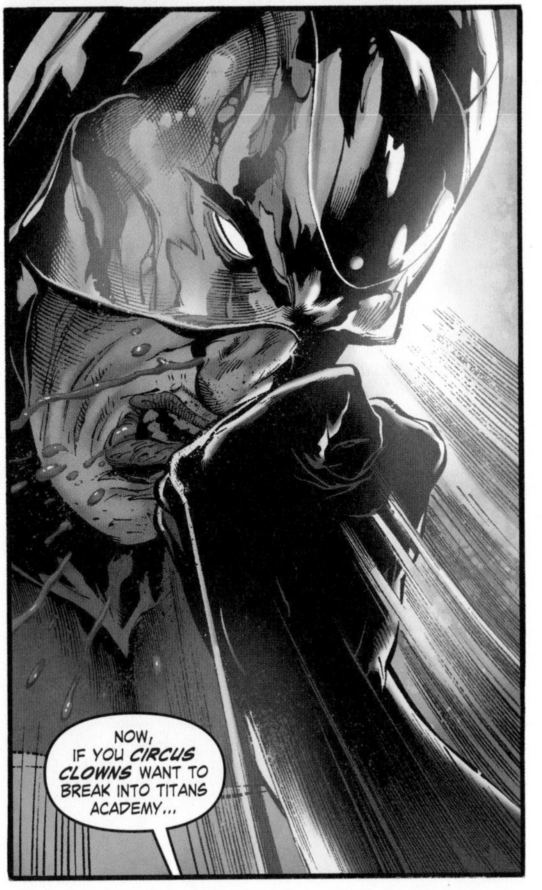
NOW, IF YOU CIRCUS CLOWNS WANT TO BREAK INTO TITANS ACADEMY...

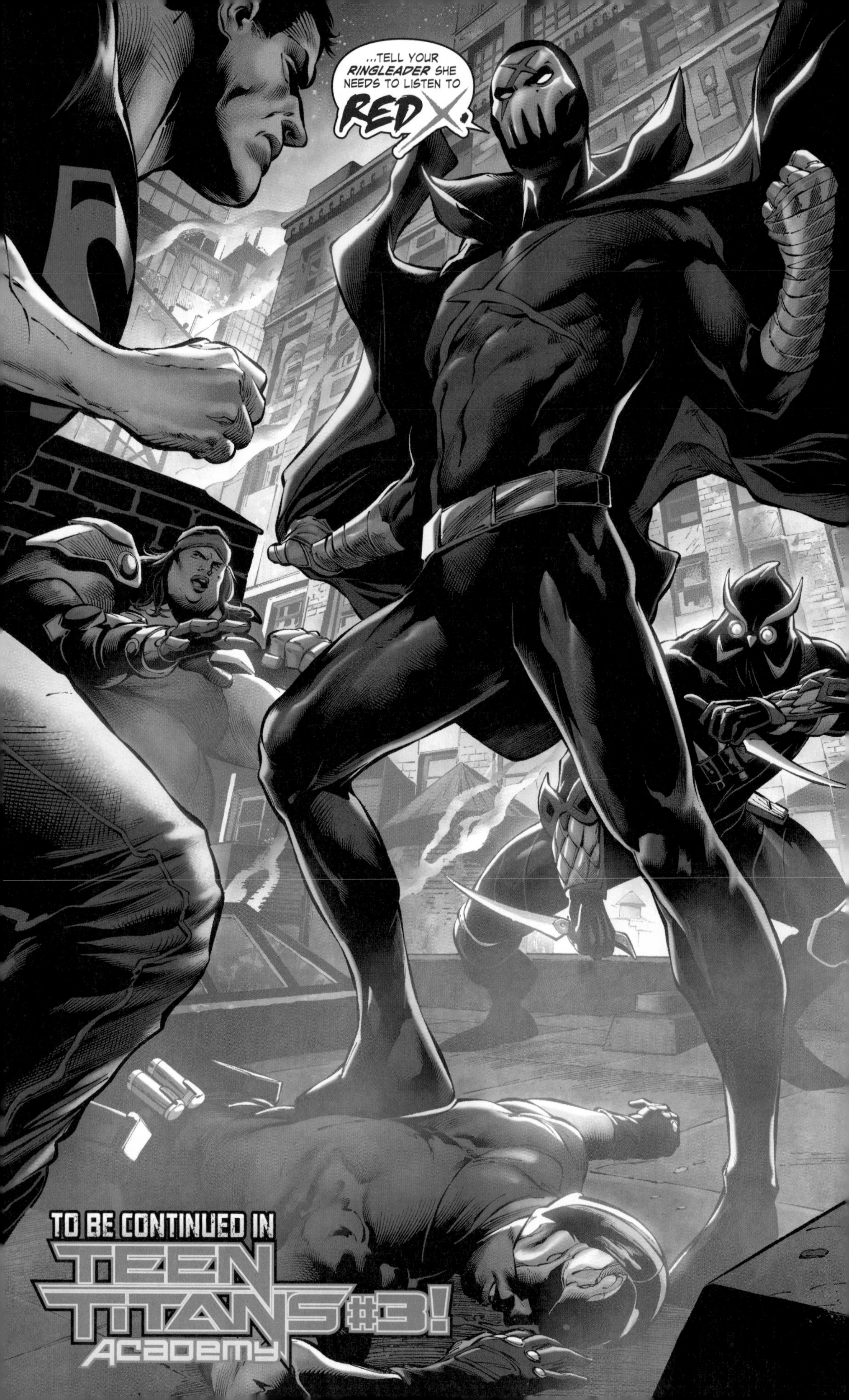
...TELL YOUR RINGLEADER SHE NEEDS TO LISTEN TO RED X.
TO BE CONTINUED IN TEEN TITANS ACADEMY #3!

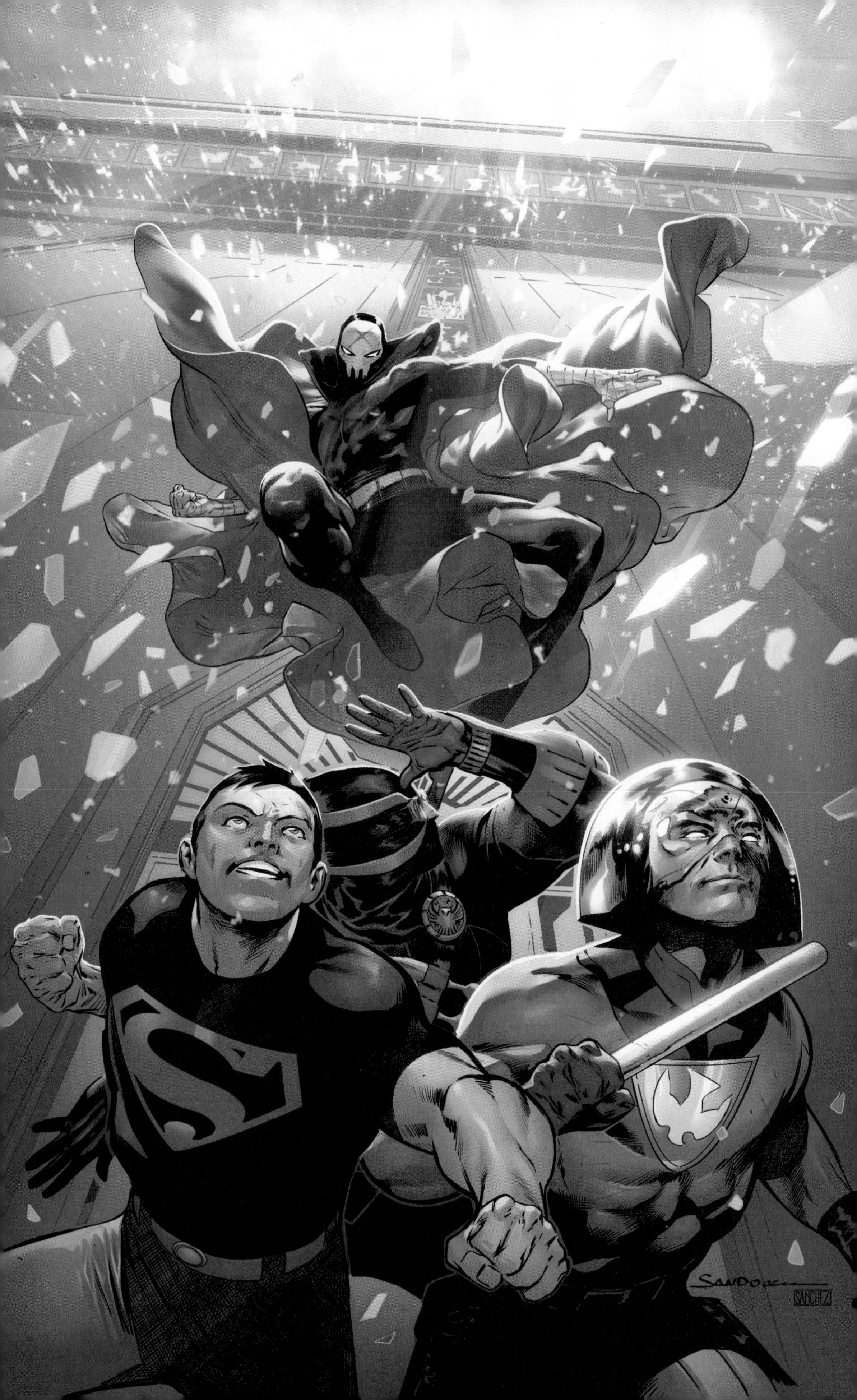
SANCHEZ

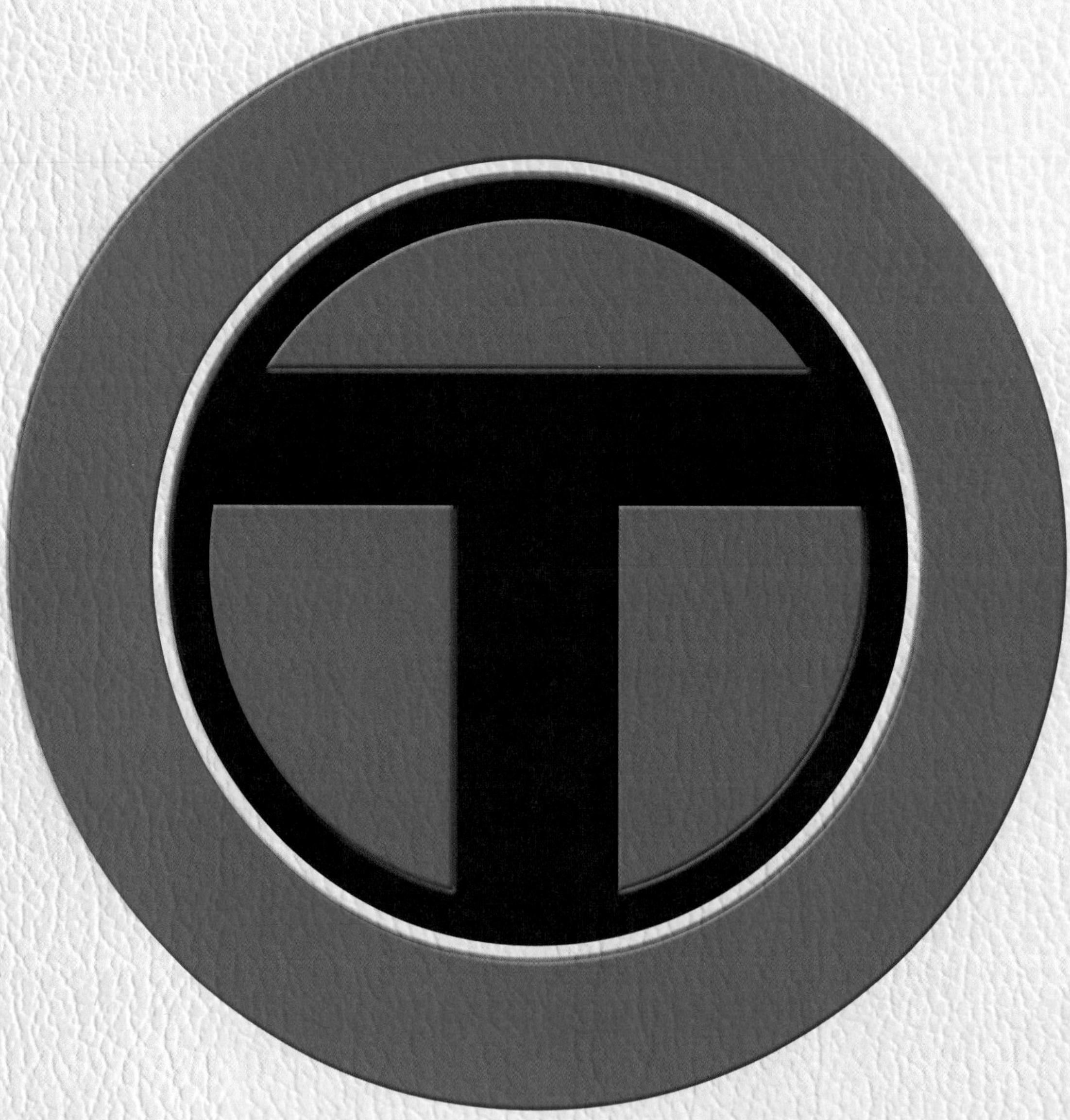

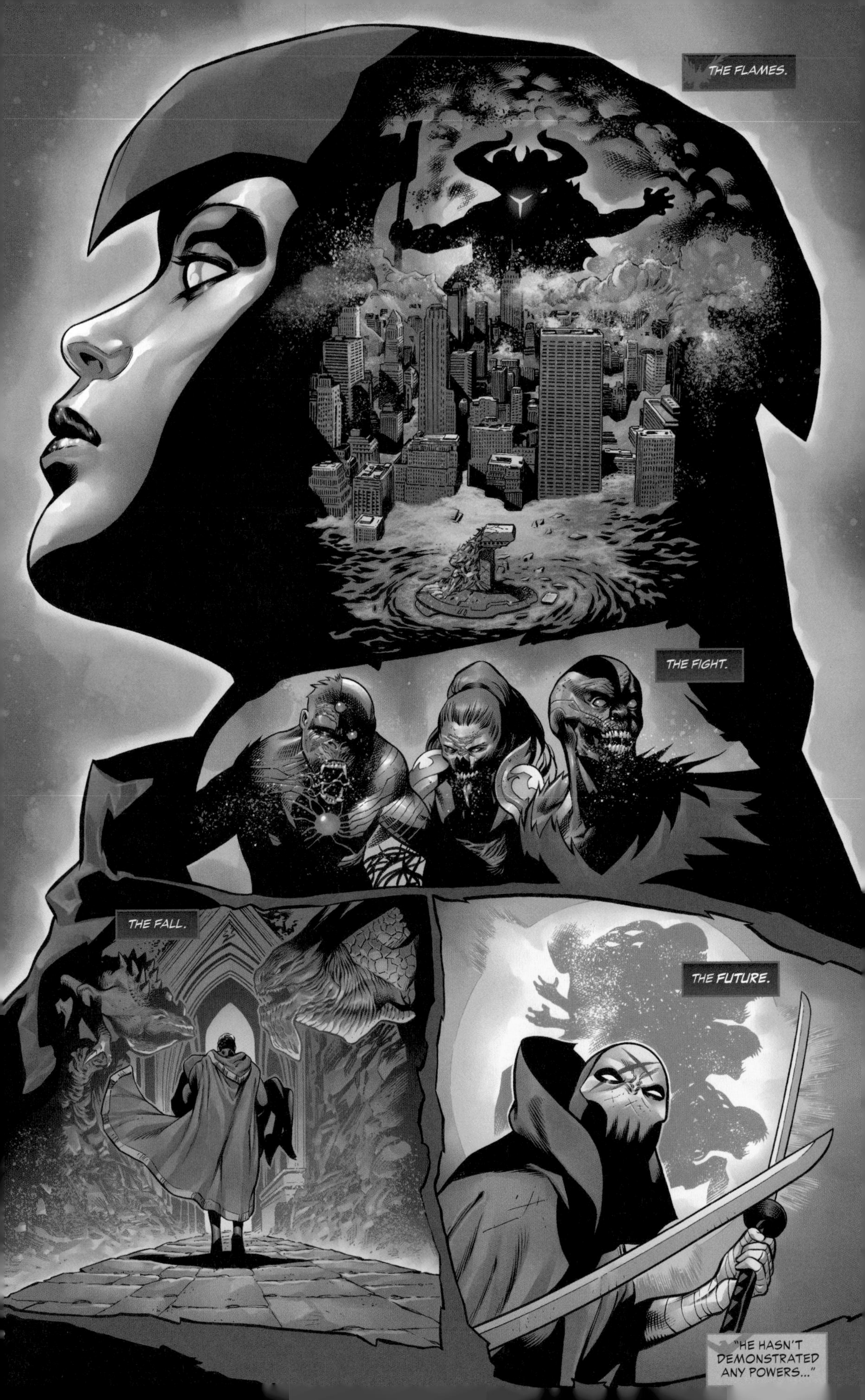
THE FLAMES.
THE FIGHT.
THE FALL.
THE FUTURE.
"HE HASN'T DEMONSTRATED ANY POWERS..."

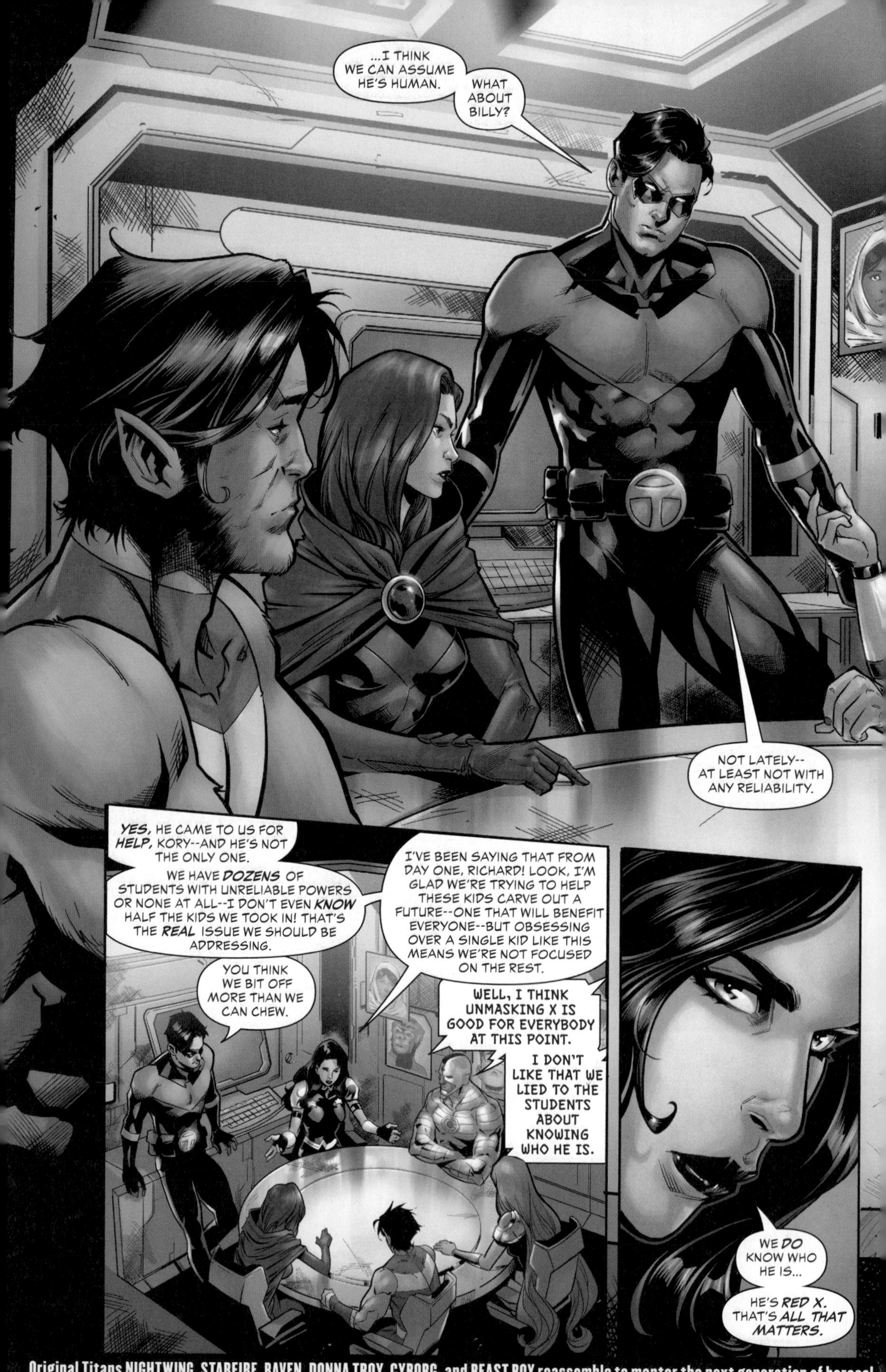
...I THINK WE CAN ASSUME HE'S HUMAN.
WHAT ABOUT BILLY?
NOT LATELY-- AT LEAST NOT WITH ANY RELIABILITY.
YES, HE CAME TO US FOR HELP, KORY--AND HE'S NOT THE ONLY ONE.
WE HAVE DOZENS OF STUDENTS WITH UNRELIABLE POWERS OR NONE AT ALL--I DON'T EVEN KNOW HALF THE KIDS WE TOOK IN! THAT'S THE REAL ISSUE WE SHOULD BE ADDRESSING.
YOU THINK WE BIT OFF MORE THAN WE CAN CHEW.
I'VE BEEN SAYING THAT FROM DAY ONE, RICHARD! LOOK, I'M GLAD WE'RE TRYING TO HELP THESE KIDS CARVE OUT A FUTURE--ONE THAT WILL BENEFIT EVERYONE--BUT OBSESSING OVER A SINGLE KID LIKE THIS MEANS WE'RE NOT FOCUSED ON THE REST.
WELL, I THINK UNMASKING X IS GOOD FOR EVERYBODY AT THIS POINT.
I DON'T LIKE THAT WE LIED TO THE STUDENTS ABOUT KNOWING WHO HE IS.
WE DO KNOW WHO HE IS...
HE'S RED X. THAT'S ALL THAT MATTERS.

Original Titans NIGHTWING, STARFIRE, RAVEN, DONNA TROY, CYBORG, and BEAST BOY reassemble to mentor the next generation of heroes! Now, TEEN TITANS ACADEMY opens its doors to a new crop of gifted youngsters eager to earn their place on the team's permanent roster, innocent of the many treacherous challenges they will face—in and out of school—over the months and years to come.

NEED FOR SPEED 2:

EXTRACTION

TIM SHERIDAN
writer

RAFA SANDOVAL
penciller

JORDI TARRAGONA
inker

MAX RAYNOR
artist (pp. 2-4, 7-9)

ALEJANDRO SANCHEZ
colorist

ALEX SINCLAIR
colorist (pp. 2-4, 7-9)

ROB LEIGH
letterer

SANDOVAL & SANCHEZ
cover

PHILIP TAN &
ELMER SANTOS
variant cover

DIEGO LOPEZ
associate editor

MIKE COTTON
editor

JAMIE S. RICH
group editor

SUPERBOY created by Jerry Siegel.
By special arrangement with the Jerry Siegel family.

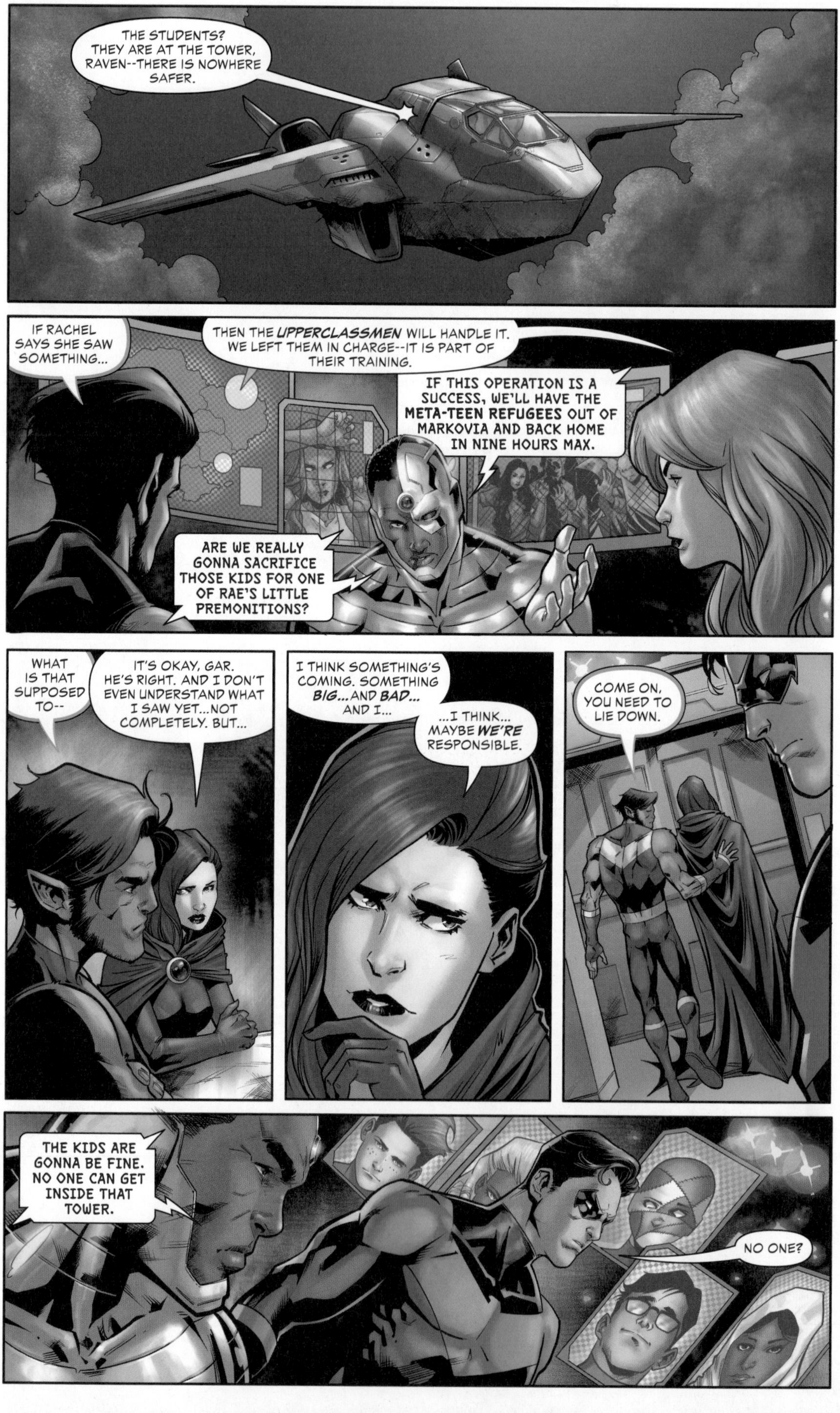
THE STUDENTS? THEY ARE AT THE TOWER, RAVEN--THERE IS NOWHERE SAFER.
IF RACHEL SAYS SHE SAW SOMETHING...
THEN THE UPPERCLASSMEN WILL HANDLE IT. WE LEFT THEM IN CHARGE--IT IS PART OF THEIR TRAINING.
IF THIS OPERATION IS A SUCCESS, WE'LL HAVE THE META-TEEN REFUGEES OUT OF MARKOVIA AND BACK HOME IN NINE HOURS MAX.
ARE WE REALLY GONNA SACRIFICE THOSE KIDS FOR ONE OF RAE'S LITTLE PREMONITIONS?
WHAT IS THAT SUPPOSED TO--
IT'S OKAY, GAR. HE'S RIGHT. AND I DON'T EVEN UNDERSTAND WHAT I SAW YET...NOT COMPLETELY. BUT...
I THINK SOMETHING'S COMING. SOMETHING BIG...AND BAD... AND I...
...I THINK... MAYBE WE'RE RESPONSIBLE.
COME ON, YOU NEED TO LIE DOWN.
THE KIDS ARE GONNA BE FINE. NO ONE CAN GET INSIDE THAT TOWER.
NO ONE?

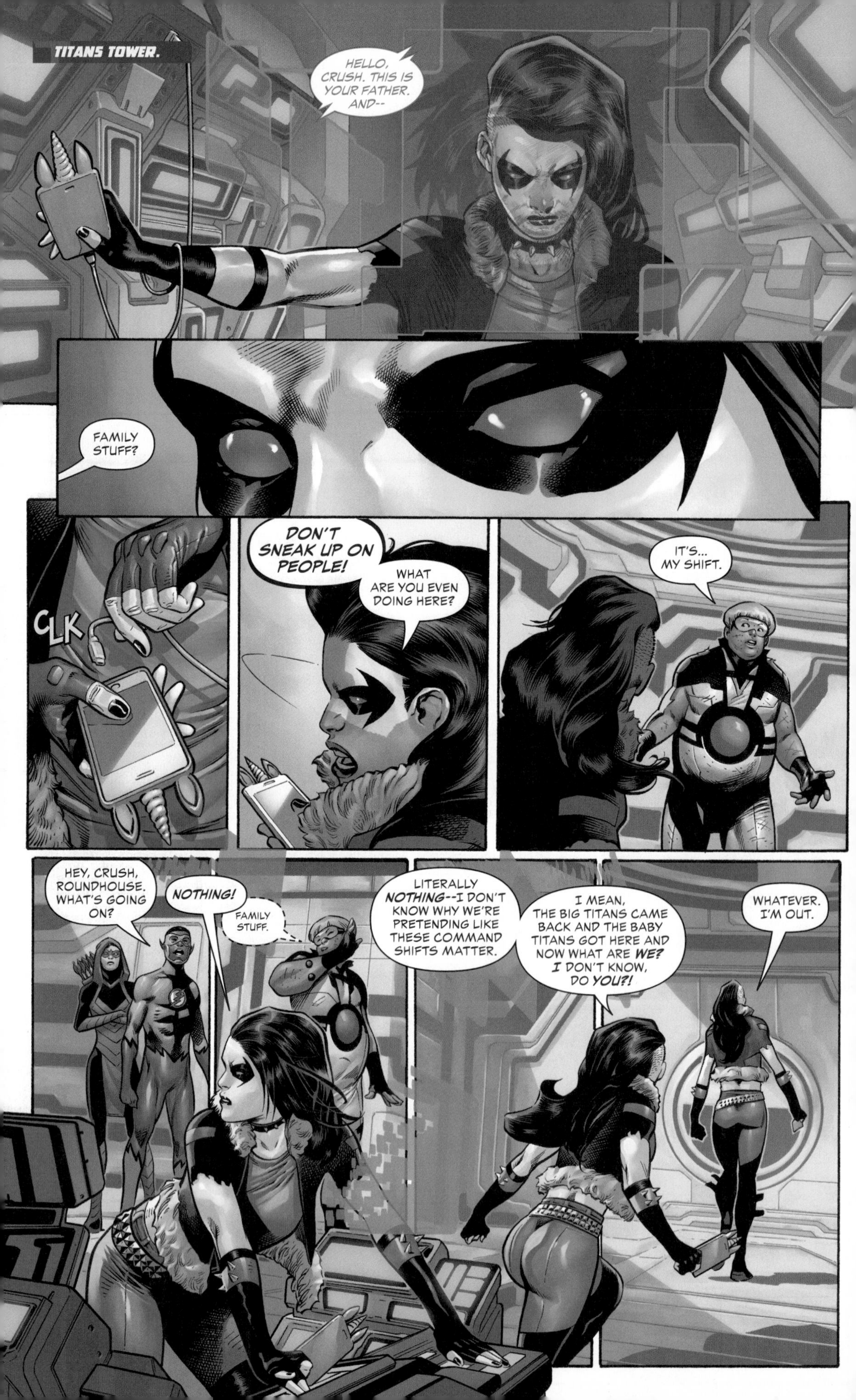

TITANS TOWER.
HELLO, CRUSH. THIS IS YOUR FATHER. AND--
FAMILY STUFF?
CLK
DON'T SNEAK UP ON PEOPLE!
WHAT ARE YOU EVEN DOING HERE?
IT'S... MY SHIFT.
HEY, CRUSH, ROUNDHOUSE. WHAT'S GOING ON?
NOTHING!
FAMILY STUFF.
LITERALLY NOTHING--I DON'T KNOW WHY WE'RE PRETENDING LIKE THESE COMMAND SHIFTS MATTER.
I MEAN, THE BIG TITANS CAME BACK AND THE BABY TITANS GOT HERE AND NOW WHAT ARE WE? I DON'T KNOW, DO YOU?!
WHATEVER. I'M OUT.

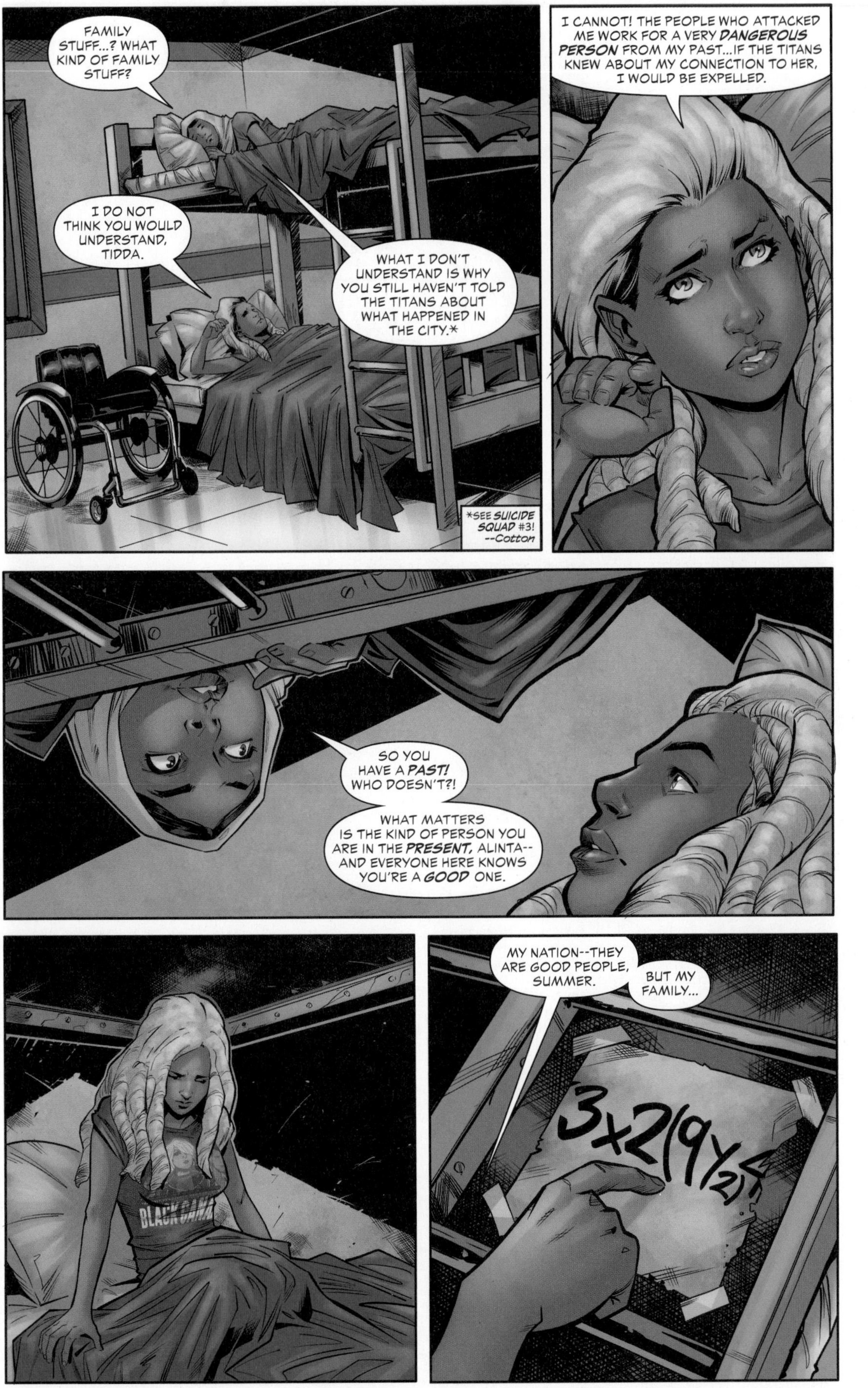

FAMILY STUFF...? WHAT KIND OF FAMILY STUFF?
I DO NOT THINK YOU WOULD UNDERSTAND, TIDDA.
WHAT I DON'T UNDERSTAND IS WHY YOU STILL HAVEN'T TOLD THE TITANS ABOUT WHAT HAPPENED IN THE CITY.*
*SEE SUICIDE SQUAD #3! --Cotton
I CANNOT! THE PEOPLE WHO ATTACKED ME WORK FOR A VERY DANGEROUS PERSON FROM MY PAST...IF THE TITANS KNEW ABOUT MY CONNECTION TO HER, I WOULD BE EXPELLED.
SO YOU HAVE A PAST! WHO DOESN'T?!
WHAT MATTERS IS THE KIND OF PERSON YOU ARE IN THE PRESENT, ALINTA--AND EVERYONE HERE KNOWS YOU'RE A GOOD ONE.
MY NATION--THEY ARE GOOD PEOPLE, SUMMER.
BUT MY FAMILY...

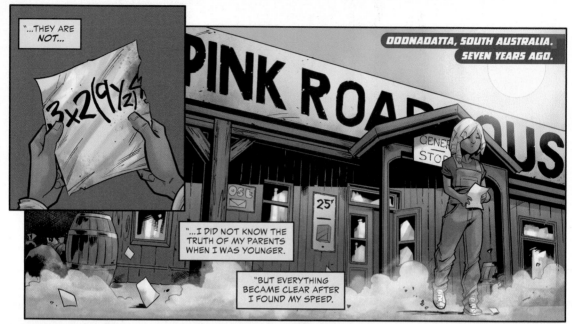

"...THEY ARE *NOT*...

"...I DID NOT KNOW THE TRUTH OF MY PARENTS WHEN I WAS YOUNGER.

"BUT EVERYTHING BECAME CLEAR AFTER I FOUND MY SPEED.

OODNADATTA, SOUTH AUSTRALIA. SEVEN YEARS AGO.

"IT WAS LIKE MAGIC-- OR A *MIRACLE*. ALL I HAD TO DO WAS REMEMBER THE CHARACTERS, IN THE RIGHT ORDER, FROM THE PAPER I FOUND.

"IT DID NOT WORK FOR EVERYONE...BUT IT WORKED FOR *ME*.

"EVEN THOUGH I COULD NOT SUSTAIN THEM FOR LONG, MY BURSTS OF SPEED WOULD, AS MY PARENTS PUT IT, 'OPEN UP NEW ROADS FOR THE FAMILY BUSINESS.'

"AND I WAS SO HAPPY TO HELP THEM.

"WHAT I DID NOT KNOW WAS THAT THEIR 'BUSINESS' WAS TRAFFICKING IN *STOLEN GOODS*.

"I WAS THEIR *RUNNER*, DELIVERING MESSAGES, PACKAGES, INSTANTLY ACROSS THE OUTBACK TO THEIR VARIOUS... ASSOCIATES.

"...UNTIL THE DAY I LOST MY FIRST LEGS."

"YOU NEVER TALK ABOUT THAT. WHAT HAPPENED?"

MY PARENTS HAD MANY DEBTS... WHEN THEY COULD NOT REPAY...

OH NO. ALINTA, I HAD NO IDEA.

AFTERWARD, I WAS LEFT FOR DEAD...

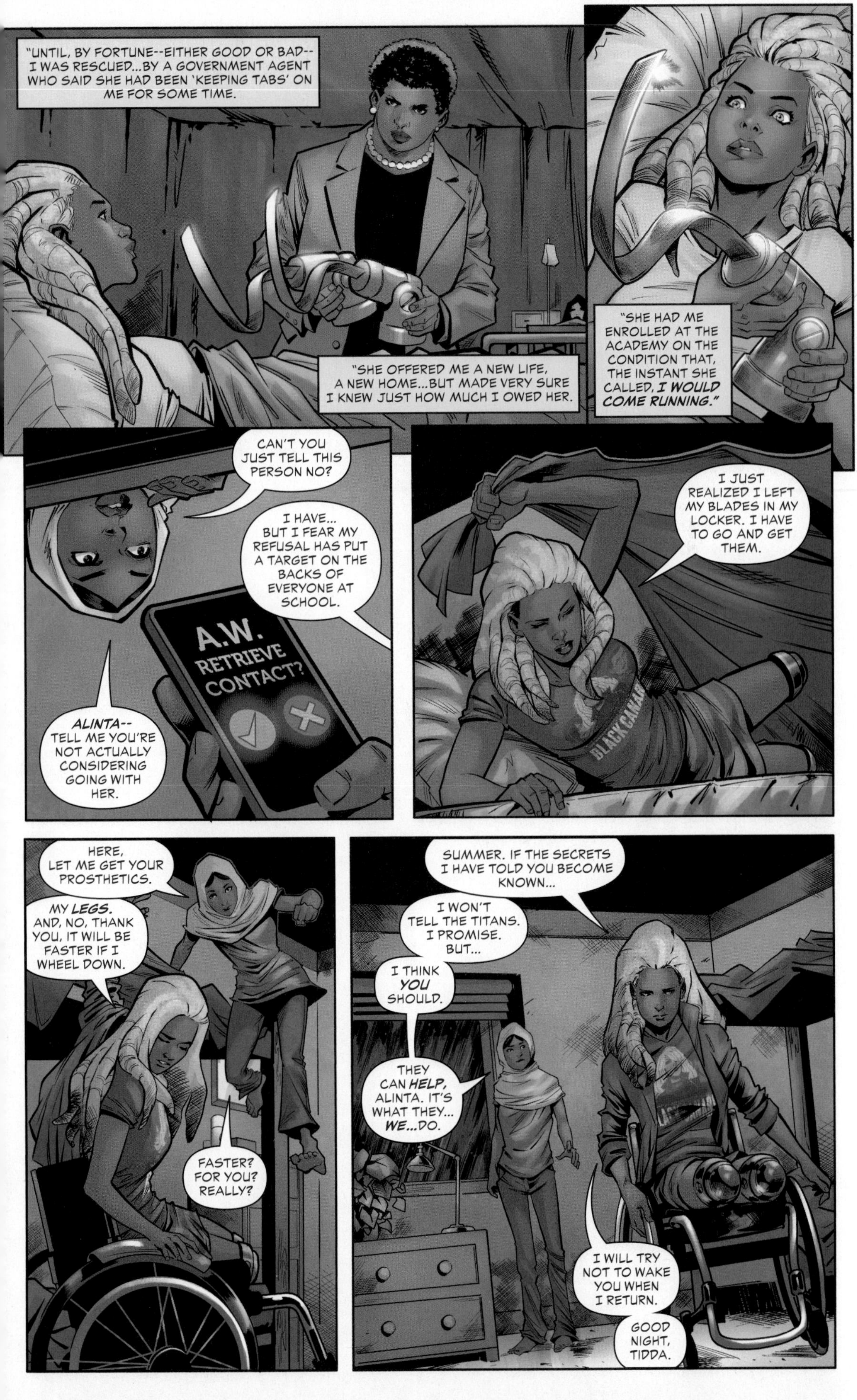

"UNTIL, BY FORTUNE--EITHER GOOD OR BAD--I WAS RESCUED...BY A GOVERNMENT AGENT WHO SAID SHE HAD BEEN 'KEEPING TABS' ON ME FOR SOME TIME.
"SHE OFFERED ME A NEW LIFE, A NEW HOME...BUT MADE VERY SURE I KNEW JUST HOW MUCH I OWED HER.
"SHE HAD ME ENROLLED AT THE ACADEMY ON THE CONDITION THAT, THE INSTANT SHE CALLED, ***I WOULD COME RUNNING."***
CAN'T YOU JUST TELL THIS PERSON NO?
I HAVE... BUT I FEAR MY REFUSAL HAS PUT A TARGET ON THE BACKS OF EVERYONE AT SCHOOL.
A.W.
RETRIEVE CONTACT?
ALINTA-- TELL ME YOU'RE NOT ACTUALLY CONSIDERING GOING WITH HER.
I JUST REALIZED I LEFT MY BLADES IN MY LOCKER. I HAVE TO GO AND GET THEM.
BLACK CANAR
HERE, LET ME GET YOUR PROSTHETICS.
MY ***LEGS.*** AND, NO, THANK YOU, IT WILL BE FASTER IF I WHEEL DOWN.
FASTER? FOR YOU? REALLY?
SUMMER. IF THE SECRETS I HAVE TOLD YOU BECOME KNOWN...
I WON'T TELL THE TITANS. I PROMISE. BUT...
I THINK ***YOU*** SHOULD.
THEY CAN ***HELP,*** ALINTA. IT'S WHAT THEY... ***WE...***DO.
I WILL TRY NOT TO WAKE YOU WHEN I RETURN.
GOOD NIGHT, TIDDA.

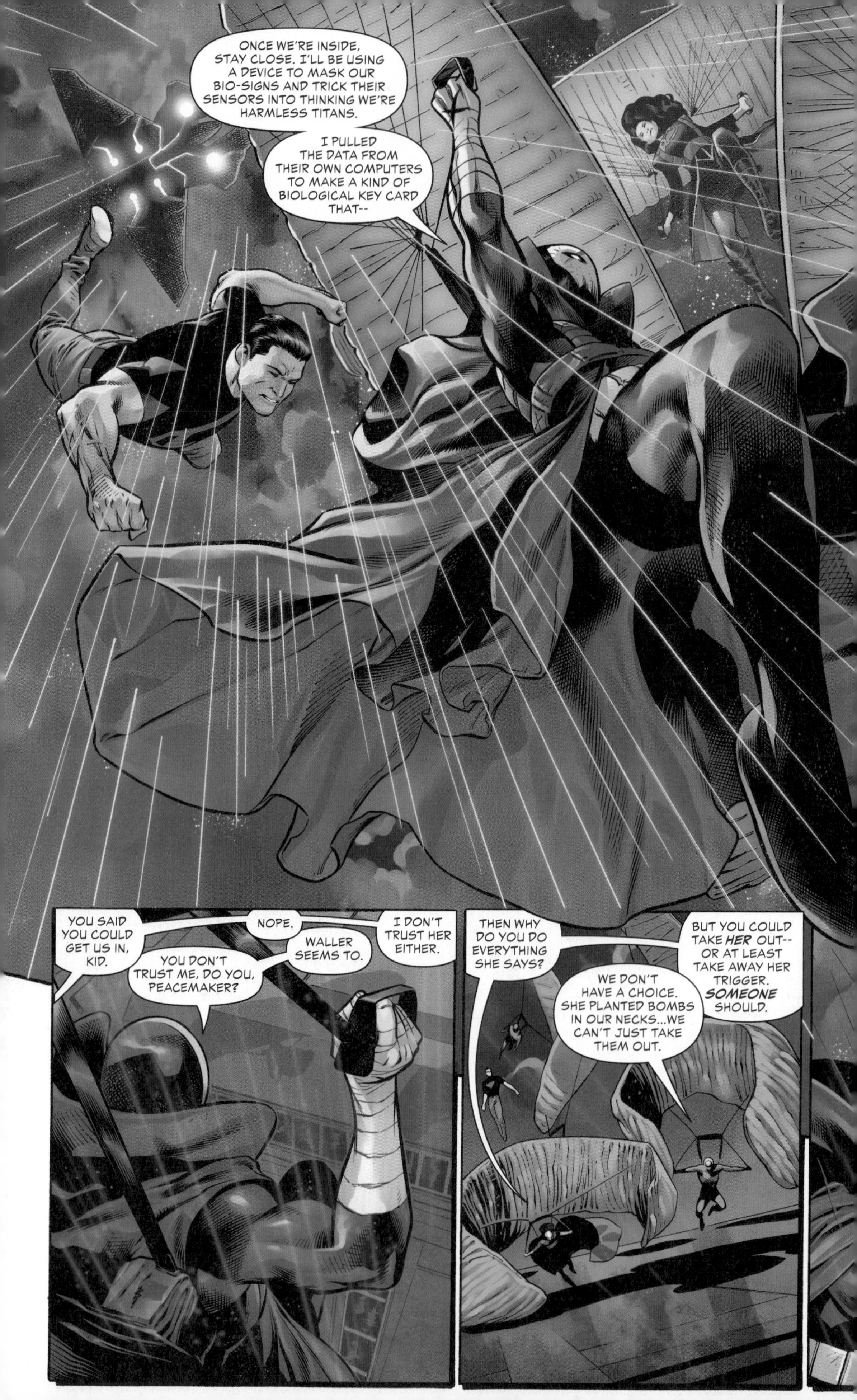
ONCE WE'RE INSIDE, STAY CLOSE. I'LL BE USING A DEVICE TO MASK OUR BIO-SIGNS AND TRICK THEIR SENSORS INTO THINKING WE'RE HARMLESS TITANS.
I PULLED THE DATA FROM THEIR OWN COMPUTERS TO MAKE A KIND OF BIOLOGICAL KEY CARD THAT--
YOU SAID YOU COULD GET US IN, KID.
YOU DON'T TRUST ME, DO YOU, PEACEMAKER?
NOPE.
WALLER SEEMS TO.
I DON'T TRUST HER EITHER.
THEN WHY DO YOU DO EVERYTHING SHE SAYS?
WE DON'T HAVE A CHOICE. SHE PLANTED BOMBS IN OUR NECKS...WE CAN'T JUST TAKE THEM OUT.
BUT YOU COULD TAKE ***HER*** OUT-- OR AT LEAST TAKE AWAY HER TRIGGER. ***SOMEONE*** SHOULD.

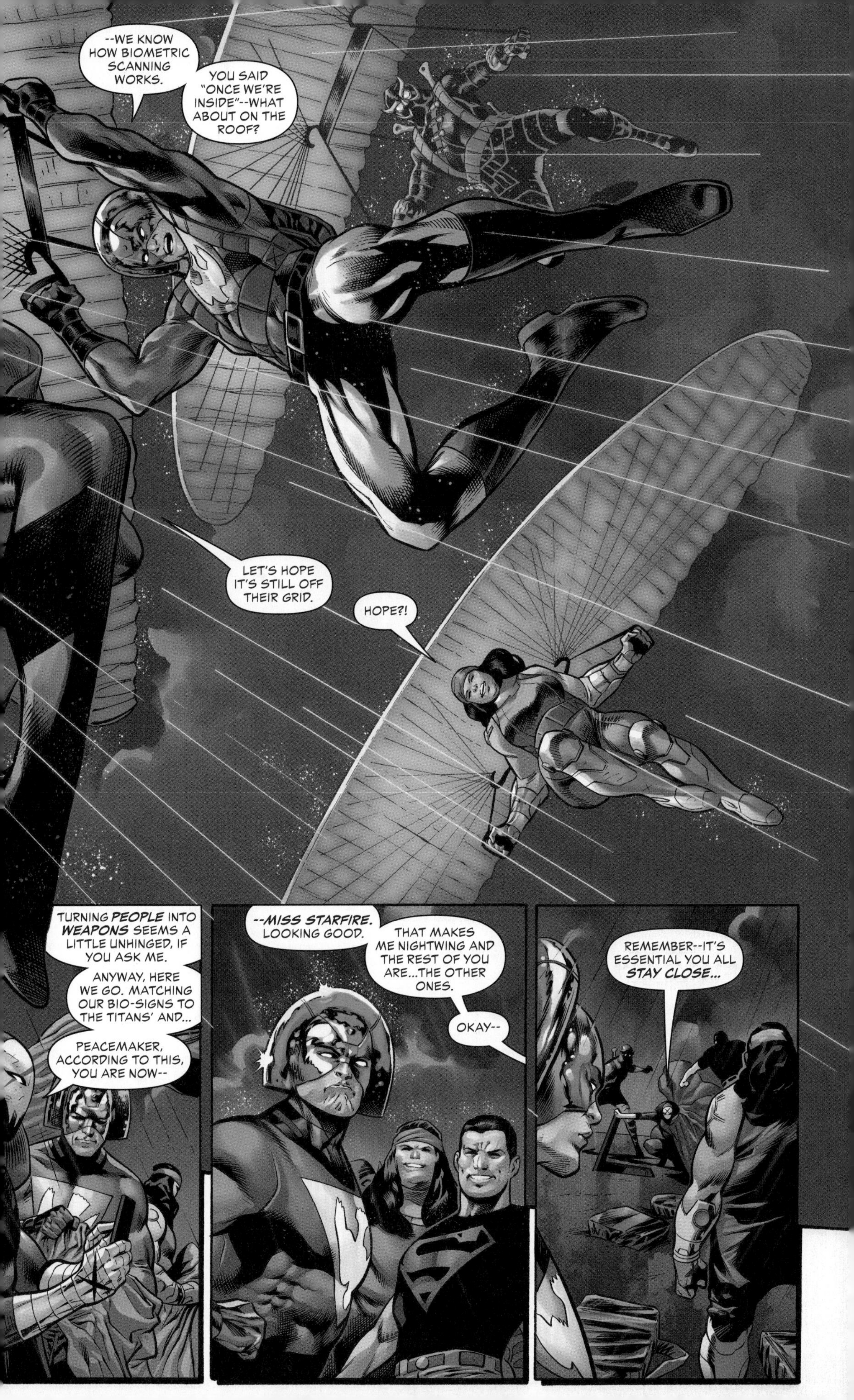
--WE KNOW HOW BIOMETRIC SCANNING WORKS.
YOU SAID "ONCE WE'RE INSIDE"--WHAT ABOUT ON THE ROOF?
LET'S HOPE IT'S STILL OFF THEIR GRID.
HOPE?!
TURNING PEOPLE INTO WEAPONS SEEMS A LITTLE UNHINGED, IF YOU ASK ME.
ANYWAY, HERE WE GO. MATCHING OUR BIO-SIGNS TO THE TITANS' AND...
PEACEMAKER, ACCORDING TO THIS, YOU ARE NOW--
--MISS STARFIRE. LOOKING GOOD.
THAT MAKES ME NIGHTWING AND THE REST OF YOU ARE...THE OTHER ONES.
OKAY--
REMEMBER--IT'S ESSENTIAL YOU ALL STAY CLOSE...

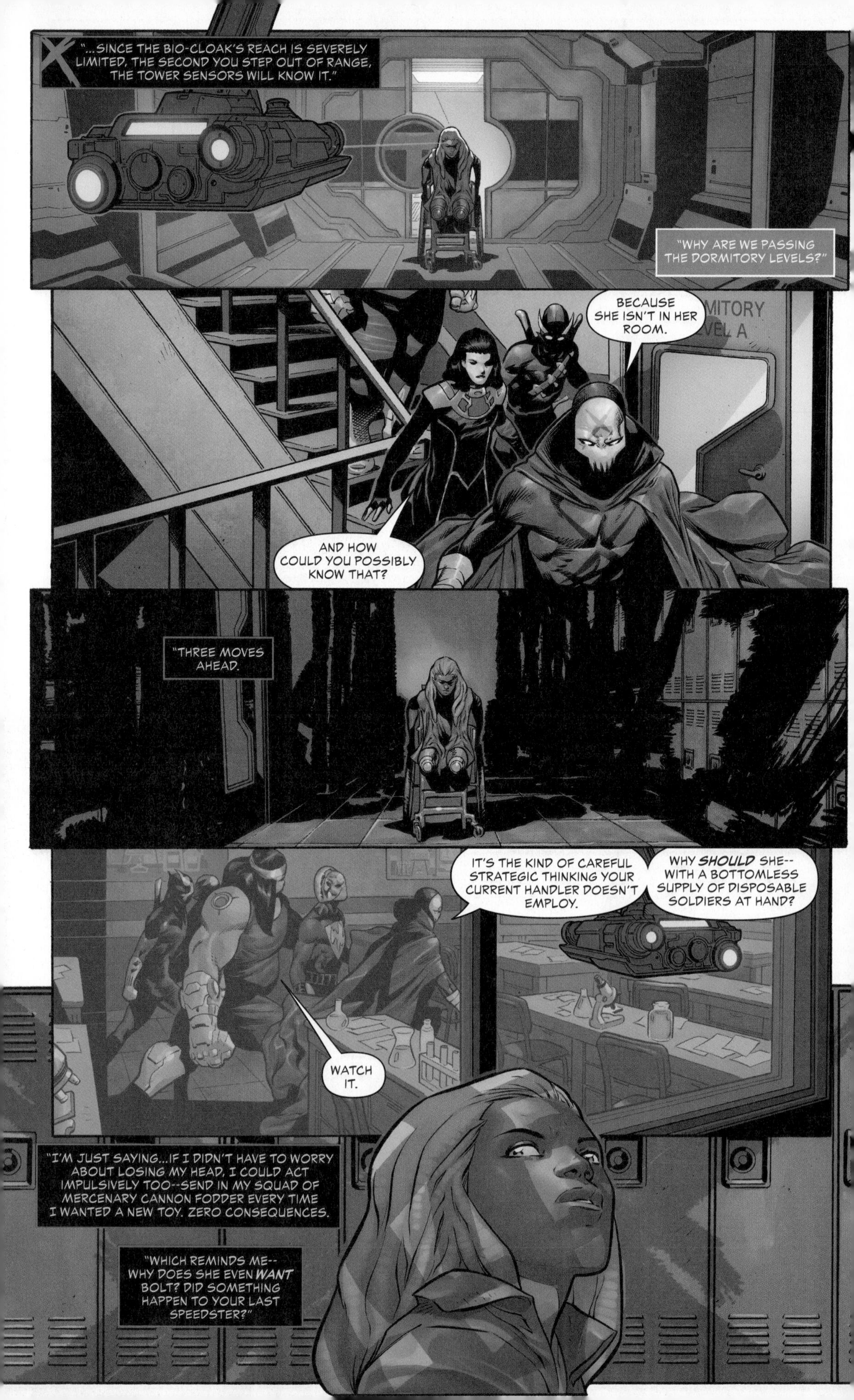
"...SINCE THE BIO-CLOAK'S REACH IS SEVERELY LIMITED, THE SECOND YOU STEP OUT OF RANGE, THE TOWER SENSORS WILL KNOW IT."
"WHY ARE WE PASSING THE DORMITORY LEVELS?"
BECAUSE SHE ISN'T IN HER ROOM.
AND HOW COULD YOU POSSIBLY KNOW THAT?
"THREE MOVES AHEAD.
IT'S THE KIND OF CAREFUL STRATEGIC THINKING YOUR CURRENT HANDLER DOESN'T EMPLOY.
WHY SHOULD SHE-- WITH A BOTTOMLESS SUPPLY OF DISPOSABLE SOLDIERS AT HAND?
WATCH IT.
"I'M JUST SAYING...IF I DIDN'T HAVE TO WORRY ABOUT LOSING MY HEAD, I COULD ACT IMPULSIVELY TOO--SEND IN MY SQUAD OF MERCENARY CANNON FODDER EVERY TIME I WANTED A NEW TOY. ZERO CONSEQUENCES.
"WHICH REMINDS ME-- WHY DOES SHE EVEN WANT BOLT? DID SOMETHING HAPPEN TO YOUR LAST SPEEDSTER?"

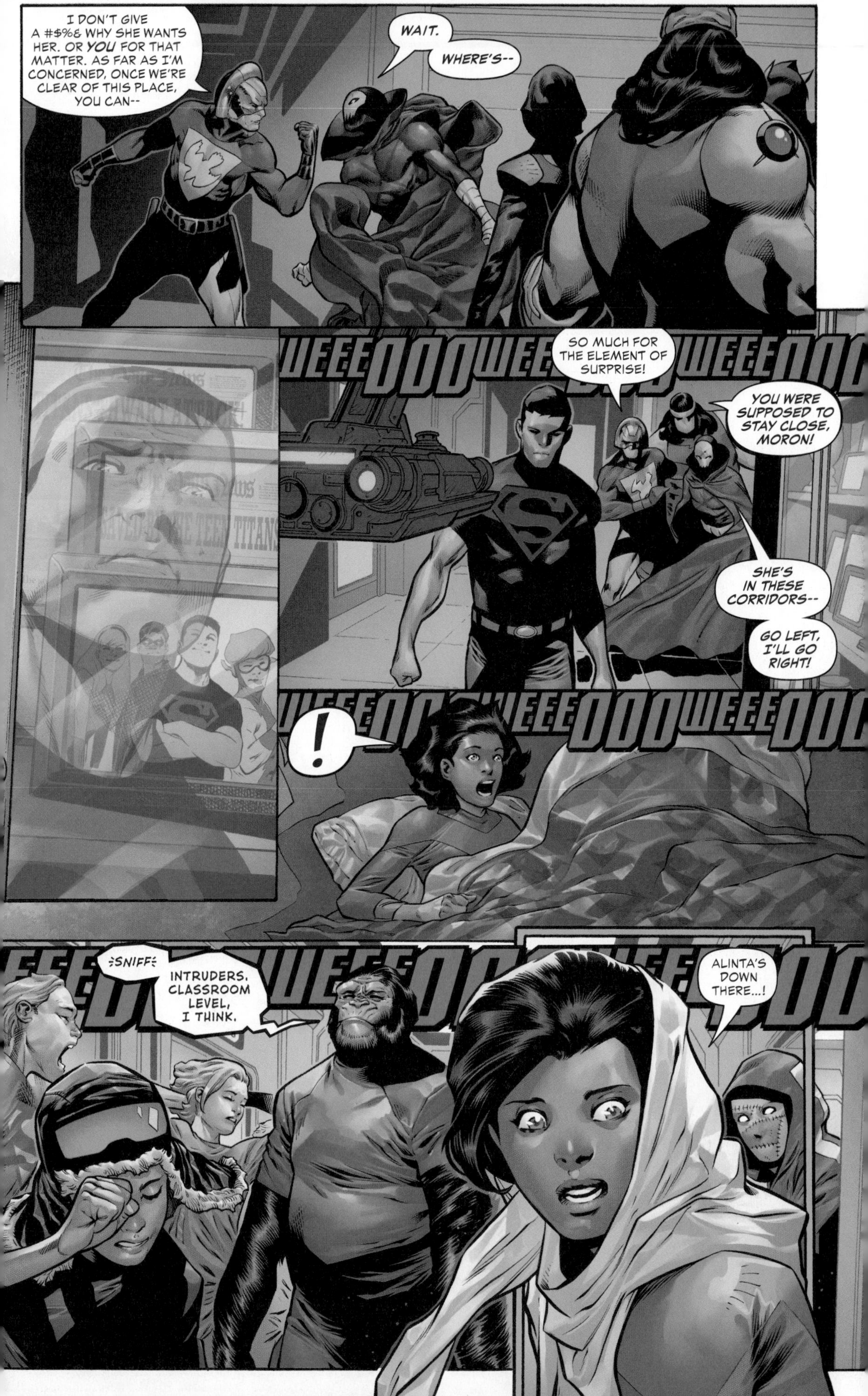
I DON'T GIVE A #$%& WHY SHE WANTS HER. OR YOU FOR THAT MATTER. AS FAR AS I'M CONCERNED, ONCE WE'RE CLEAR OF THIS PLACE, YOU CAN--
WAIT.
WHERE'S--
WEEEOOOWEEEOOOWEEEOOO
SO MUCH FOR THE ELEMENT OF SURPRISE!
YOU WERE SUPPOSED TO STAY CLOSE, MORON!
SHE'S IN THESE CORRIDORS--
GO LEFT, I'LL GO RIGHT!
WEEEOOOWEEEOOOWEEEOOO
!
SNIFF
INTRUDERS. CLASSROOM LEVEL, I THINK.
ALINTA'S DOWN THERE...!

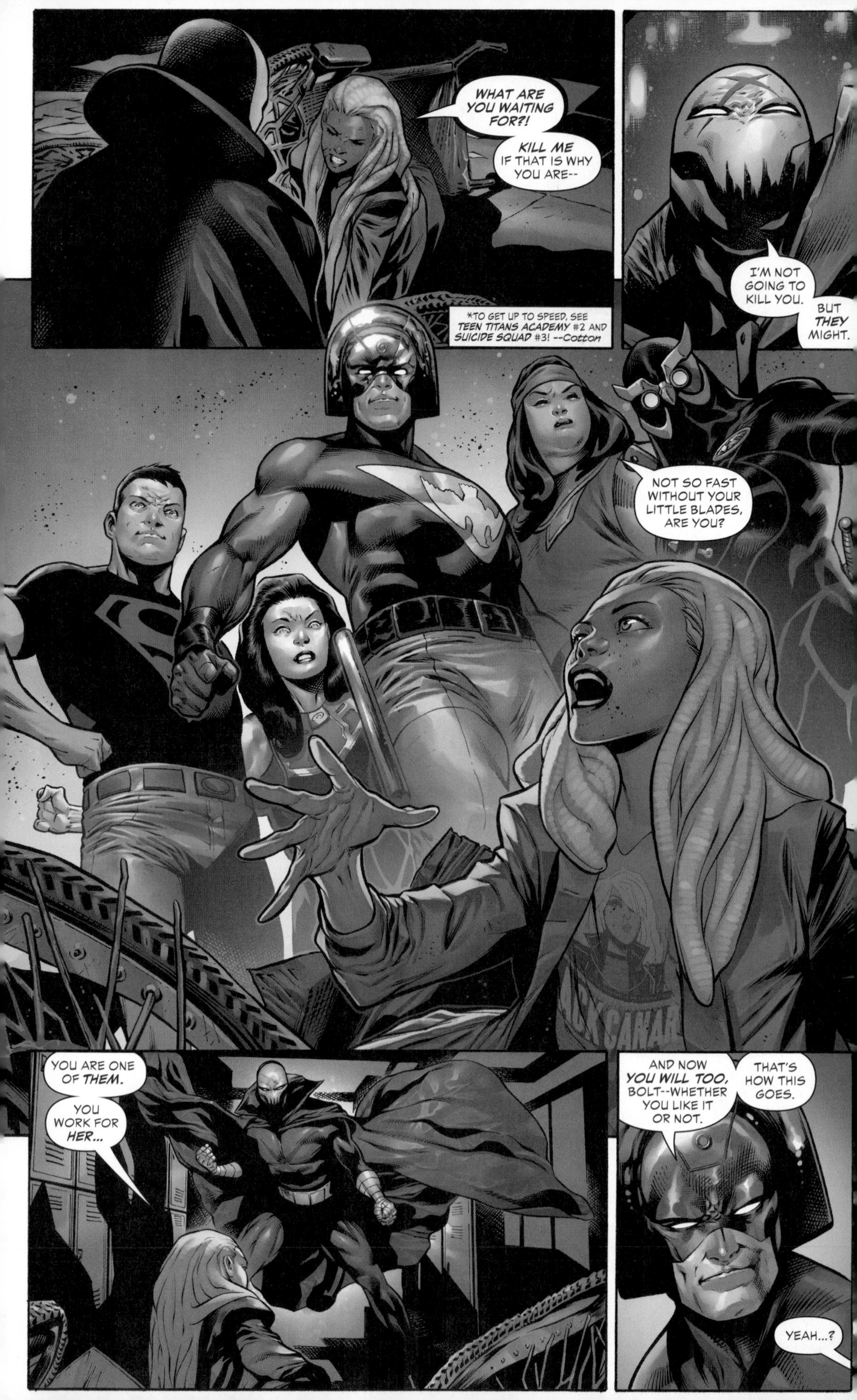
WHAT ARE YOU WAITING FOR?!
KILL ME IF THAT IS WHY YOU ARE--
I'M NOT GOING TO KILL YOU.
BUT THEY MIGHT.
*TO GET UP TO SPEED, SEE TEEN TITANS ACADEMY #2 AND SUICIDE SQUAD #3! --Cotton
NOT SO FAST WITHOUT YOUR LITTLE BLADES, ARE YOU?
YOU ARE ONE OF THEM.
YOU WORK FOR HER...
AND NOW YOU WILL TOO, BOLT--WHETHER YOU LIKE IT OR NOT.
THAT'S HOW THIS GOES.
YEAH...?

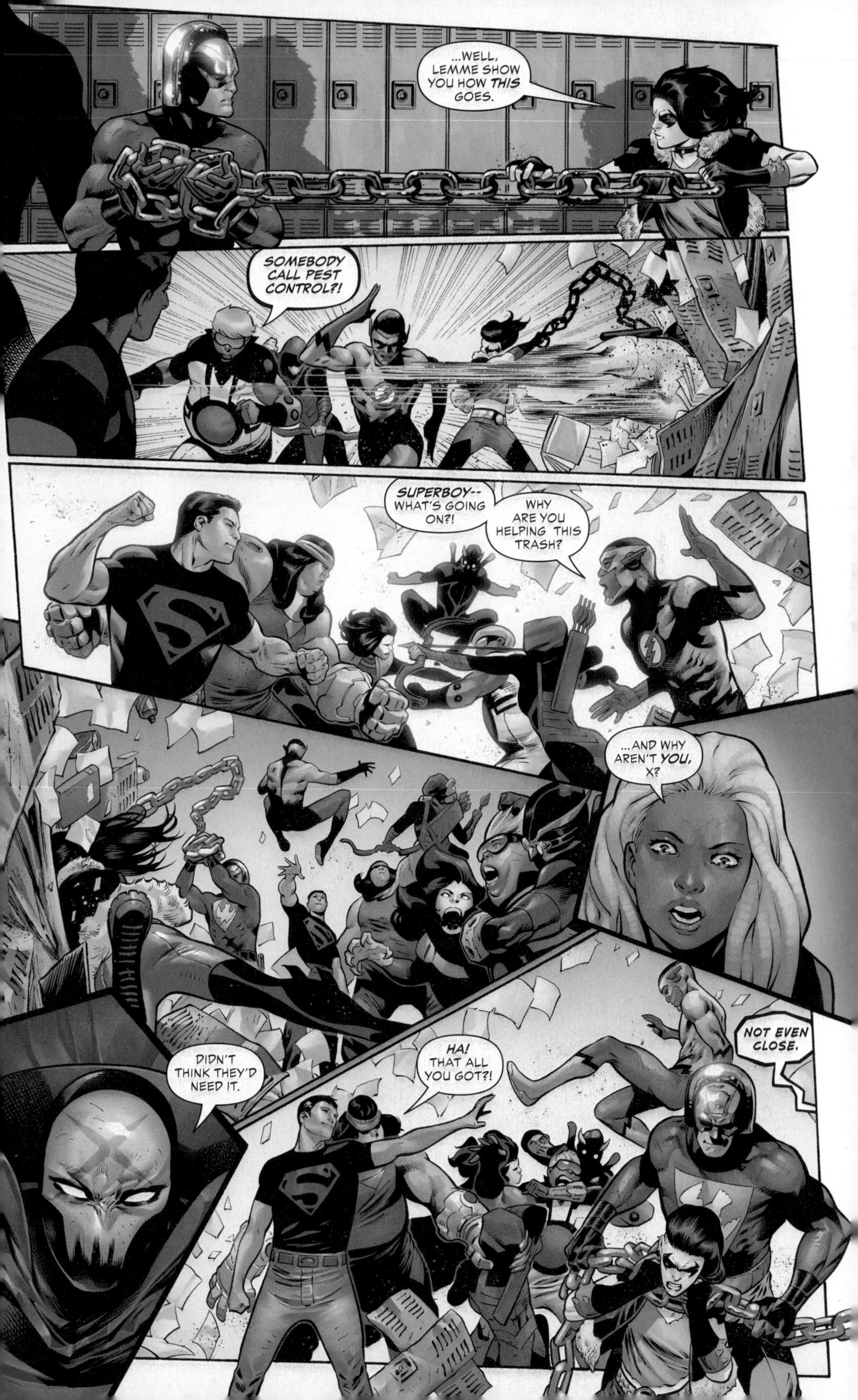
...WELL, LEMME SHOW YOU HOW THIS GOES.
SOMEBODY CALL PEST CONTROL?!
SUPERBOY-- WHAT'S GOING ON?!
WHY ARE YOU HELPING THIS TRASH?
...AND WHY AREN'T YOU, X?
DIDN'T THINK THEY'D NEED IT.
HA! THAT ALL YOU GOT?!
NOT EVEN CLOSE.

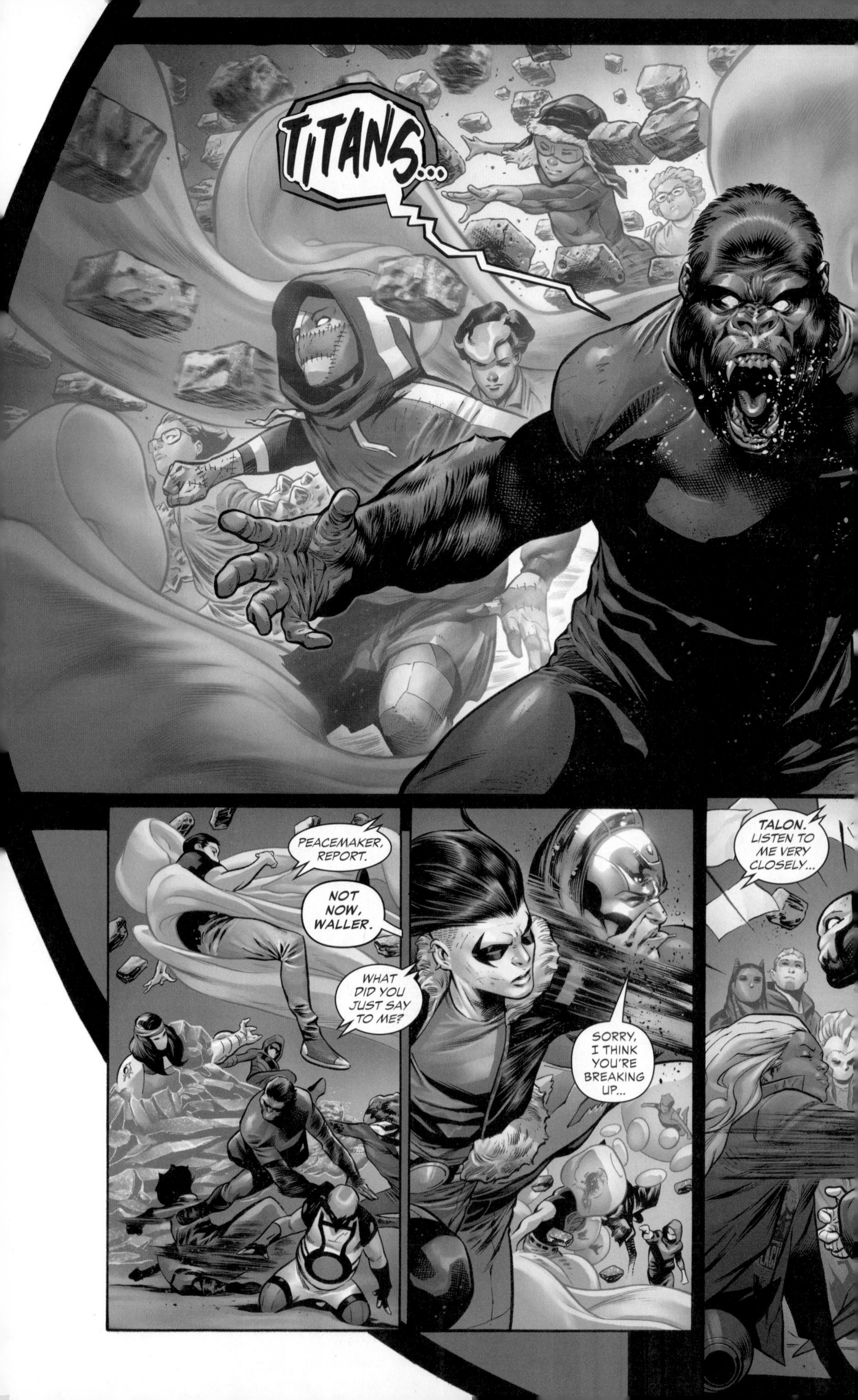
TITANS...
PEACEMAKER, REPORT.
NOT NOW, WALLER.
WHAT DID YOU JUST SAY TO ME?
SORRY, I THINK YOU'RE BREAKING UP...
TALON. LISTEN TO ME VERY CLOSELY...

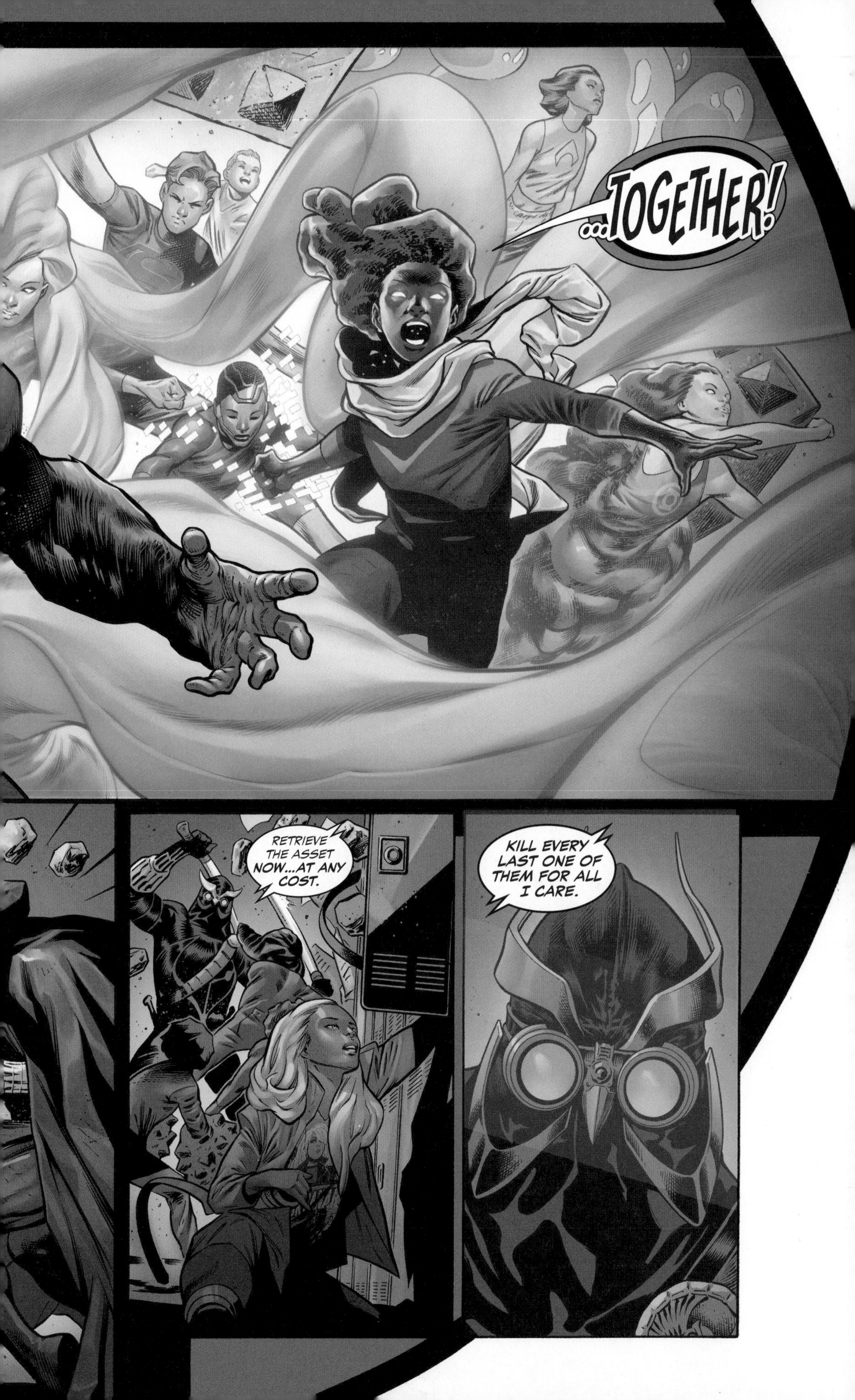

...TOGETHER!
RETRIEVE THE ASSET NOW...AT ANY COST.
KILL EVERY LAST ONE OF THEM FOR ALL I CARE.

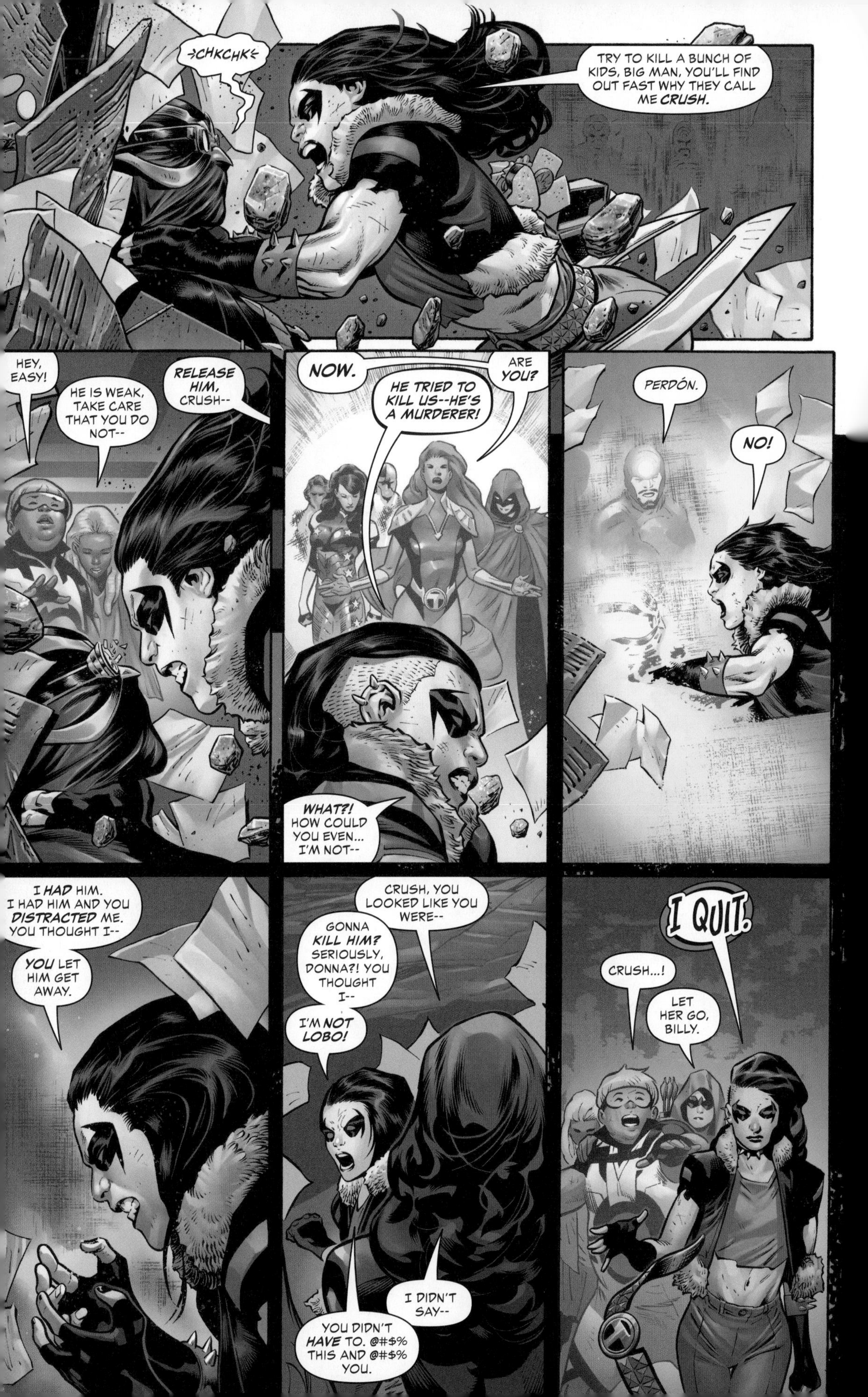

CHKCHK
TRY TO KILL A BUNCH OF KIDS, BIG MAN, YOU'LL FIND OUT FAST WHY THEY CALL ME CRUSH.
HEY, EASY!
HE IS WEAK, TAKE CARE THAT YOU DO NOT--
RELEASE HIM, CRUSH--
NOW.
ARE YOU?
HE TRIED TO KILL US--HE'S A MURDERER!
WHAT?! HOW COULD YOU EVEN... I'M NOT--
PERDÓN.
NO!
I HAD HIM. I HAD HIM AND YOU DISTRACTED ME. YOU THOUGHT I--
YOU LET HIM GET AWAY.
CRUSH, YOU LOOKED LIKE YOU WERE--
GONNA KILL HIM? SERIOUSLY, DONNA?! YOU THOUGHT I--
I'M NOT LOBO!
I DIDN'T SAY--
YOU DIDN'T HAVE TO. @#$% THIS AND @#$% YOU.
I QUIT.
CRUSH...!
LET HER GO, BILLY.

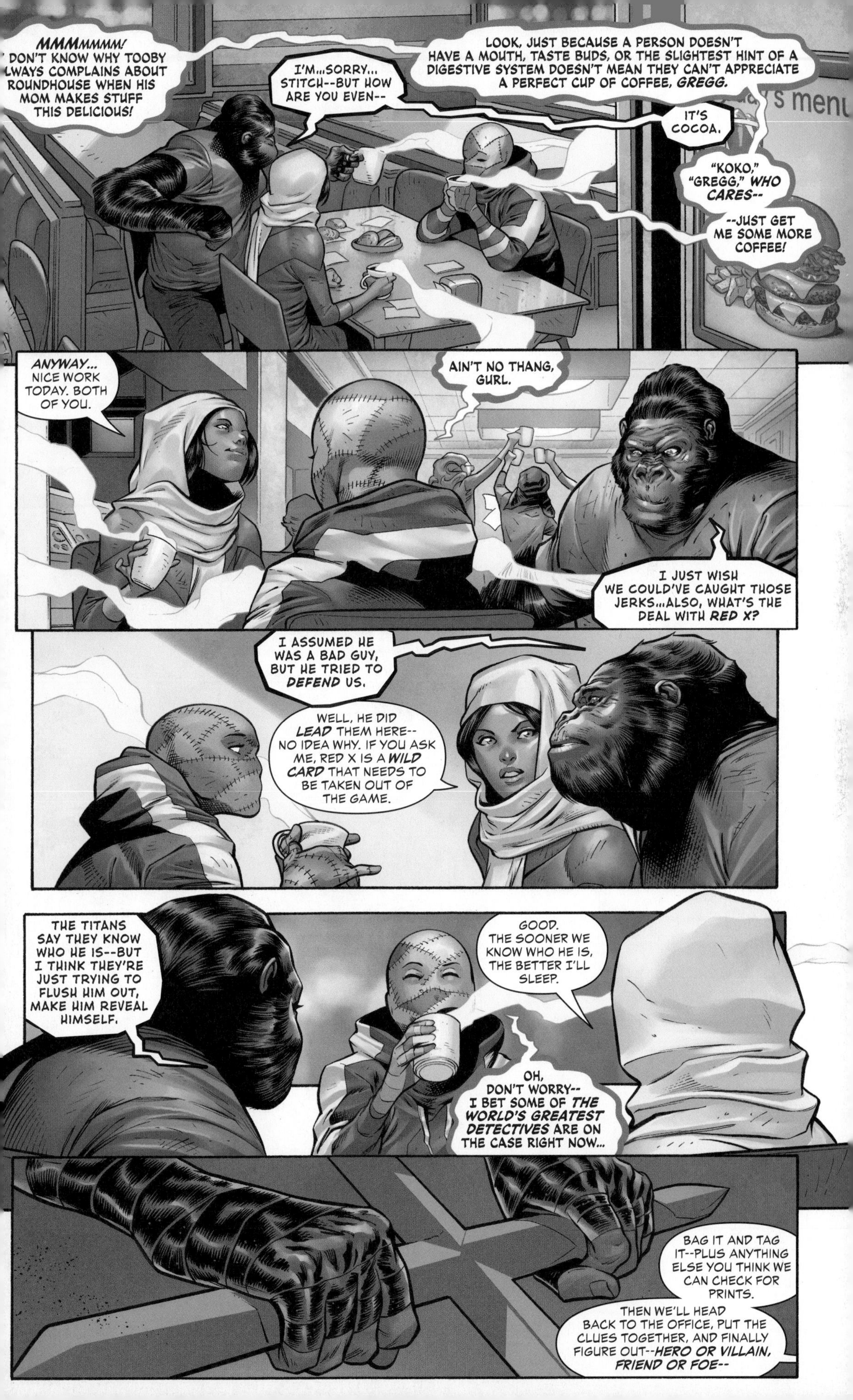
MMMmmmm!
' DON'T KNOW WHY TOOBY LWAYS COMPLAINS ABOUT ROUNDHOUSE WHEN HIS MOM MAKES STUFF THIS DELICIOUS!
I'M...SORRY... STITCH--BUT HOW ARE YOU EVEN--
LOOK, JUST BECAUSE A PERSON DOESN'T HAVE A MOUTH, TASTE BUDS, OR THE SLIGHTEST HINT OF A DIGESTIVE SYSTEM DOESN'T MEAN THEY CAN'T APPRECIATE A PERFECT CUP OF COFFEE, GREGG.
IT'S COCOA.
"KOKO," "GREGG," WHO CARES--
--JUST GET ME SOME MORE COFFEE!
ANYWAY... NICE WORK TODAY. BOTH OF YOU.
AIN'T NO THANG, GURL.
I JUST WISH WE COULD'VE CAUGHT THOSE JERKS...ALSO, WHAT'S THE DEAL WITH RED X?
I ASSUMED HE WAS A BAD GUY, BUT HE TRIED TO DEFEND US.
WELL, HE DID LEAD THEM HERE-- NO IDEA WHY. IF YOU ASK ME, RED X IS A WILD CARD THAT NEEDS TO BE TAKEN OUT OF THE GAME.
THE TITANS SAY THEY KNOW WHO HE IS--BUT I THINK THEY'RE JUST TRYING TO FLUSH HIM OUT, MAKE HIM REVEAL HIMSELF.
GOOD. THE SOONER WE KNOW WHO HE IS, THE BETTER I'LL SLEEP.
OH, DON'T WORRY-- I BET SOME OF THE WORLD'S GREATEST DETECTIVES ARE ON THE CASE RIGHT NOW...
BAG IT AND TAG IT--PLUS ANYTHING ELSE YOU THINK WE CAN CHECK FOR PRINTS.
THEN WE'LL HEAD BACK TO THE OFFICE, PUT THE CLUES TOGETHER, AND FINALLY FIGURE OUT--HERO OR VILLAIN, FRIEND OR FOE--

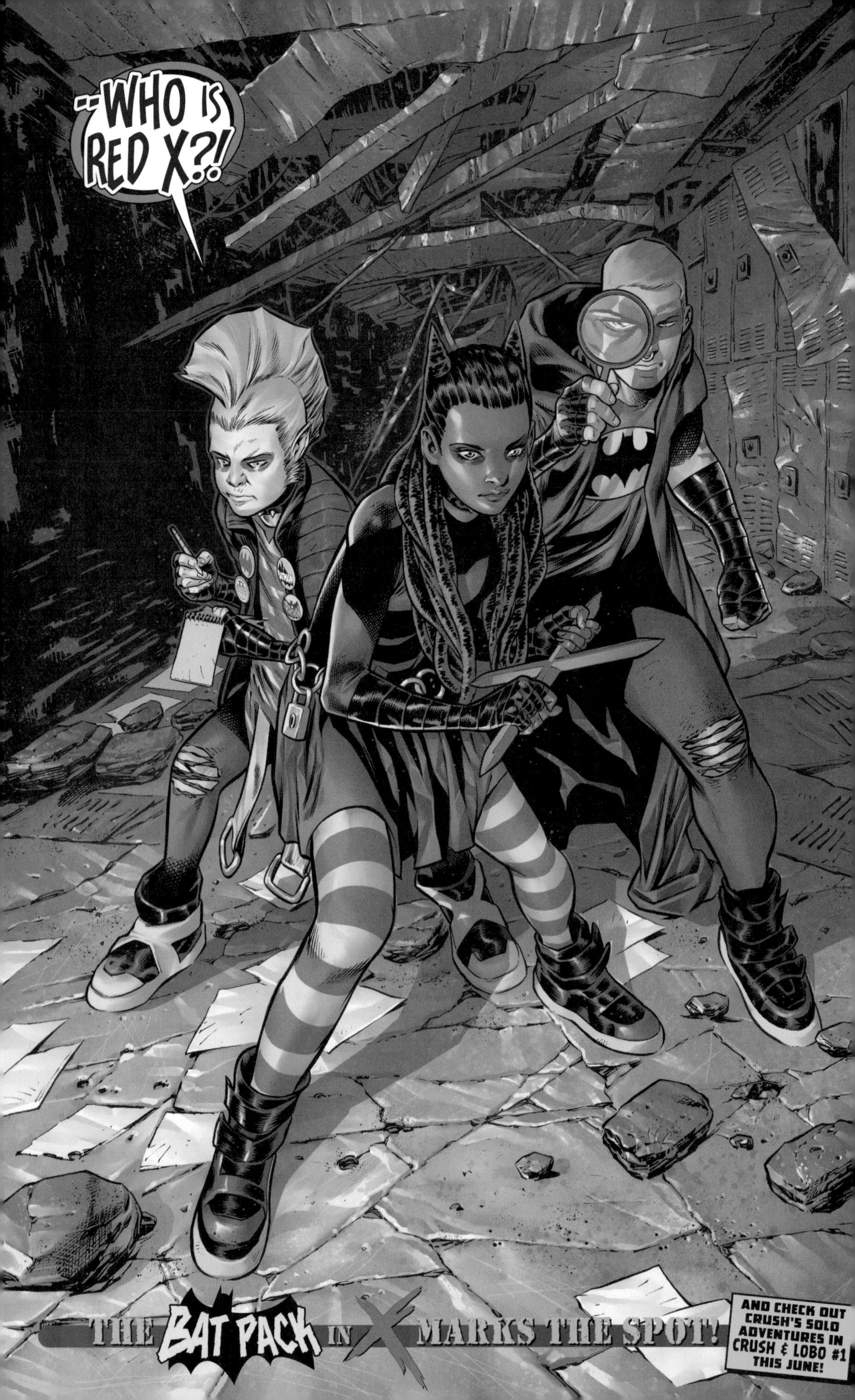
--WHO IS RED X?!
THE BAT PACK IN X MARKS THE SPOT!
AND CHECK OUT CRUSH'S SOLO ADVENTURES IN CRUSH & LOBO #1 THIS JUNE!

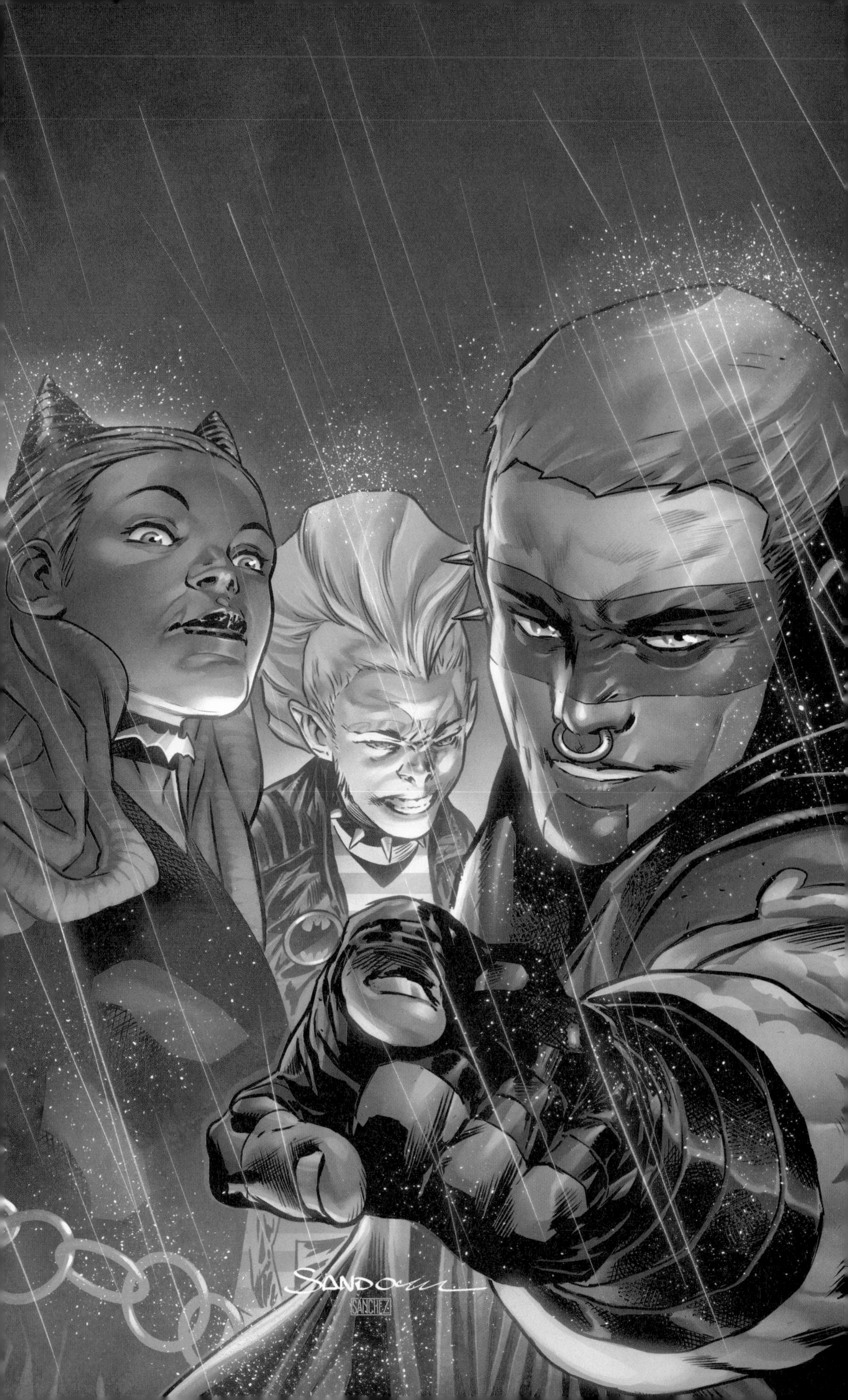
SANCHEZ

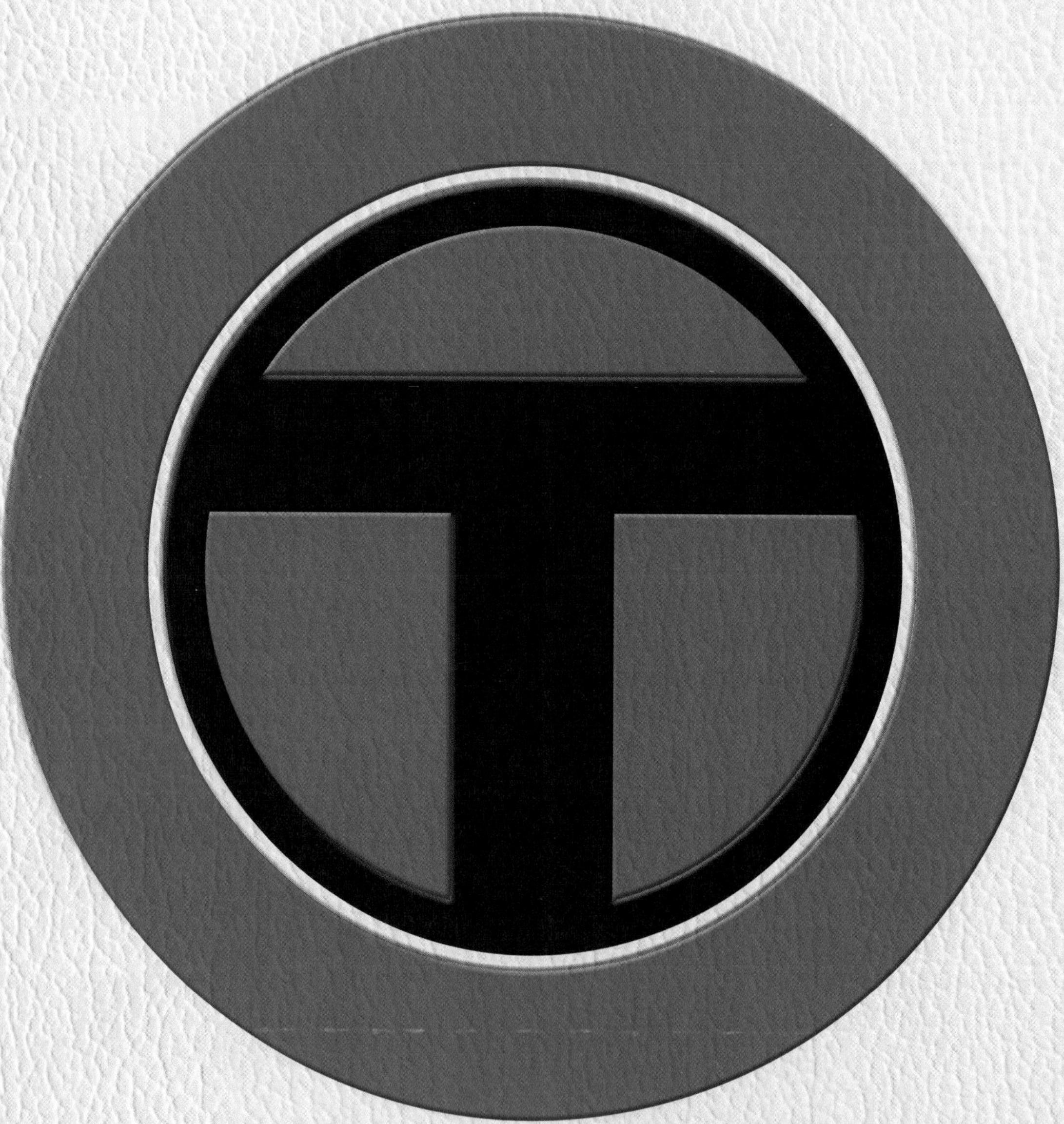

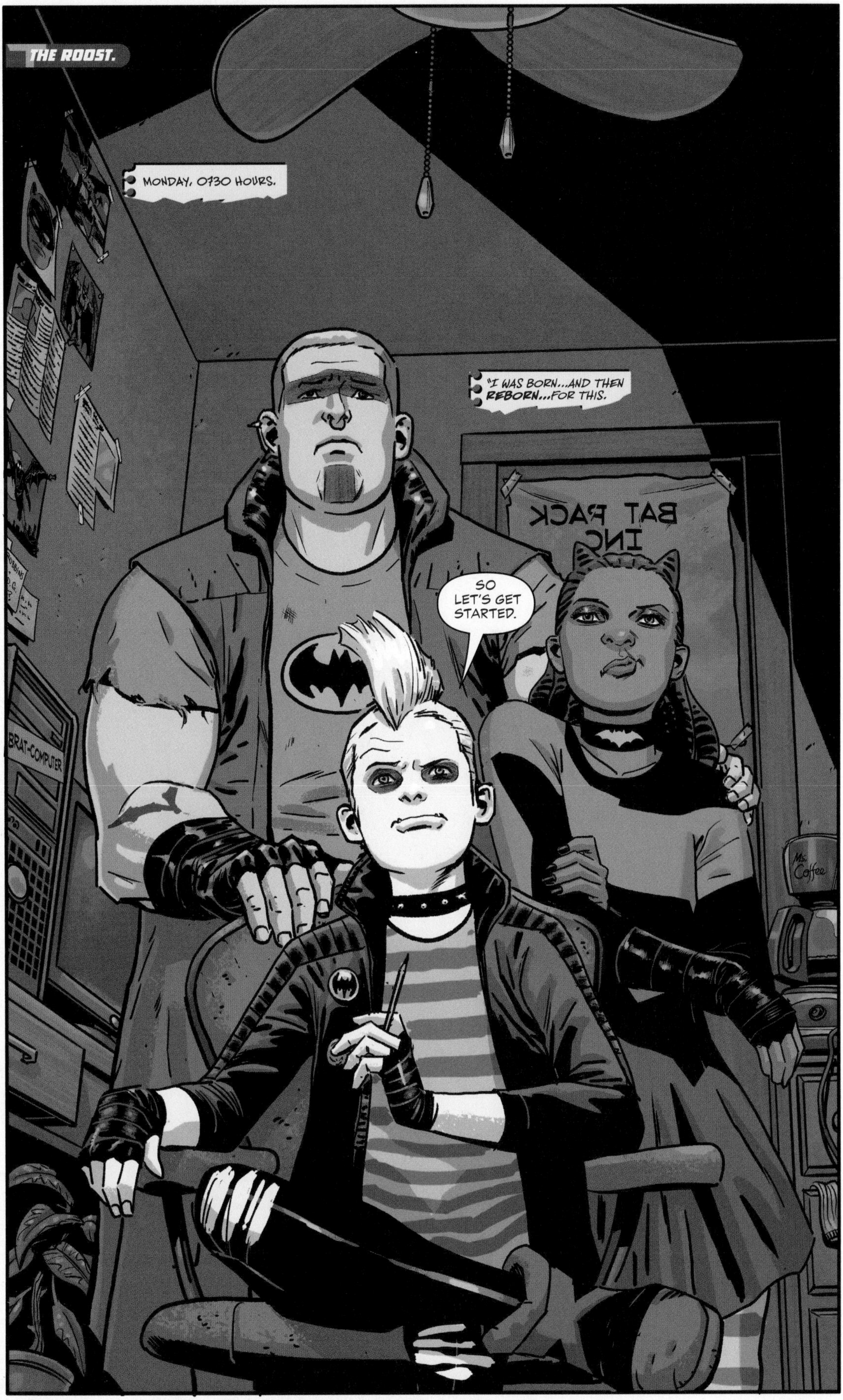
THE ROOST.
MONDAY, 0730 HOURS.
"I WAS BORN...AND THEN REBORN...FOR THIS.
SO LET'S GET STARTED.
BRAT-COMPUTER
Ms. Coffee

"I'D STUDIED EVERY MOVE MADE BY THE *DARK KNIGHT*.

"THE WORLD'S GREATEST DETECTIVE.

TEEN TITANS ACADEMY *Presents: The* BAT PACK *in*

X MARKS THE SPOT!

TIM SHERIDAN
writer

STEVE LIEBER
artist

DAVE STEWART
colorist

ROB LEIGH
letterer

STEPHEN
BYRNE
pride variant cover

RAFA
SANDOVAL
cover

ALEJANDRO
SANCHEZ

PHILIP
TAN
variant cover

ELMER
SANTOS

DIEGO
LOPEZ
assoc. editor

MIKE
COTTON
editor

JAMIE S.
RICH
group editor

The "Progress" Pride flag in the DC Logo designed by DANIEL QUASAR

From the halls of TEEN TITANS ACADEMY, through the darque doors of existential ennui, emerges the world's greatest team of junior nihilist detectives: THE BAT PACK! Together, brainy BRATGIRL, chilling CHUPACABRA, and the mighty MEGABAT are on the case, following the clues, wherever they may lead, to solve the freakiest mysteries the universe has ever known!...or, ya know, whatever. Ugh.

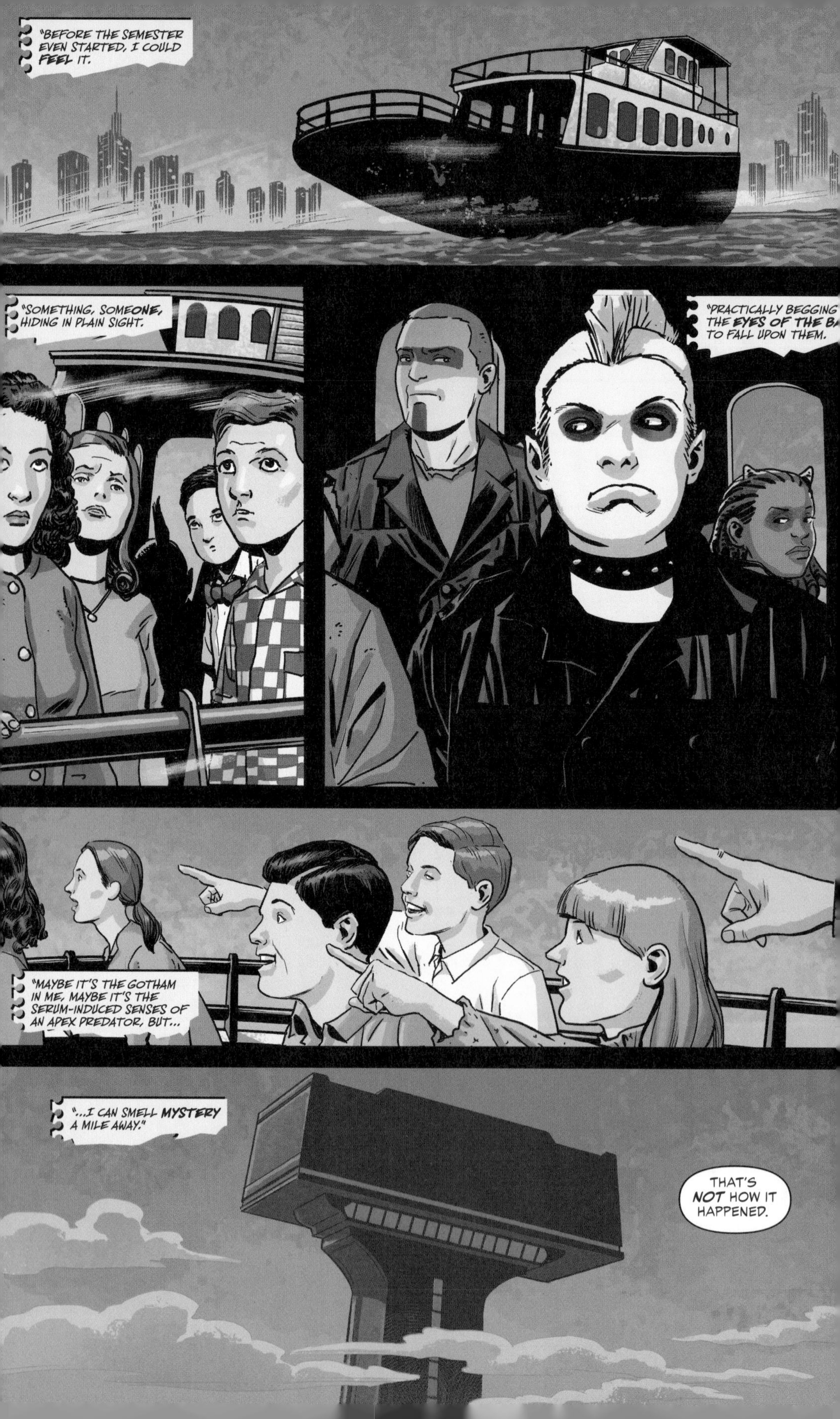
"BEFORE THE SEMESTER EVEN STARTED, I COULD FEEL IT.
"SOMETHING, SOMEONE, HIDING IN PLAIN SIGHT.
"PRACTICALLY BEGGING THE EYES OF THE B
TO FALL UPON THEM.
"MAYBE IT'S THE GOTHAM IN ME, MAYBE IT'S THE SERUM-INDUCED SENSES OF AN APEX PREDATOR, BUT...
"...I CAN SMELL MYSTERY A MILE AWAY."
THAT'S NOT HOW IT HAPPENED.

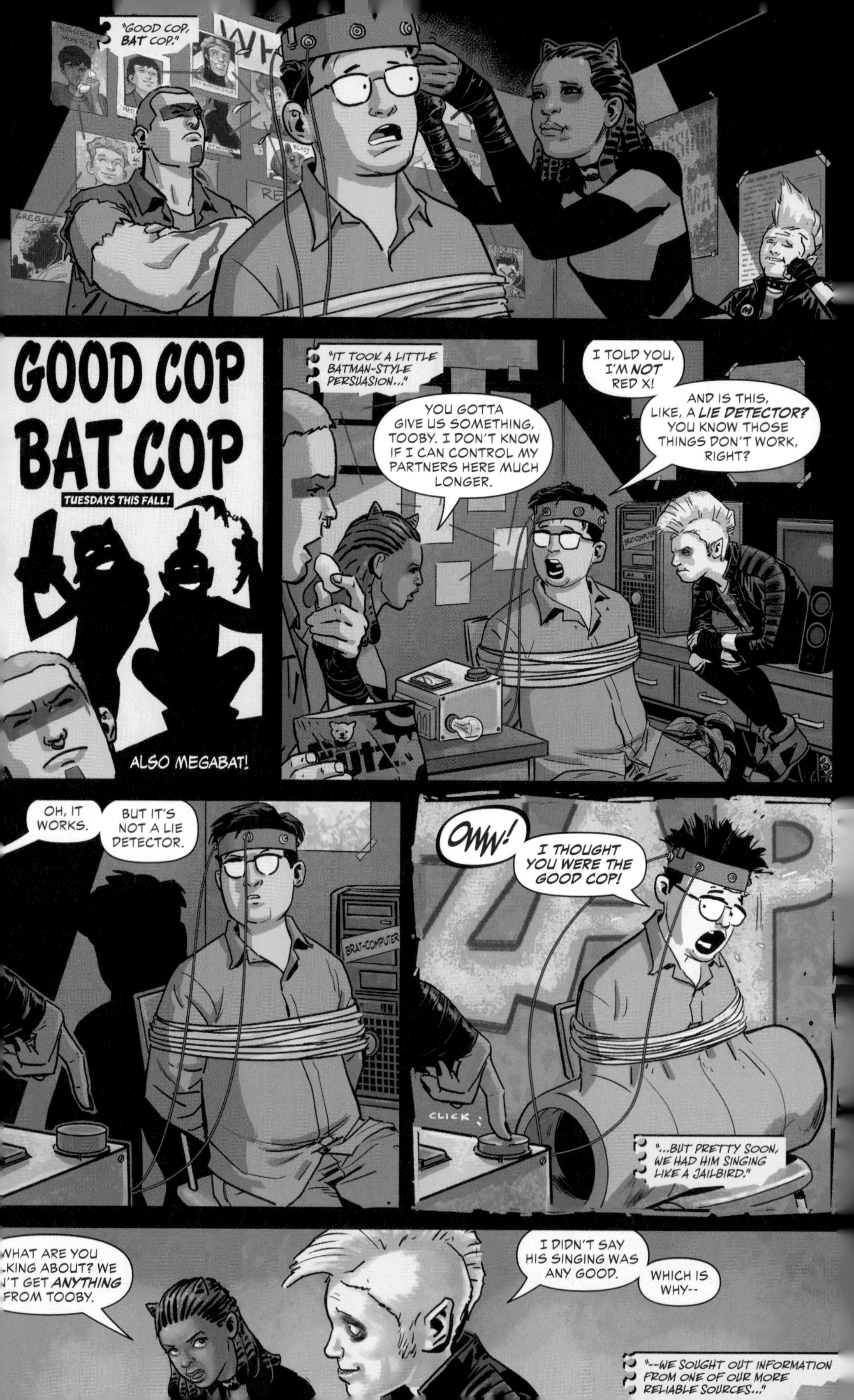

"GOOD COP, **BAT** COP."
GOOD COP BAT COP
TUESDAYS THIS FALL!
ALSO MEGABAT!
"IT TOOK A LITTLE BATMAN-STYLE PERSUASION..."
YOU GOTTA GIVE US SOMETHING, TOOBY. I DON'T KNOW IF I CAN CONTROL MY PARTNERS HERE MUCH LONGER.
I TOLD YOU, I'M **NOT** RED X!
AND IS THIS, LIKE, A ***LIE DETECTOR?*** YOU KNOW THOSE THINGS DON'T WORK, RIGHT?
BRAT-COMPUTER
OH, IT WORKS.
BUT IT'S NOT A LIE DETECTOR.
BRAT-COMPUTER
OWW!
I THOUGHT YOU WERE THE GOOD COP!
CLICK
"...BUT PRETTY SOON, WE HAD HIM SINGING LIKE A JAILBIRD."
WHAT ARE YOU
LKING ABOUT? WE
N'T GET ***ANYTHING***
FROM TOOBY.
I DIDN'T SAY HIS SINGING WAS ANY GOOD.
WHICH IS WHY--
"--WE SOUGHT OUT INFORMATION FROM ONE OF OUR MORE RELIABLE SOURCES..."

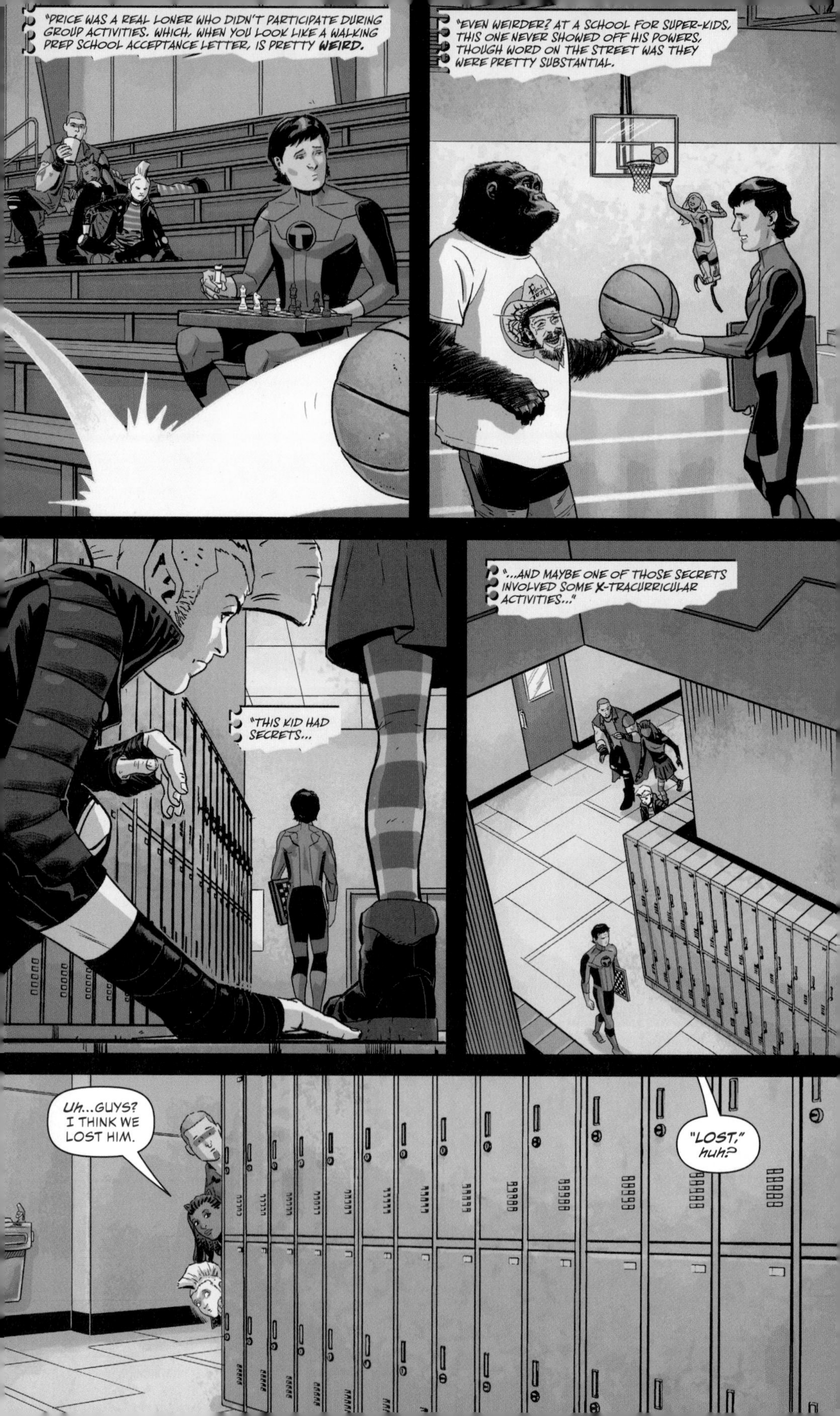
"PRICE WAS A REAL LONER WHO DIDN'T PARTICIPATE DURING GROUP ACTIVITIES. WHICH, WHEN YOU LOOK LIKE A WALKING PREP SCHOOL ACCEPTANCE LETTER, IS PRETTY WEIRD.
"EVEN WEIRDER? AT A SCHOOL FOR SUPER-KIDS, THIS ONE NEVER SHOWED OFF HIS POWERS, THOUGH WORD ON THE STREET WAS THEY WERE PRETTY SUBSTANTIAL.
"THIS KID HAD SECRETS...
"...AND MAYBE ONE OF THOSE SECRETS INVOLVED SOME X-TRACURRICULAR ACTIVITIES..."
Uh...GUYS? I THINK WE LOST HIM.
"LOST," huh?

DETENTION:
a chance to stop and
think about what you've done.

"IT TURNS OUT, DETENTION REALLY *IS* A CHANCE TO STOP AND THINK ABOUT WHAT YOU'VE DONE..."

"...AND ALL *WE'D* DONE IS CHASE OUR OWN TAIL THE ENTIRE INVESTIGATION. WE WERE NOWHERE, AND WE KNEW IT."

"THE BASIC FACTS: X DOWNLOADED UNKNOWN FILES FROM THE TOWER'S CLASSIFIED MAINFRAME, THEN WORKED WITH A *POSSIBLE TERRORIST GROUP* TO KIDNAP BOLT BEFORE SWITCHING SIDES TO DEFEND HER AND THE REST OF THE STUDENT BODY.*"

"*A BIG BREAK THAT, *MAYBE*, WAS RIGHT IN FRONT OF US."

"*HOW DID WE NOT THINK OF *HIM* BEFORE? CLASSIC BULLY, QUICK TO ANGER, WITH AN OBVIOUS, YET *MYSTERIOUS*, CHIP ON HIS SHOULDER."

"ASIDE FROM A COUPLE MORE RANDOM SIGHTINGS, THAT'S ALL WE HAD."

TOOBY

STITCH

PHATT

IS HE FRIEND? FOE? OUT-OF-CONTROL CLASS PRANK?

WE NEED A BIG BREAK, YOU GUYS-- AND *SOON*.

*SEE *TTA* #3 AND *SUICIDE SQUAD* #3. --Cotton

"IF THERE WAS ONE NAME-BRAND ANGRY LONER AT THE *TITANS SCHOOL FOR GIFTED YOUNGSTERS*, IT WAS BRICK PETTIROSSO.

"THIS KID WAS ABSOLUTELY HIDING SOMETHING. CLEVERLY STASHED AWAY, WRAPPED UP SOMEWHERE OUT OF SIGHT.

"IF WE COULD GET OUR HANDS ON WHATEVER THAT WAS--"

IT'S *NOT* BRICK...

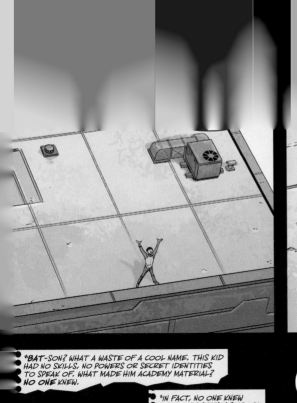

"*BAT-SON? WHAT A WASTE OF A COOL NAME. THIS KID HAD NO SKILLS. NO POWERS OR SECRET IDENTITIES TO SPEAK OF. WHAT MADE HIM ACADEMY MATERIAL? NO ONE KNEW.*

"*IN FACT, NO ONE KNEW MUCH OF ANYTHING ABOUT BILLY BATSON...*"

LOOK AT THIS VIDEO OF X FROM TWO MONTHS AGO.

COULD BE THE SAME GUY.

GO BACK TO THE LIVE FEED...

LET'S SEE IF WE CAN READ BILLY'S LIPS, FIGURE OUT WHAT HE'S--

THAT'S ODD.

VISUAL'S DOWN--SOME KIND OF SUDDEN ELECTRICAL INTERFERENCE...

WHAT THE HECK IS HAPPENING UP THERE?!

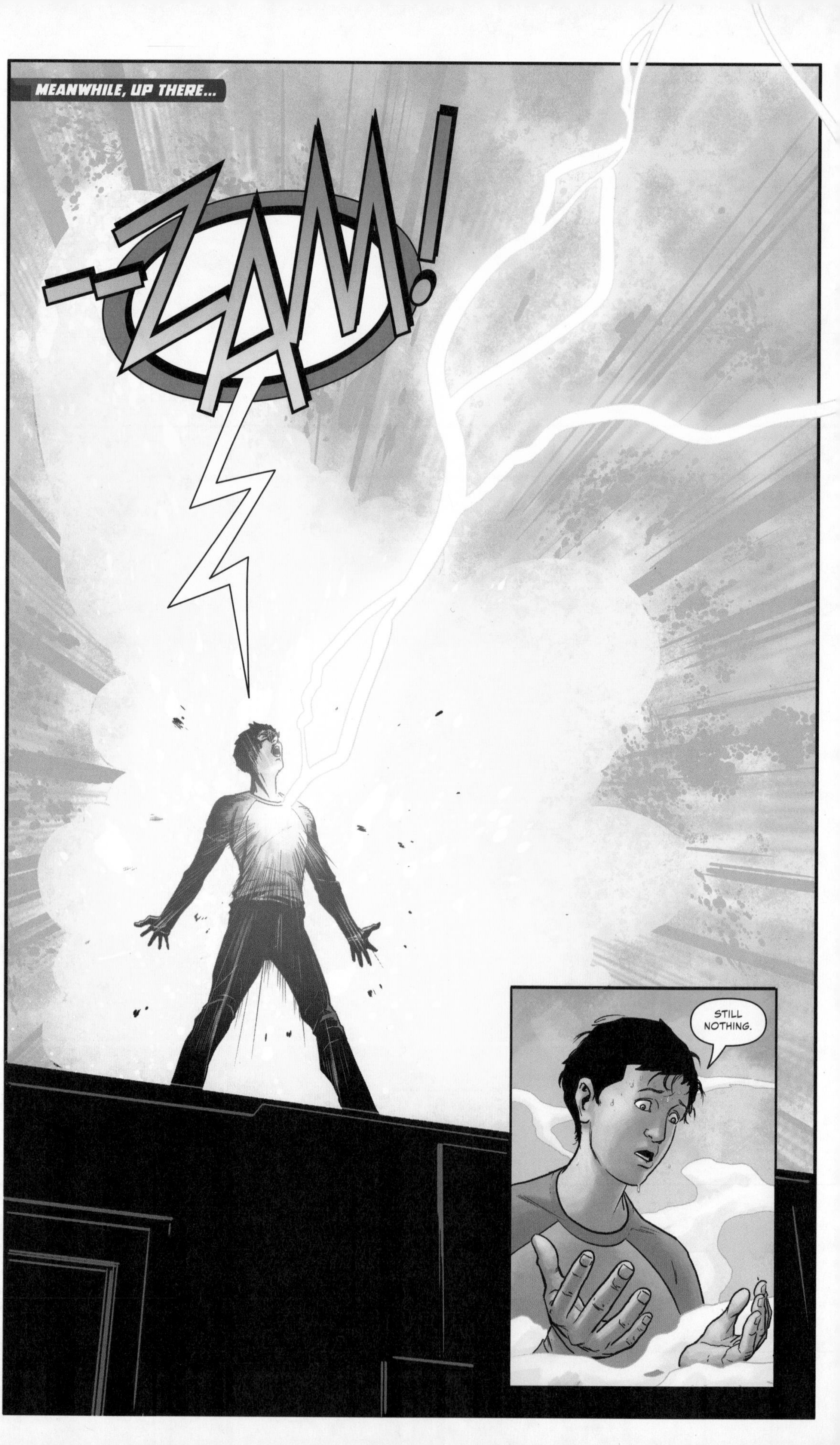
MEANWHILE, UP THERE...
-ZAM!
STILL NOTHING.

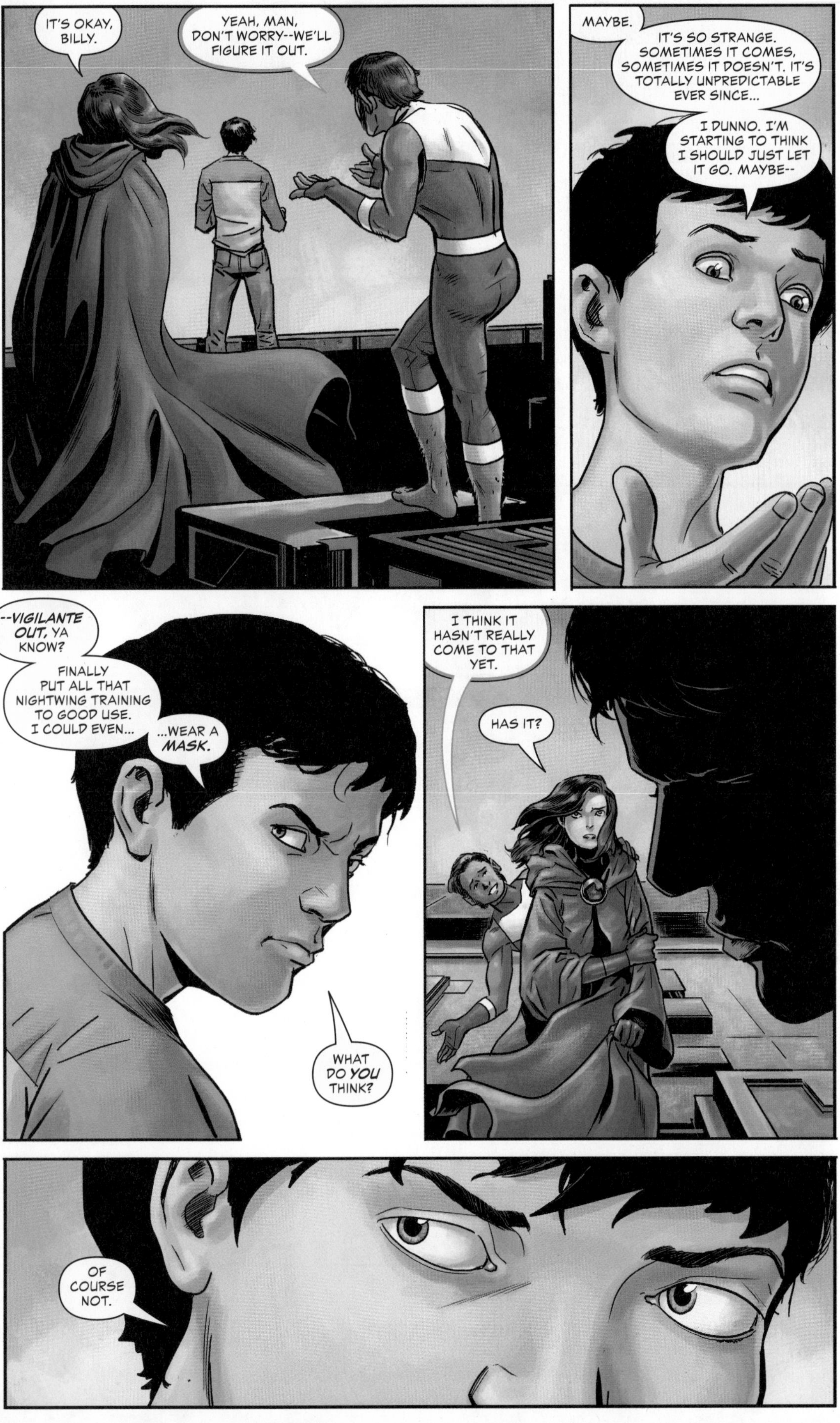
IT'S OKAY, BILLY.
YEAH, MAN, DON'T WORRY--WE'LL FIGURE IT OUT.
MAYBE.
IT'S SO STRANGE. SOMETIMES IT COMES, SOMETIMES IT DOESN'T. IT'S TOTALLY UNPREDICTABLE EVER SINCE...
I DUNNO. I'M STARTING TO THINK I SHOULD JUST LET IT GO. MAYBE--
--VIGILANTE OUT, YA KNOW?
FINALLY PUT ALL THAT NIGHTWING TRAINING TO GOOD USE. I COULD EVEN...
...WEAR A MASK.
WHAT DO YOU THINK?
I THINK IT HASN'T REALLY COME TO THAT YET.
HAS IT?
OF COURSE NOT.

"SINCE BRATGIRL COULDN'T REESTABLISH THE VISUAL LINK TO THE ROOF, WE HAD ABSOLUTELY NO IDEA WHAT HAPPENED UP THERE."

"SO AFTER DETENTION, WE PAID A VISIT TO BILLY'S PLACE, WHERE WE MET ONE MIGUEL MONTEZ."

B. BATSON
M. MONTEZ

NO, I UNDERSTAND COMPLETELY. YOU THREE WANT TO SEARCH OUR ROOM AS PART OF SOME TOP SECRET UNDERGROUND INVESTIGATION YOU'RE CONDUCTING.

GOT IT.

B. BATSON
M. MONTEZ

SLAM

B. BATSON
M. MONTEZ

YIKES.

THE DOOR WASN'T OPEN LONG ENOUGH TO COMPLETE MY SCAN.

B. BATSON
M. MONTEZ

YOU CAN SCAN MY STUFF IF YOU WANT.

M. RADLEY
B. PETTIROSSO

I MEAN, LIKE, IF IT'S FOR SCIENCE, OR WHATEVER.

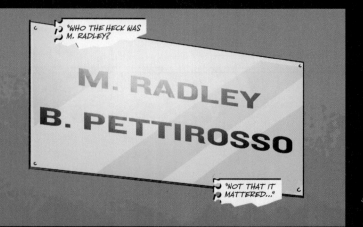

"WHO THE HECK WAS M. RADLEY?"

M. RADLEY
B. PETTIROSSO

"NOT THAT IT MATTERED..."

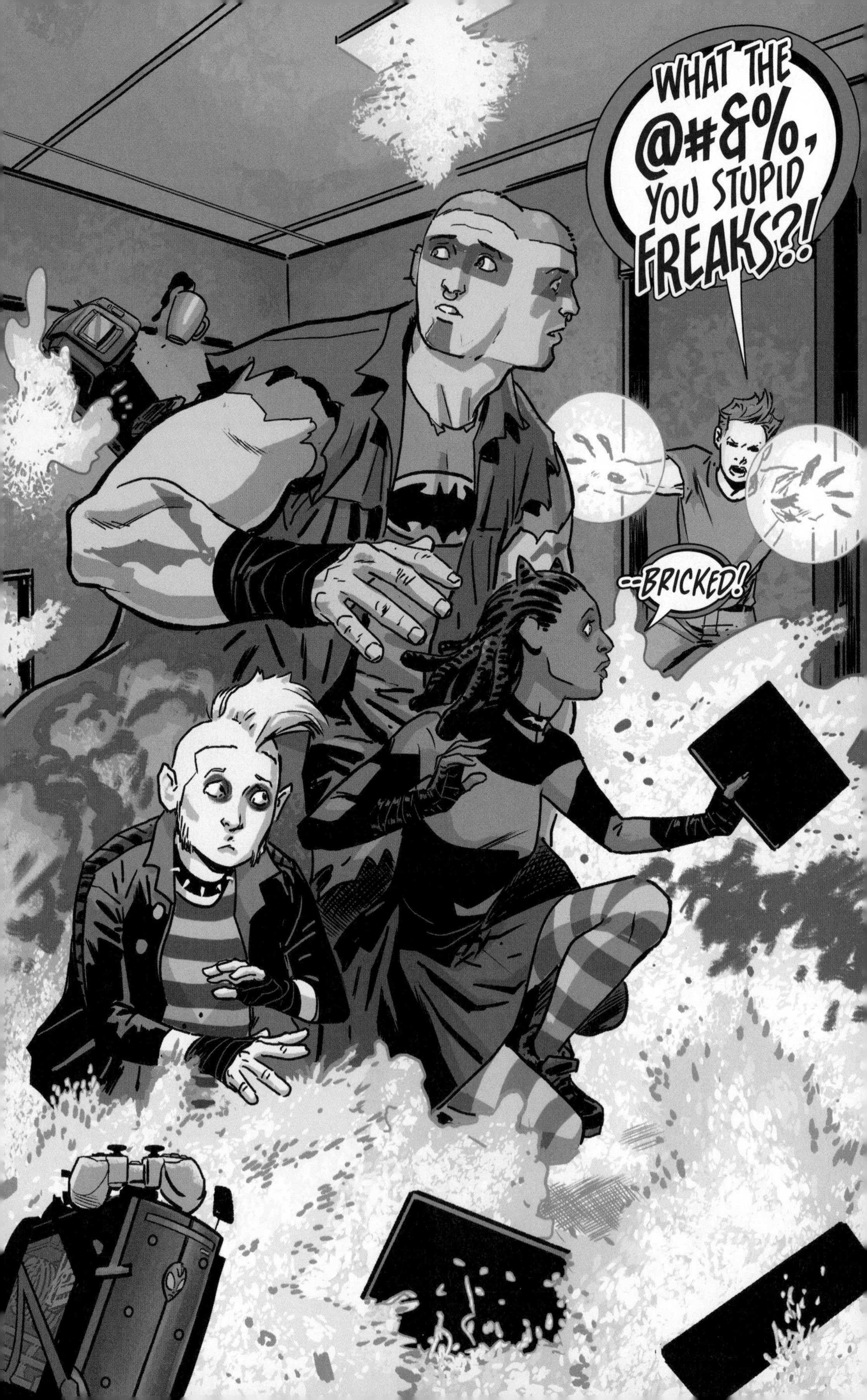
WHAT THE @#&%, YOU STUPID FREAKS?!
--BRICKED!

...IS **NOT** RED X.

HEY! DON'T SNEAK UP!

WHAT IS THIS? HAVE YOU GUYS BEEN DOING YOUR OWN LITTLE INVESTIGATION?

DIEGO, MERISSA, LUCAS--LISTEN TO ME. **STAY AWAY FROM THIS.**

WE DON'T KNOW IF THIS NEW RED X IS ON OUR SIDE, OUT FOR HIMSELF...OR WORKING FOR SOMEONE MUCH WORSE. IT'S THE **NOT KNOWING** THAT MAKES HIM A DANGER TO US.

THAT'S WHY WE'RE GONNA UNMASK HIM! IN FRONT OF YOU, IN FRONT OF EVERYONE.

NO. THIS ISN'T UP FOR DISCUSSION. STAY AWAY FROM IT. GO BACK TO YOUR STUDIES AND IF YOU SO MUCH AS **HEAR** ABOUT RED X, YOU BRING IT TO US. THAT'S **FINAL.**

NOW GET BACK TO YOUR ROOMS.

*THE OVERLORDS HAD SPOKEN.

*THEY WANTED US OFF THE CASE, AND TO STEER CLEAR OF--

DO YOU GUYS SMELL... **BRIMSTONE?**

BILLY!

THERE YOU ARE! MIGUEL SAID YOU WERE ALL LOOKING FOR ME?

Uhhh...

...NOPE?

REALLY. *Huh*. OKAY. WELL...THEN I GUESS I'LL SEE YOU AROUND?

FOR SURE.

HE KNOWS WE KNOW!

AND NOW *HE* KNOWS *WE* KNOW HE KNOWS WE KNOW!

HE'S **THREE MOVES AHEAD...** AND YOU KNOW WHAT THAT MEANS...

BILLY BATSON IS **DEFINITELY--**

KLIK

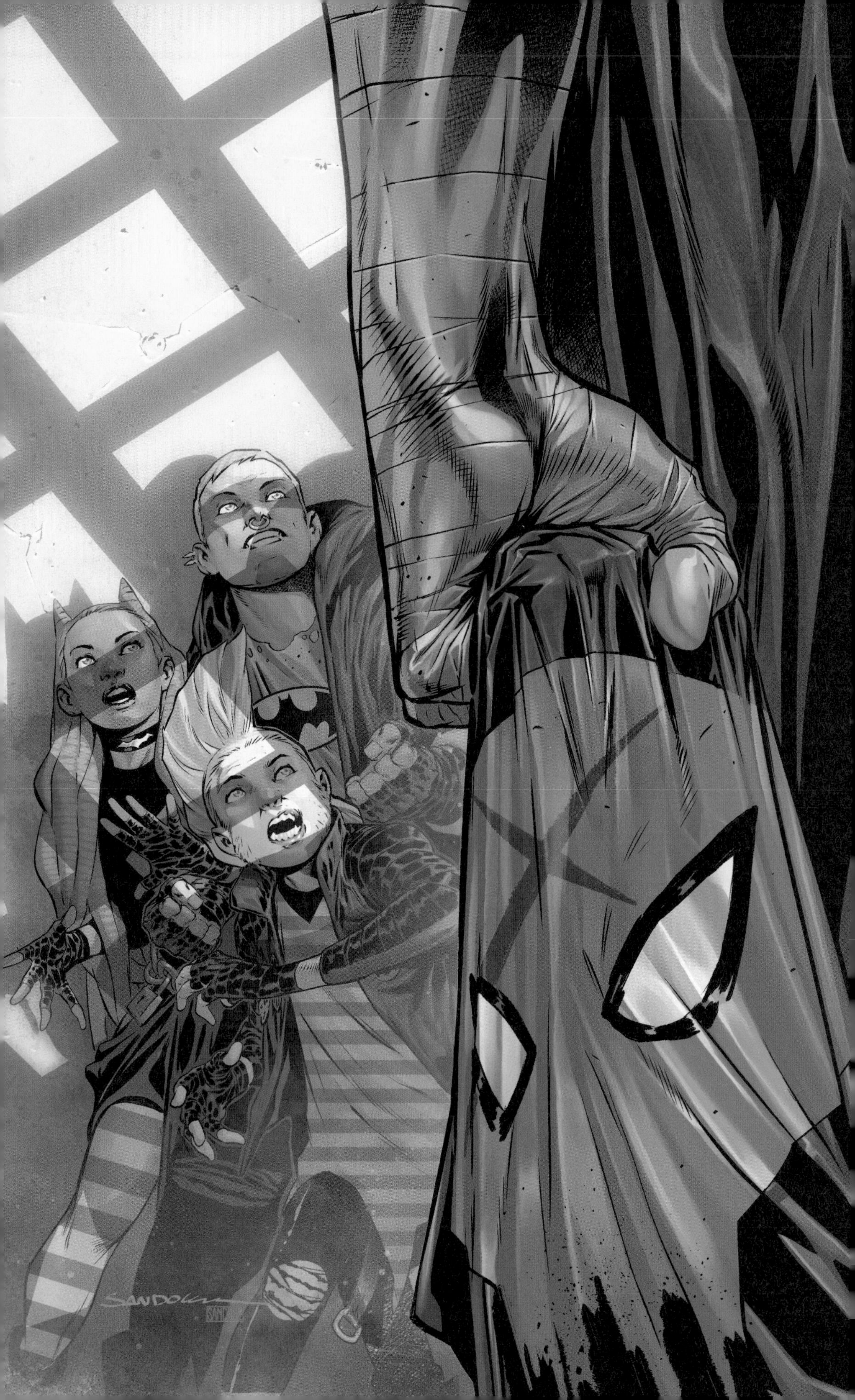

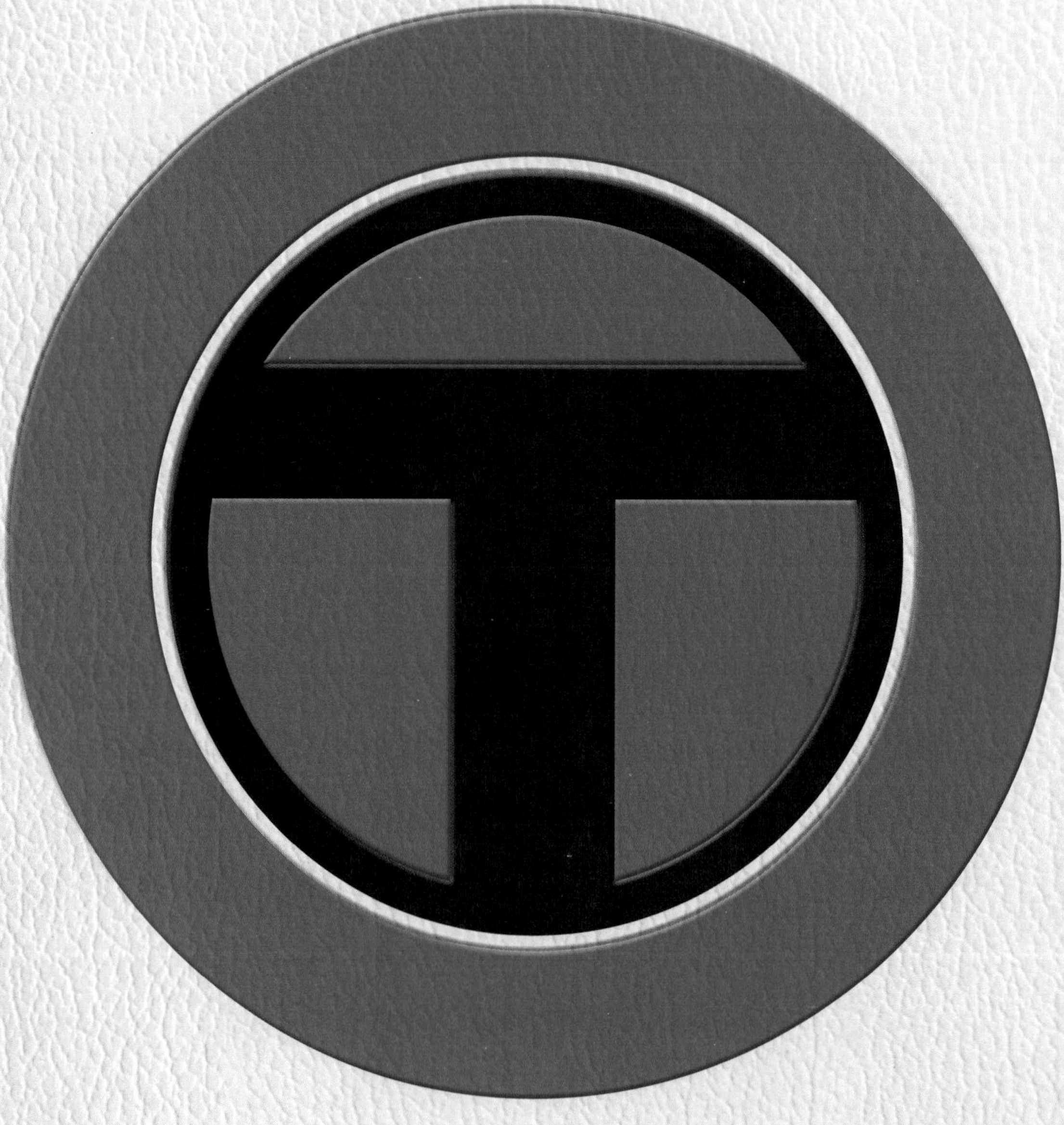

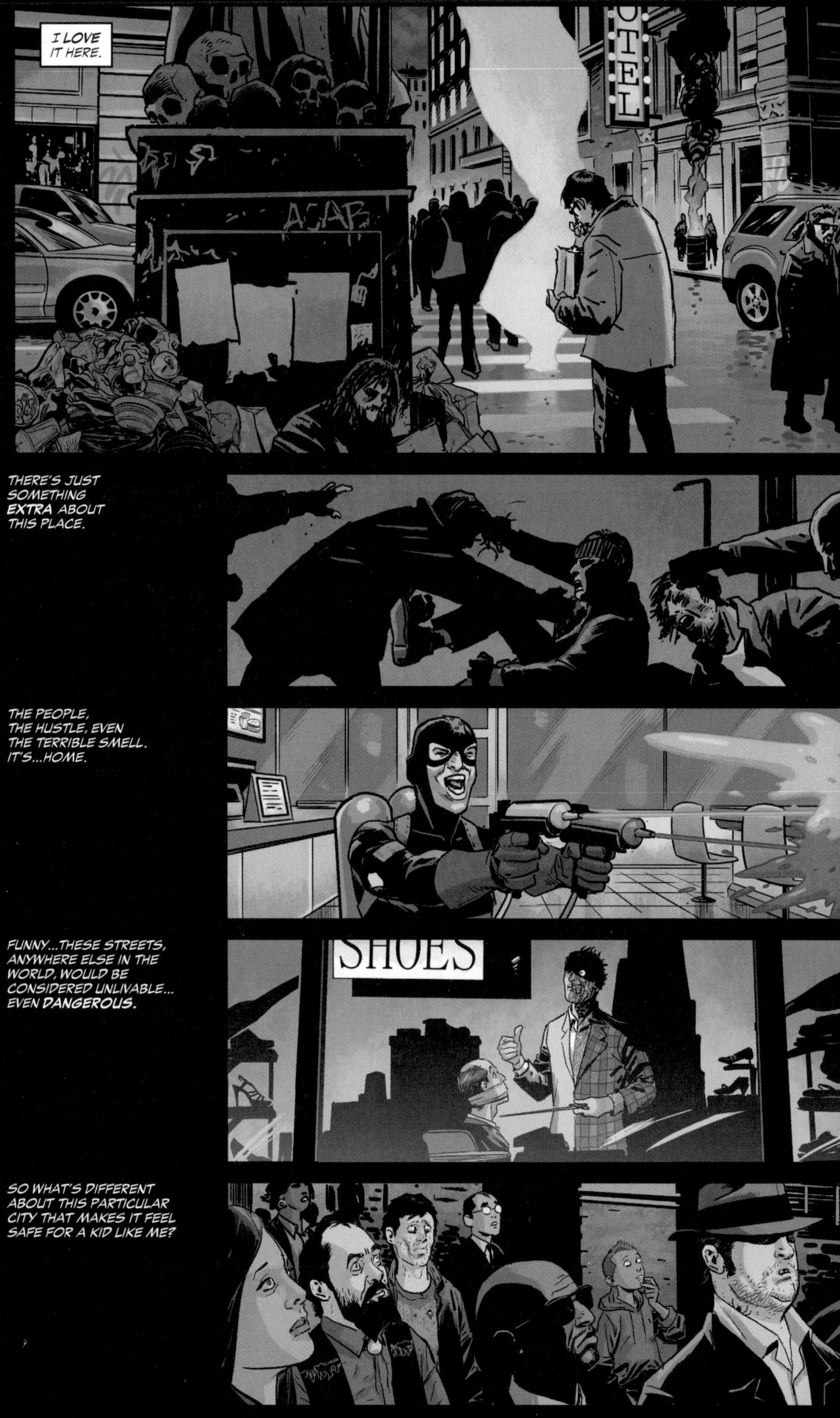
I LOVE IT HERE.
THERE'S JUST SOMETHING **EXTRA** ABOUT THIS PLACE.
THE PEOPLE, THE HUSTLE, EVEN THE TERRIBLE SMELL. IT'S...HOME.
FUNNY...THESE STREETS, ANYWHERE ELSE IN THE WORLD, WOULD BE CONSIDERED UNLIVABLE... EVEN **DANGEROUS**.
SHOES
SO WHAT'S DIFFERENT ABOUT THIS PARTICULAR CITY THAT MAKES IT FEEL SAFE FOR A KID LIKE ME?

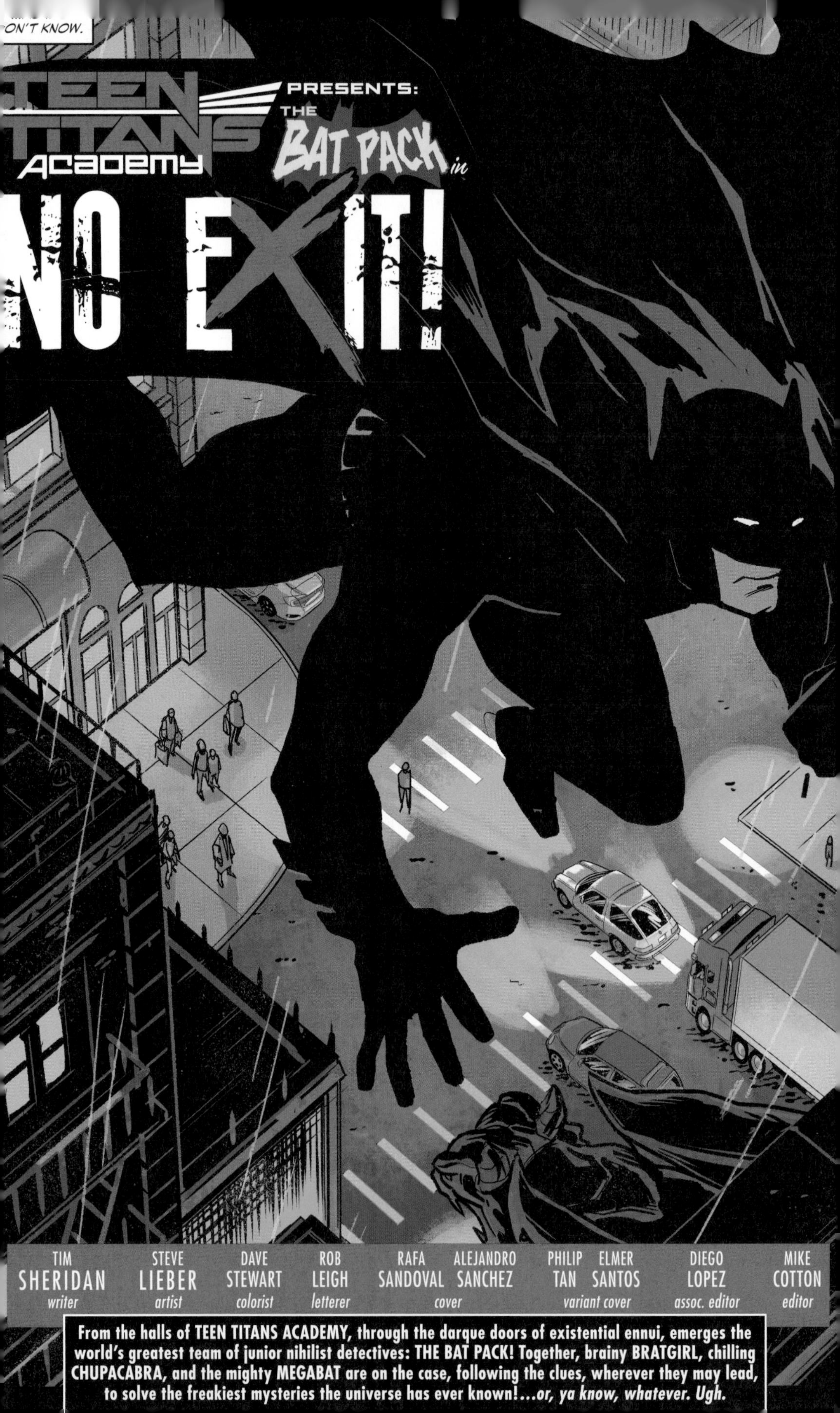
ON'T KNOW.
TEEN TITANS ACADEMY PRESENTS: THE BAT PACK in
NO EXIT!
TIM SHERIDAN writer
STEVE LIEBER artist
DAVE STEWART colorist
ROB LEIGH letterer
RAFA SANDOVAL ALEJANDRO SANCHEZ cover
PHILIP TAN ELMER SANTOS variant cover
DIEGO LOPEZ assoc. editor
MIKE COTTON editor
From the halls of TEEN TITANS ACADEMY, through the darque doors of existential ennui, emerges the world's greatest team of junior nihilist detectives: THE BAT PACK! Together, brainy BRATGIRL, chilling CHUPACABRA, and the mighty MEGABAT are on the case, following the clues, wherever they may lead, to solve the freakiest mysteries the universe has ever known!...or, ya know, whatever. Ugh.

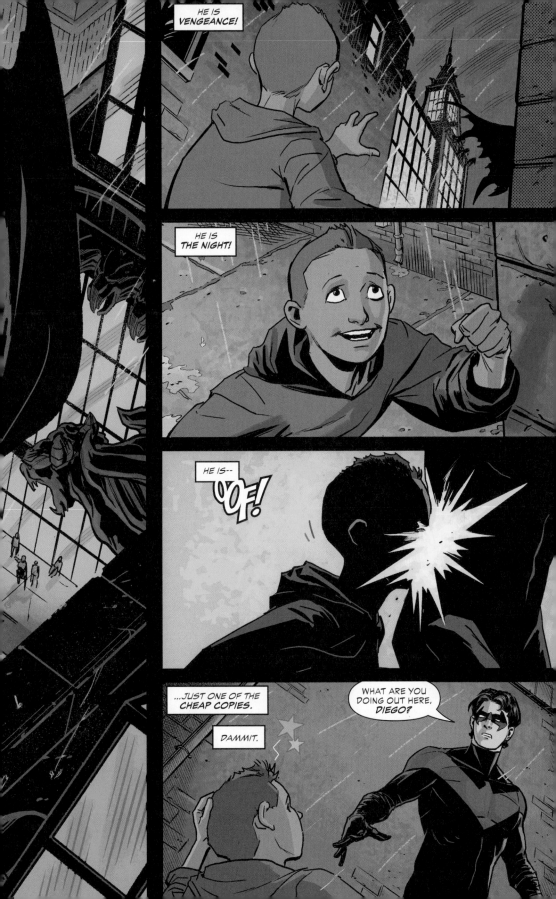

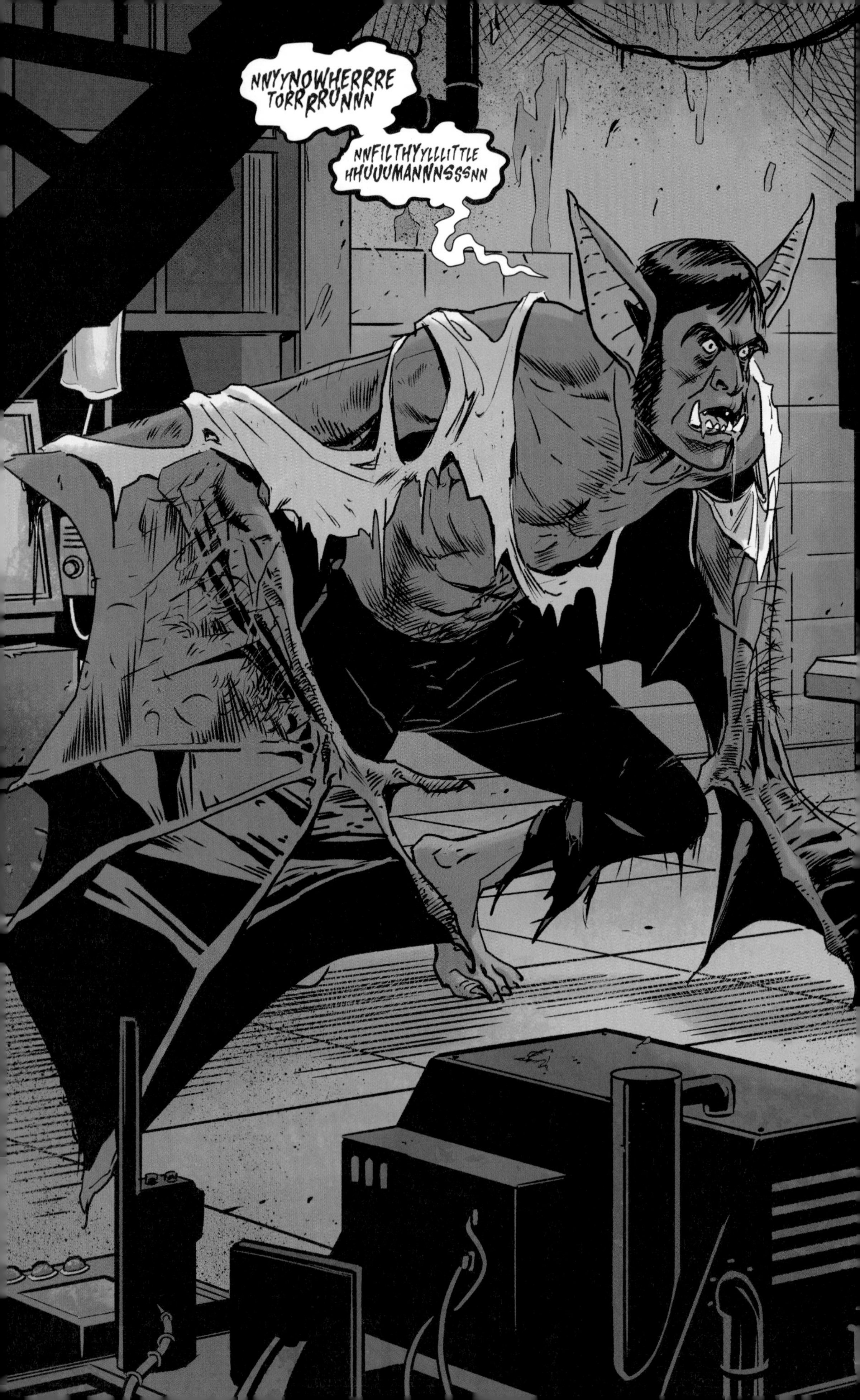
NNYYNOWHERRRE TORRRRUNNN
NNFILTHYYLLLITTLE HHUUUMANNNSSSNN

DIEGO--*CHUPACABRA*--YOU STEPPED IN AND TOOK LUCAS'S PLACE HAVING NO IDEA WHAT GRUSEL HAD IN STORE. IT WAS *STUPID* AND *RECKLESS*...BUT ALSO A LITTLE BIT *HEROIC*.

MERISSA, LUCAS... NOT ONLY DID YOU GET PAST THE BEAUMONT HOME'S TIGHT SECURITY, BUT, ON YOUR WAY HERE TO HELP, YOU MADE AN IMPORTANT STOP.

HOW DID YOU KNOW THAT?

"BECAUSE EARLIER TONIGHT, COMMISSIONER JIM GORDON RECEIVED AN ANONYMOUS TIP VIA A RATHER THICK FILE FOLDER LEFT AT POLICE HEADQUARTERS.

"THE FILE WAS FULL OF RECEIPTS FOR TRANSACTIONS THAT TIE DR. GRUSEL AND OTHERS TO THE ADMINISTRATOR OF THE BEAUMONT HOME AND IMPLICATES THEM ALL IN SOME VERY SERIOUS CHILD-TRAFFICKING, IF NOT *WORSE*, CHARGES."

"DID HE GIVE THE EVIDENCE TO BATMAN?!"

"*BATMAN* WOULD HAVE GIVEN IT TO *GORDON*--WHO'S PROBABLY ALREADY TAKEN THE ADMINISTRATOR INTO CUSTODY AND SHUT DOWN THE ORPHANAGE.

"THE POINT IS...YOU DID THE RIGHT THING."

"WAIT--*SHUT IT DOWN?* BUT WHAT ABOUT *US?*"

THERE'S ONLY A HANDFUL OF KIDS LEFT AT BEAUMONT THESE DAYS. THEY'LL BE PLACED IN FOSTER CARE...UNLESS MORE SUITABLE ARRANGEMENTS CAN BE MADE.

"*UNLESS* MORE SUITABLE ARRANGEMENTS CAN BE MADE..."

FOSTER CARE? THEY'RE GONNA SPLIT US UP, AREN'T THEY?

"...EVER BEEN TO NEW YORK?"

WHAT YOU DID TODAY WAS IMPULSIVE, BUT IT WAS ALSO IMPRESSIVE. I THINK YOU THREE MAKE QUITE THE LITTLE *BAT PACK*-- AND THAT GOT ME THINKING...

THERE'S A NEW PROJECT I'VE STARTED PLANNING WITH *MY* OLD PACK, AND, WELL...

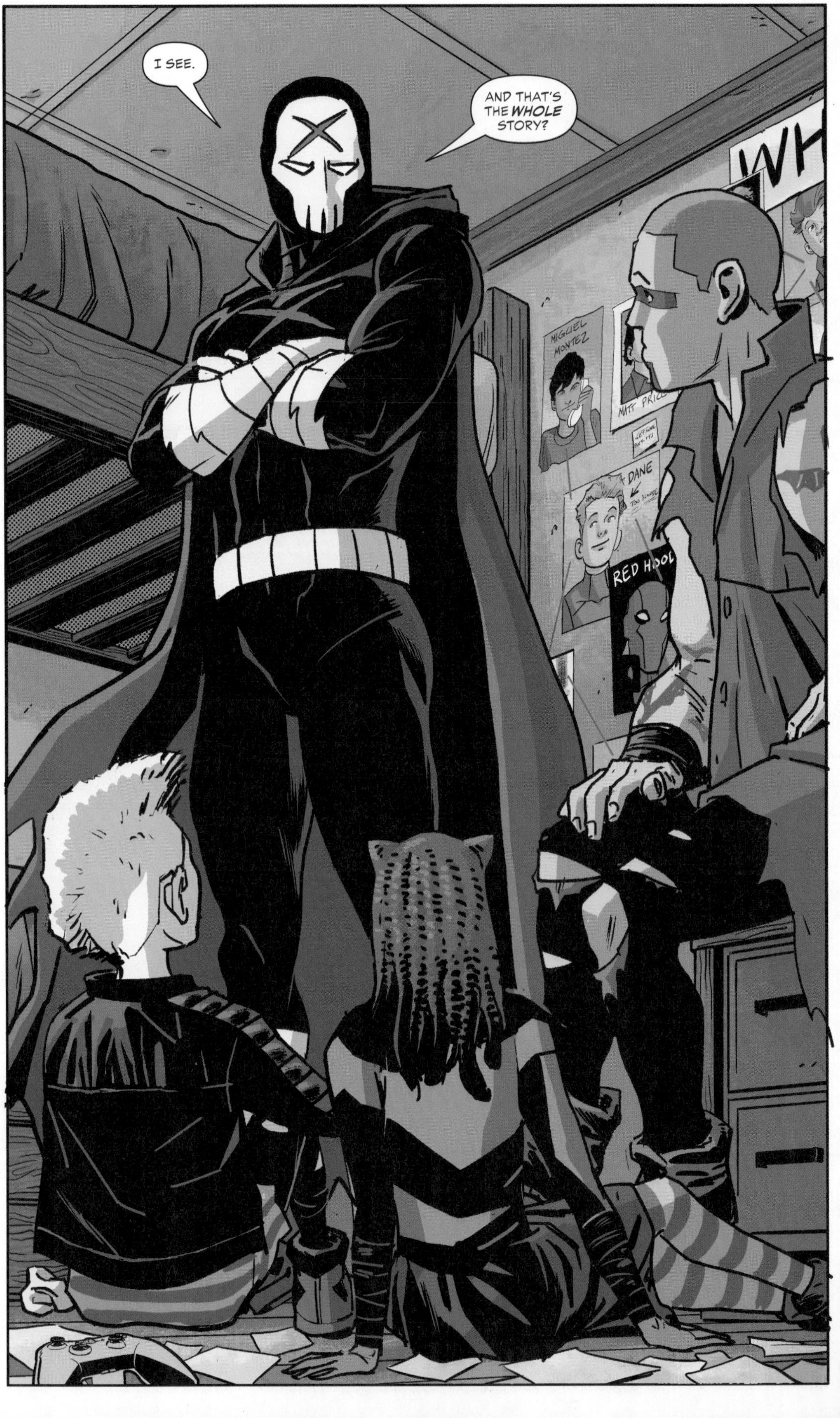
I SEE.
AND THAT'S THE *WHOLE* STORY?
MIGUEL MONTEZ
DANE
TOO BLONDE
RED HOOD

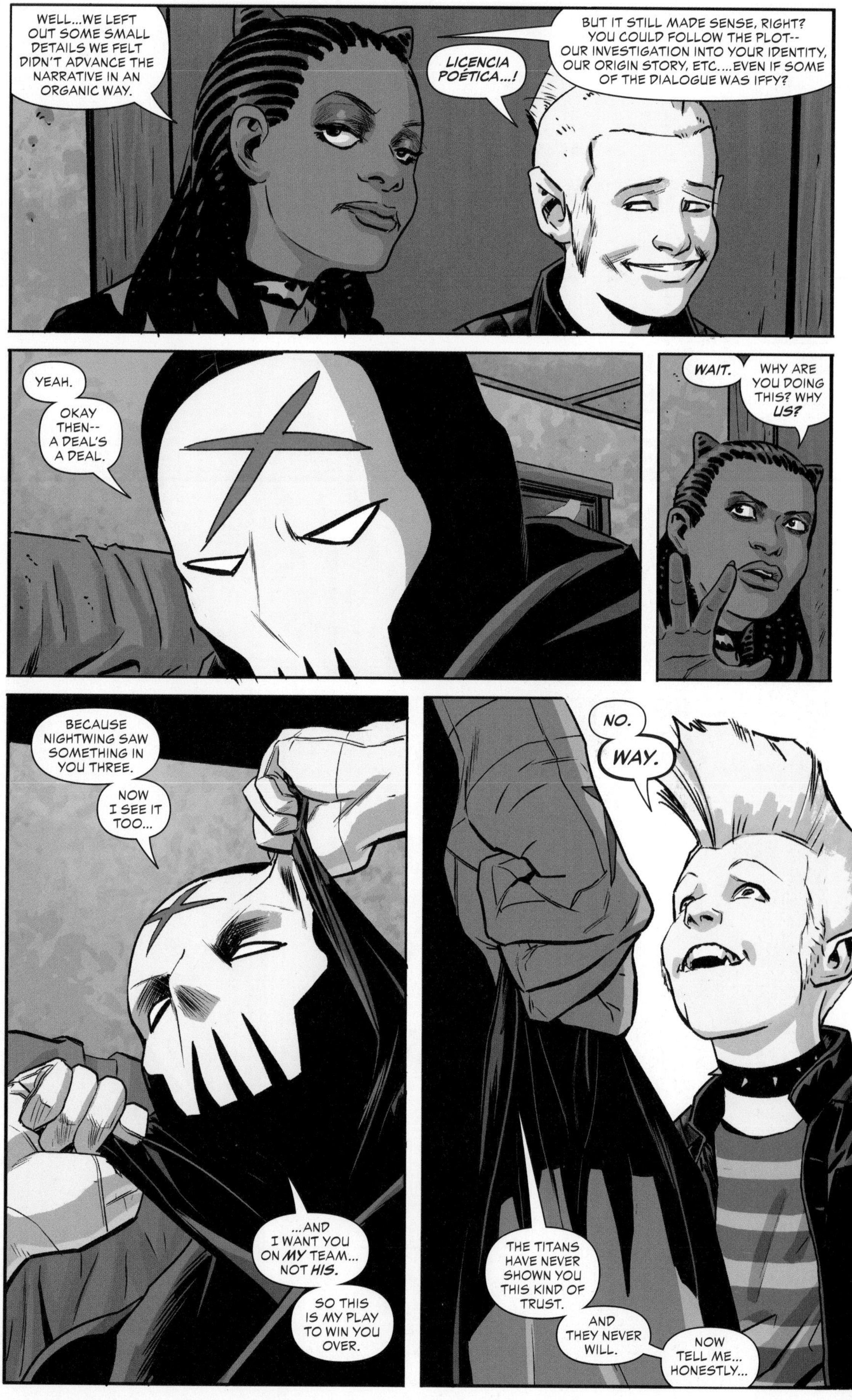
WELL...WE LEFT OUT SOME SMALL DETAILS WE FELT DIDN'T ADVANCE THE NARRATIVE IN AN ORGANIC WAY.
LICENCIA POÉTICA...!
BUT IT STILL MADE SENSE, RIGHT? YOU COULD FOLLOW THE PLOT-- OUR INVESTIGATION INTO YOUR IDENTITY, OUR ORIGIN STORY, ETC.... EVEN IF SOME OF THE DIALOGUE WAS IFFY?
YEAH.
OKAY THEN-- A DEAL'S A DEAL.
WAIT.
WHY ARE YOU DOING THIS? WHY US?
BECAUSE NIGHTWING SAW SOMETHING IN YOU THREE.
NOW I SEE IT TOO...
...AND I WANT YOU ON MY TEAM... NOT HIS.
SO THIS IS MY PLAY TO WIN YOU OVER.
NO.
WAY.
THE TITANS HAVE NEVER SHOWN YOU THIS KIND OF TRUST.
AND THEY NEVER WILL.
NOW TELL ME... HONESTLY...

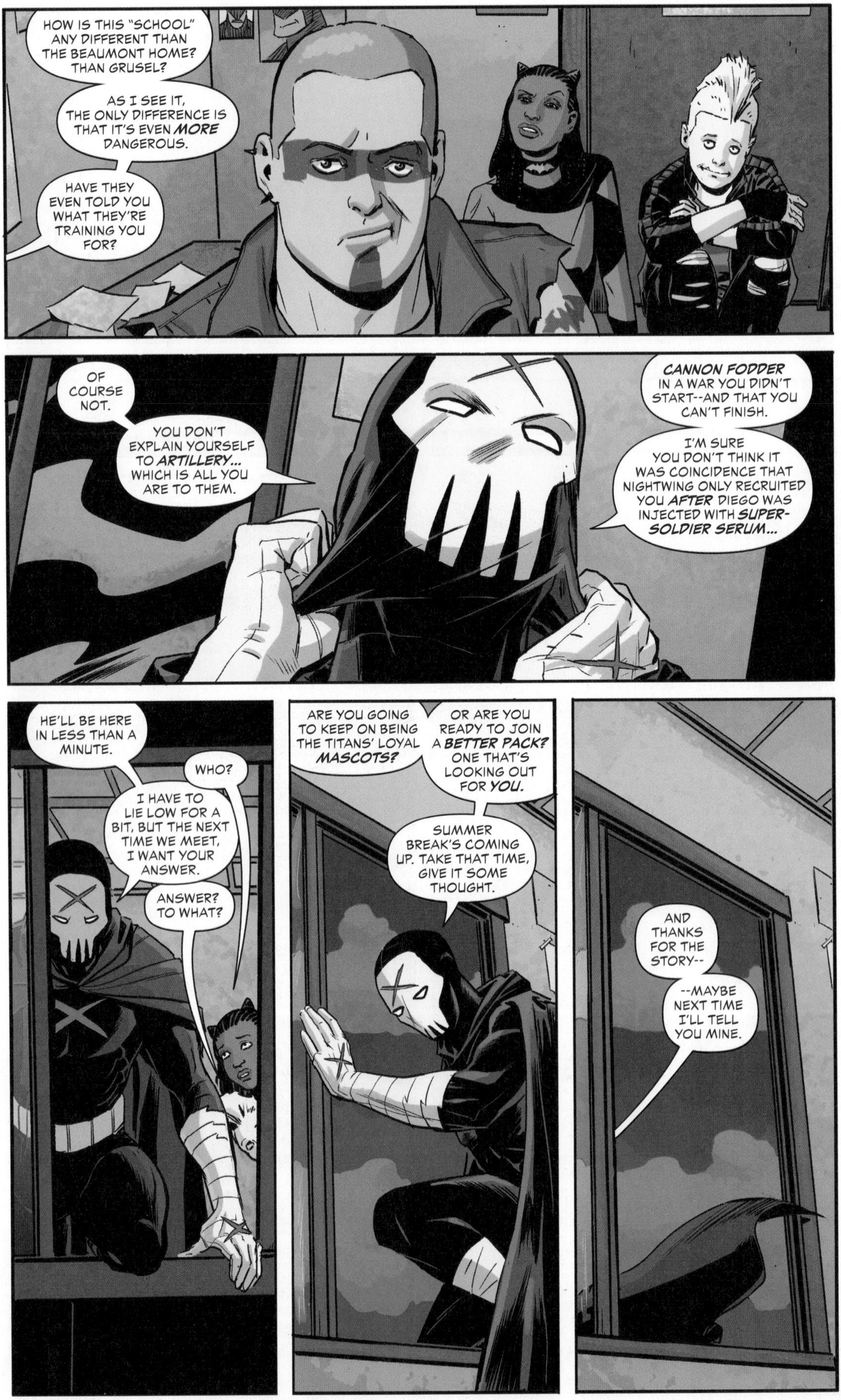
HOW IS THIS "SCHOOL" ANY DIFFERENT THAN THE BEAUMONT HOME? THAN GRUSEL?
AS I SEE IT, THE ONLY DIFFERENCE IS THAT IT'S EVEN MORE DANGEROUS.
HAVE THEY EVEN TOLD YOU WHAT THEY'RE TRAINING YOU FOR?
OF COURSE NOT.
YOU DON'T EXPLAIN YOURSELF TO ARTILLERY... WHICH IS ALL YOU ARE TO THEM.
CANNON FODDER IN A WAR YOU DIDN'T START--AND THAT YOU CAN'T FINISH.
I'M SURE YOU DON'T THINK IT WAS COINCIDENCE THAT NIGHTWING ONLY RECRUITED YOU AFTER DIEGO WAS INJECTED WITH SUPER-SOLDIER SERUM...
HE'LL BE HERE IN LESS THAN A MINUTE.
WHO?
I HAVE TO LIE LOW FOR A BIT, BUT THE NEXT TIME WE MEET, I WANT YOUR ANSWER.
ANSWER? TO WHAT?
ARE YOU GOING TO KEEP ON BEING THE TITANS' LOYAL MASCOTS?
OR ARE YOU READY TO JOIN A BETTER PACK? ONE THAT'S LOOKING OUT FOR YOU.
SUMMER BREAK'S COMING UP. TAKE THAT TIME, GIVE IT SOME THOUGHT.
AND THANKS FOR THE STORY--
--MAYBE NEXT TIME I'LL TELL YOU MINE.

TEEN TITANS ACADEMY

2021 YEARBOOK

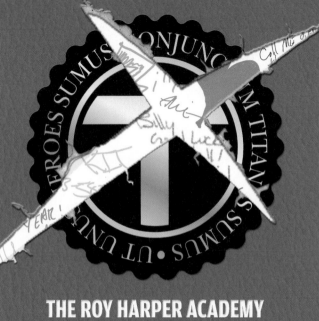

**THE ROY HARPER ACADEMY
INAUGURAL CLASS**

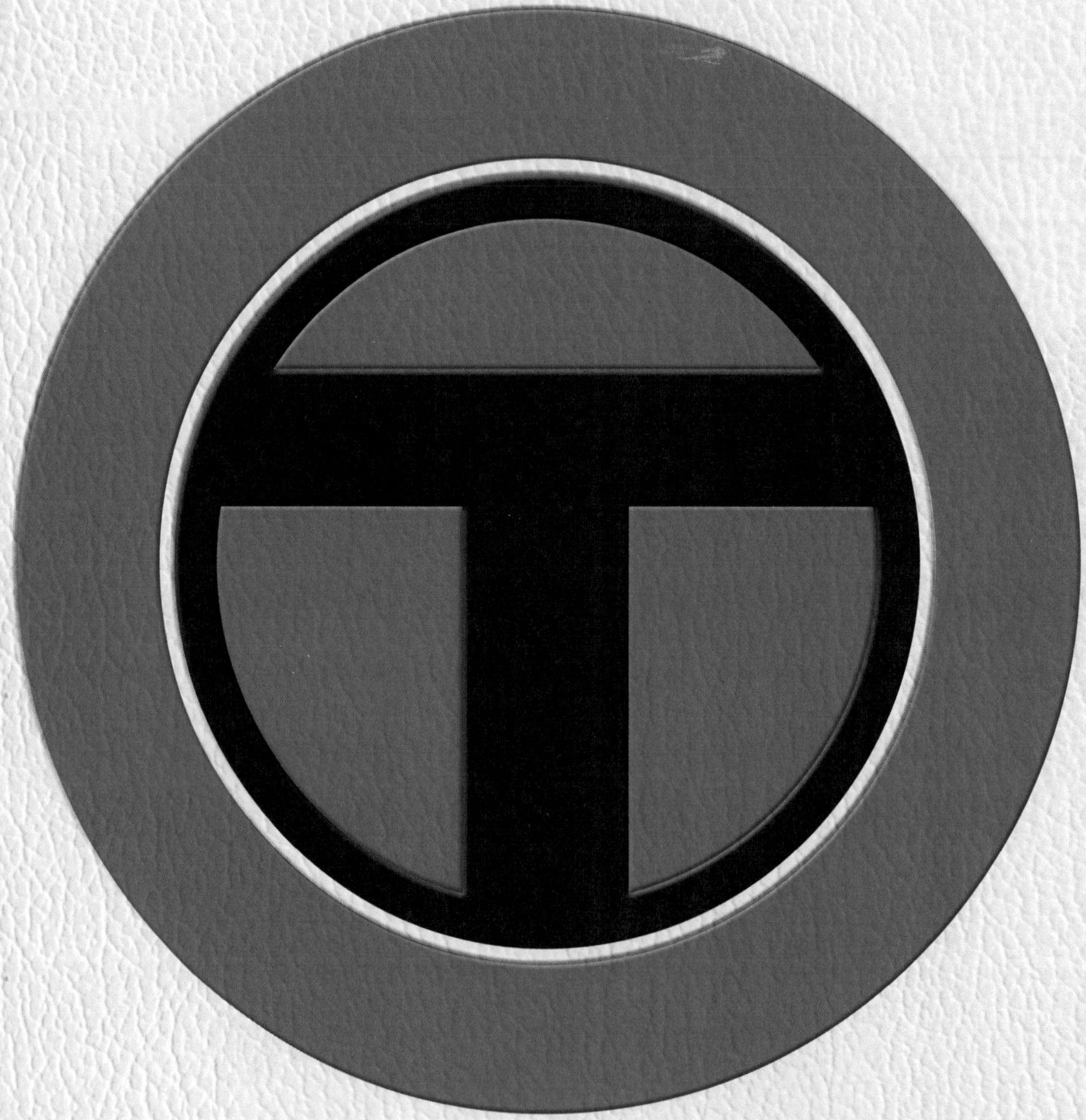

Contents

021 Yearbook Staff

DITOR: Gorilla Gregg
HOTOGRAPHER: Billy Batson
ESEARCH: Diego Perez
ESIGN: Wallace West
T SUPPORT: Merissa Cooper
ACULTY ADVISOR: Mr. Beast Boy

A LETTER FROM The Class President

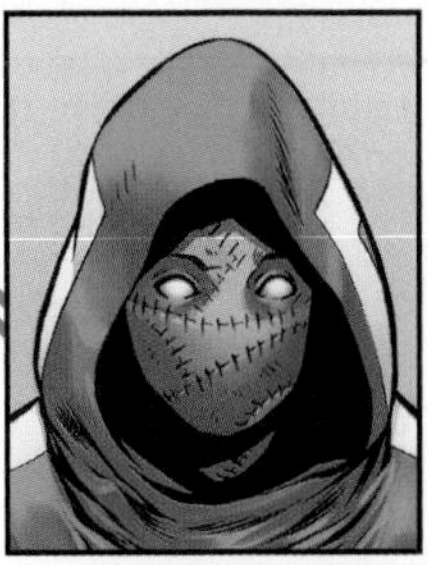

Dear Members of the Inaugural Class of the **ROY HARPER TITANS ACADEMY**,

A **JOURNEY** is about growth and change. And I don't mean all that physical growth and change so many of you, especially the boys and girls, are experiencing. Let's keep that crap in Health class where it belongs! I mean a much bigger journey—the kind our faithful teachers, the "classic" Titans, undertook. Theirs is the story of humble sidekicks who carved a path to their own identities, independent of the heroes they served. A path that started in a big T-shaped building in San Francisco and led all the way to...another big T-shaped building in New York City.

And so, as you leaf through this book, turning the page from memory to memory, call to mind the incredible journeys of those that came before us to open the doors of this school, so that one day, we could walk through them...

...as we begin journeys of our own.

BOOM. Nailed it,

PRESIDENT STITCH
(They/Them)

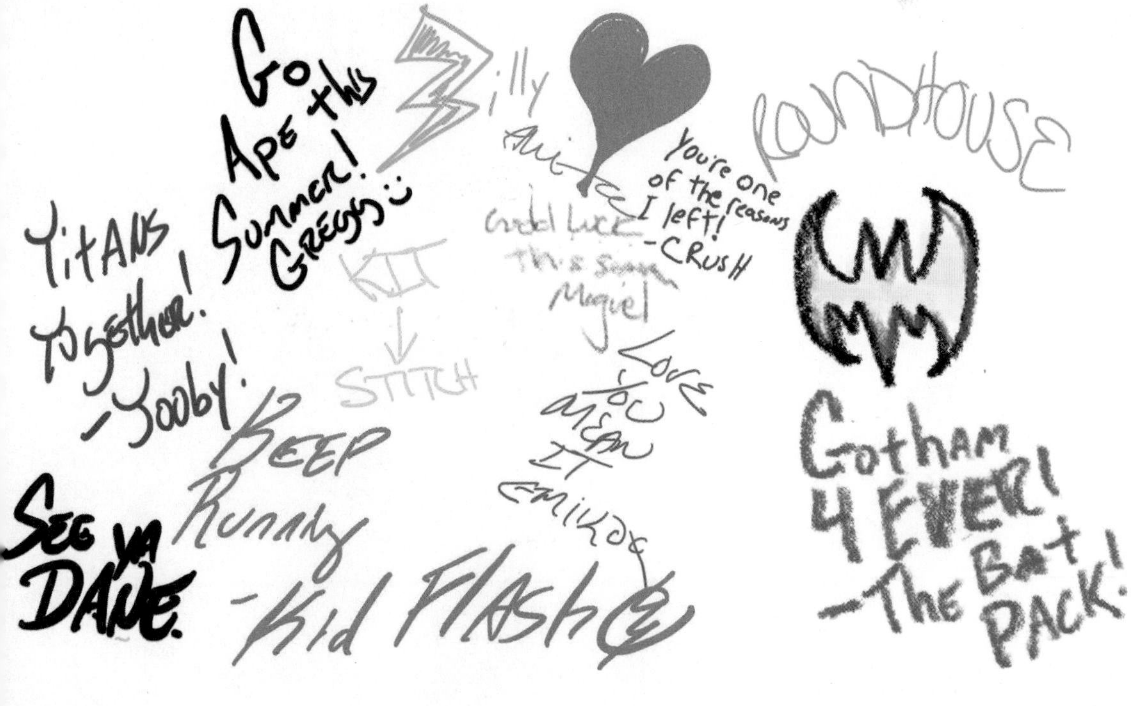

Go Ape this Summer! Greggs :)
Billy
You're one of the reasons I left! -Crush
ROUNDHOUSE
Titans together!
Kit
Stitch
Keep Runnin
-Kid Flash
See ya Dane.
Love you mean it
Emiko
Gotham 4 EVER! -The Bat Pack!

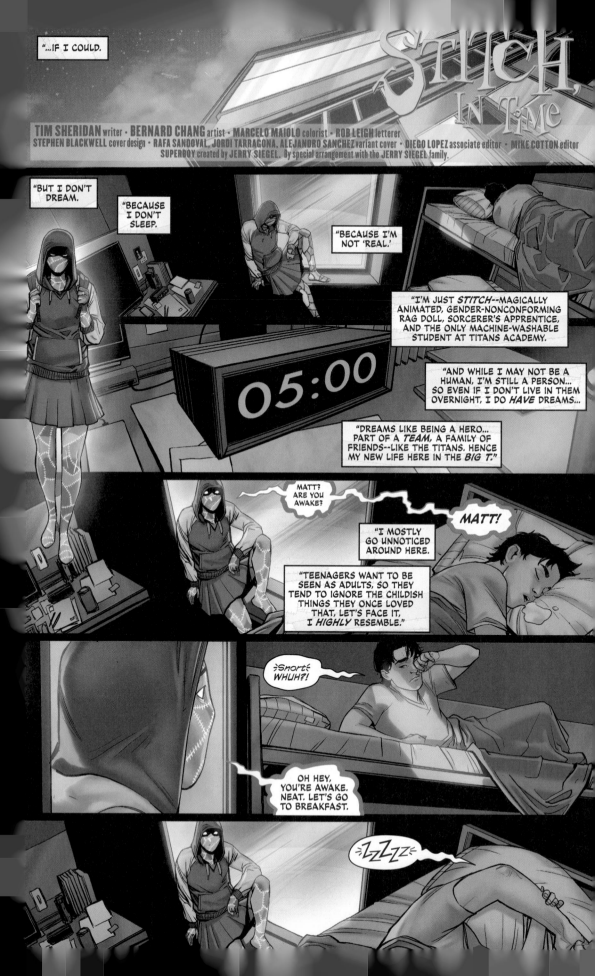

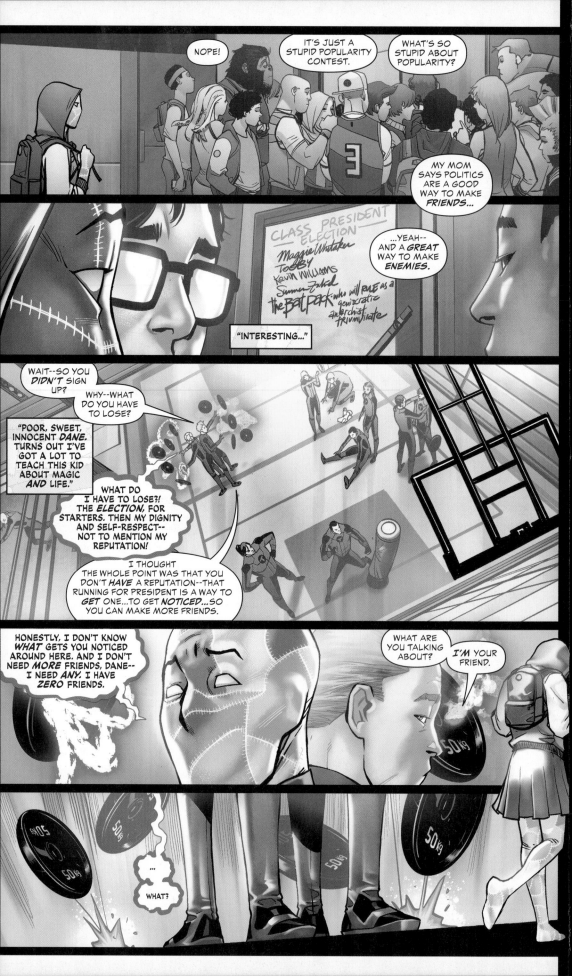

NOPE!

IT'S JUST A STUPID POPULARITY CONTEST.

WHAT'S SO STUPID ABOUT POPULARITY?

MY MOM SAYS POLITICS ARE A GOOD WAY TO MAKE *FRIENDS...*

CLASS PRESIDENT ELECTION
Maggie Whitaker
Toeby
Kevin WILLIAMS
Summer Zahid
the Bat Pack - who will RULE as a geniocratic anarchist triumvirate

...YEAH-- AND A *GREAT* WAY TO MAKE *ENEMIES.*

"INTERESTING..."

WAIT--SO YOU *DIDN'T* SIGN UP?

WHY--WHAT DO YOU HAVE TO LOSE?

"POOR, SWEET, INNOCENT *DANE.* TURNS OUT I'VE GOT A LOT TO TEACH THIS KID ABOUT MAGIC *AND* LIFE."

WHAT DO I HAVE TO LOSE?! THE *ELECTION,* FOR STARTERS. THEN MY DIGNITY AND SELF-RESPECT-- NOT TO MENTION MY REPUTATION!

I THOUGHT THE WHOLE POINT WAS THAT YOU DON'T *HAVE* A REPUTATION--THAT RUNNING FOR PRESIDENT IS A WAY TO *GET* ONE...TO GET *NOTICED*...SO YOU CAN MAKE MORE FRIENDS.

HONESTLY, I DON'T KNOW *WHAT* GETS YOU NOTICED AROUND HERE. AND I DON'T NEED *MORE* FRIENDS, DANE-- I NEED *ANY.* I HAVE *ZERO* FRIENDS.

WHAT ARE YOU TALKING ABOUT?

I'M YOUR FRIEND.

...

WHAT?

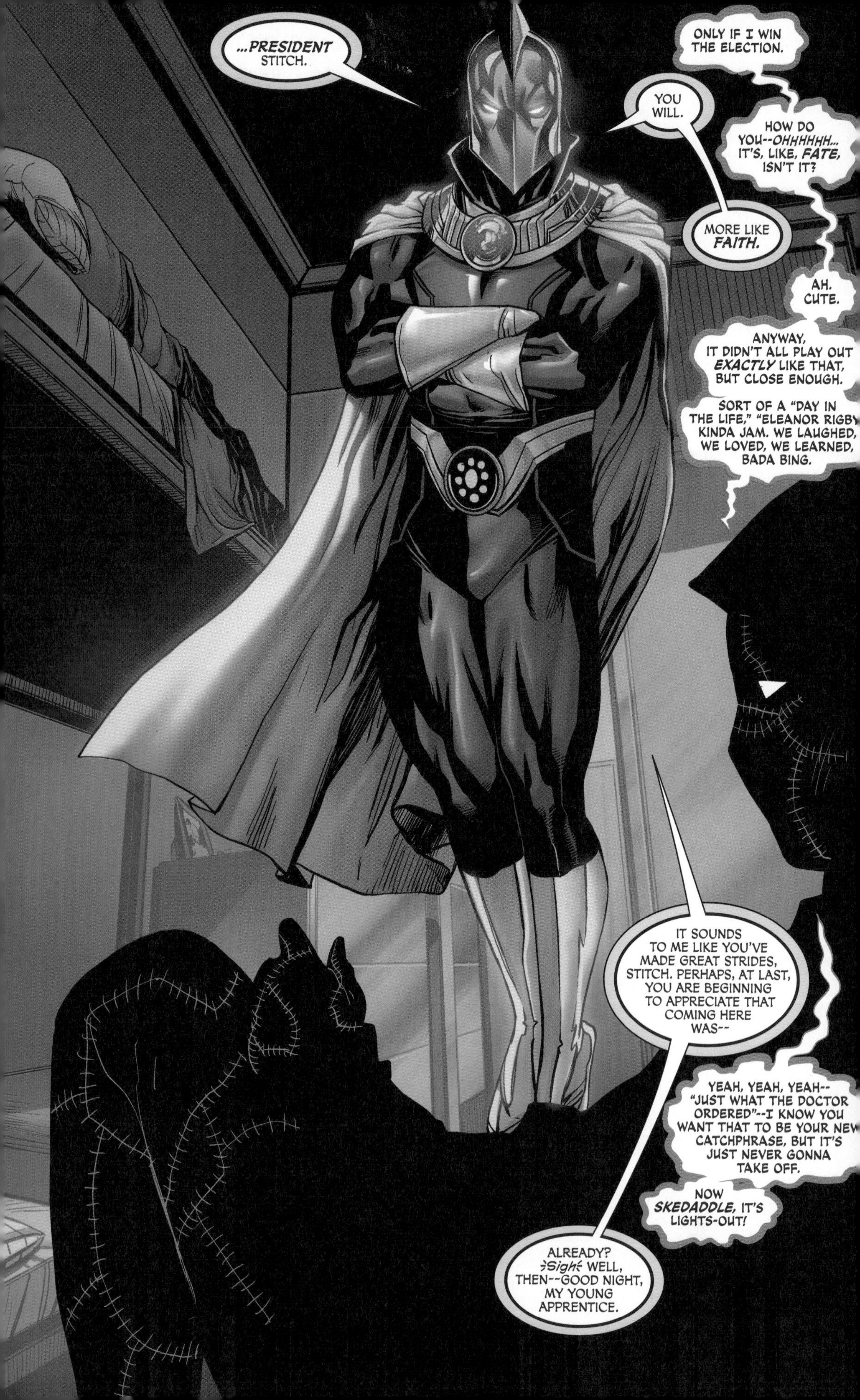
...PRESIDENT STITCH.
ONLY IF I WIN THE ELECTION.
YOU WILL.
HOW DO YOU--OHHHHHH... IT'S, LIKE, FATE, ISN'T IT?
MORE LIKE FAITH.
AH. CUTE.
ANYWAY, IT DIDN'T ALL PLAY OUT EXACTLY LIKE THAT, BUT CLOSE ENOUGH.
SORT OF A "DAY IN THE LIFE," "ELEANOR RIGBY" KINDA JAM. WE LAUGHED, WE LOVED, WE LEARNED, BADA BING.
IT SOUNDS TO ME LIKE YOU'VE MADE GREAT STRIDES, STITCH. PERHAPS, AT LAST, YOU ARE BEGINNING TO APPRECIATE THAT COMING HERE WAS--
YEAH, YEAH, YEAH--"JUST WHAT THE DOCTOR ORDERED"--I KNOW YOU WANT THAT TO BE YOUR NEW CATCHPHRASE, BUT IT'S JUST NEVER GONNA TAKE OFF.
NOW SKEDADDLE, IT'S LIGHTS-OUT!
ALREADY? Sigh WELL, THEN--GOOD NIGHT, MY YOUNG APPRENTICE.

IN *Memoriam*

This yearbook is dedicated to the memory and enduring legacy of ROY W. HARPER JR. a.k.a. "Mr. Arsenal" a.k.a. "Mr. Red Arrow (1)", a.k.a. "Mr. Speedy."

We, the students of the Roy Harper Titans Academy, wish to honor Mr. Speedy's heroic actions and sacrifice by posthumously naming him an HONORARY ADVISOR TO THE INAUGURAL CLASS.

"Sometimes an Outsider, forever a Titan, always in our hearts. Wherever you are, may you be at peace..."

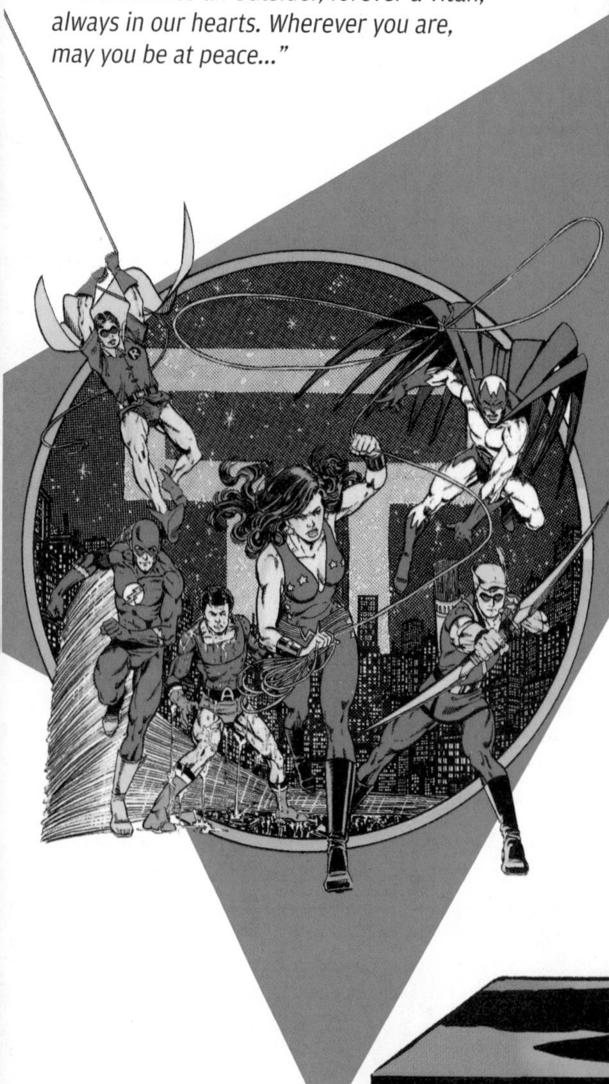

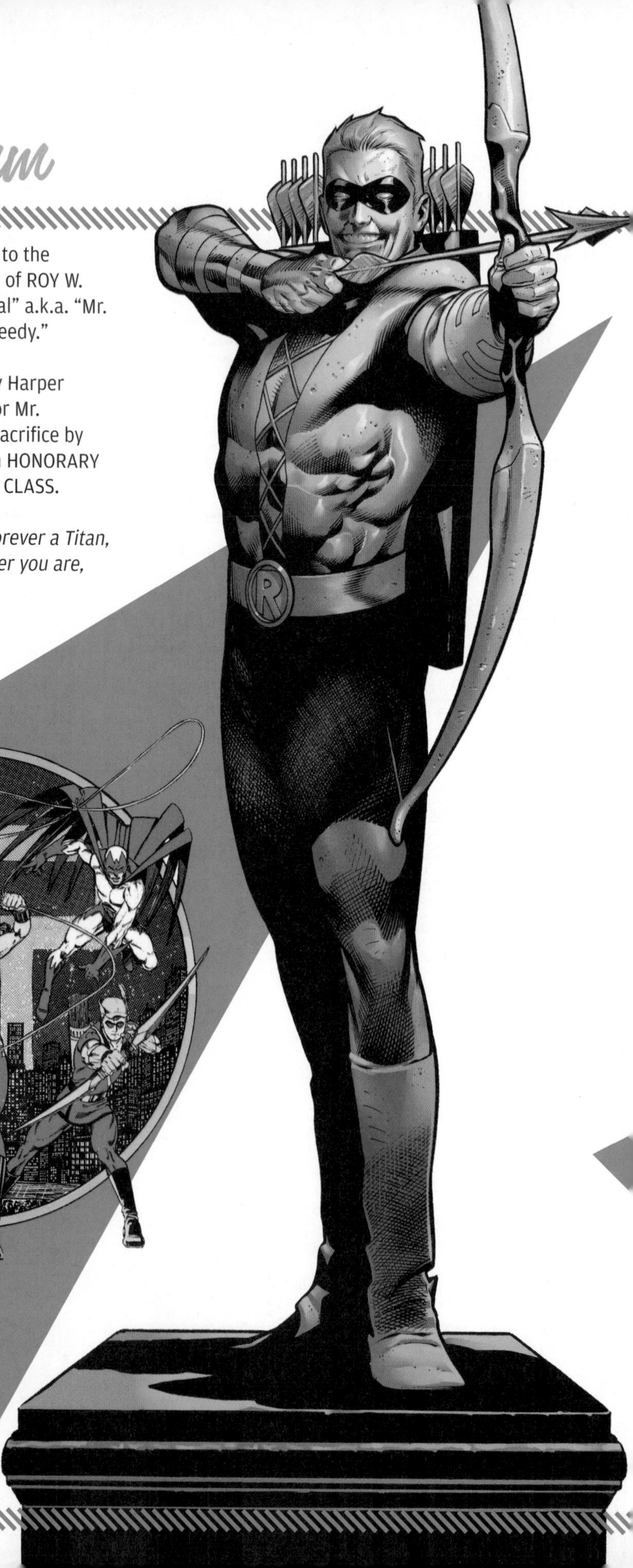

OUR *Faculty*

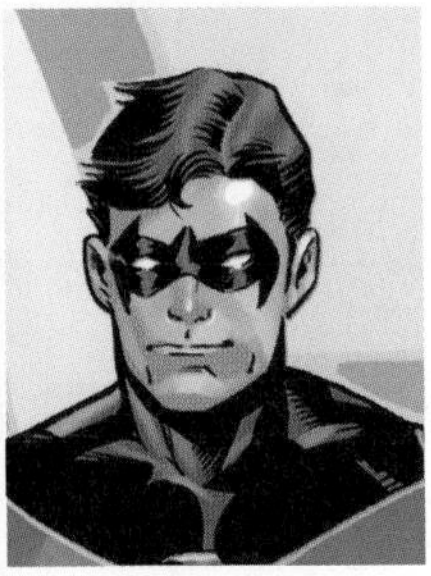

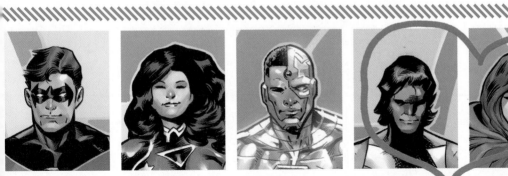

NIGHTWING
Bio not approved before print deadline.

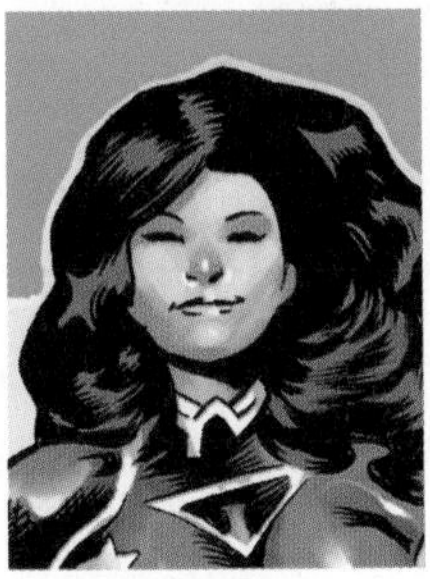

DONNA TROY
Ms. Troy's origins seem as complicated as her History of the Multiverse class, but it's in her Armed Combat Workshop that we learned the simplest lesson of all—that a REAL hero offers their foe a hand before offering a fist.

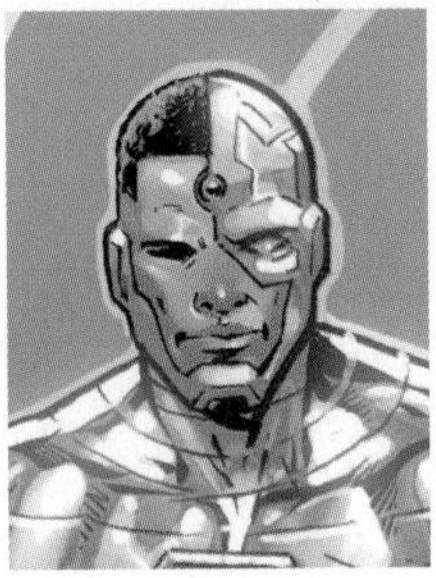

CYBORG
Part man, part machine, all heart. Students in Coach Cyborg's Home Ec class know how much of a softie this metric ton of steel and muscle can be. Whether calling plays or cooling pies, he's taught us there's no substitute for hard work and a little seasoning.

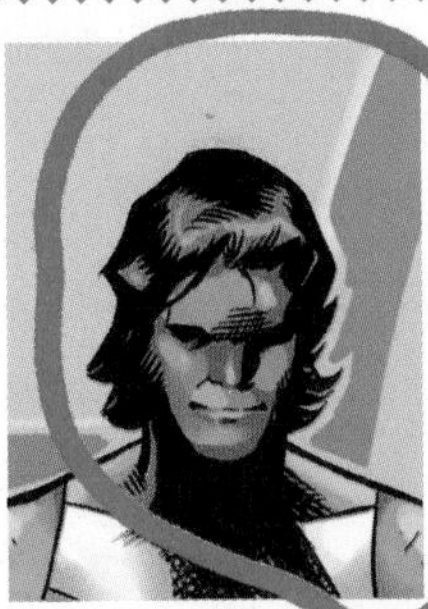

BEAST BOY
No instructor makes us laugh more than Mr. Beast Boy! And even if many of us struggle in his Intro to Acting class, who can forget his...interesting...one-man production of *Animal Farm*?

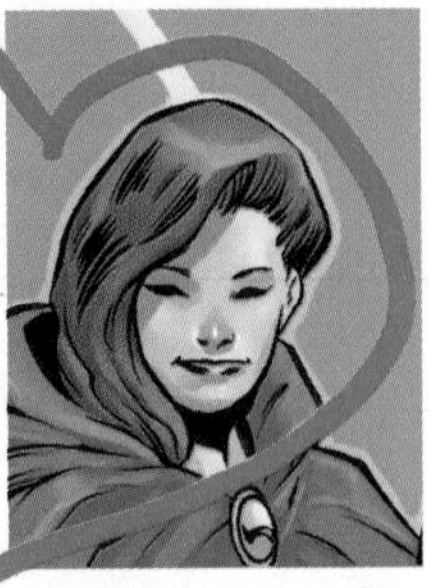

RAVEN
Our counselor and confidant, magical Ms. Raven helps shine a light in the darkness that can come with being a super teen in a super weird world. She always finds a moment to help a student in need, even if it means literally stopping time to do it...

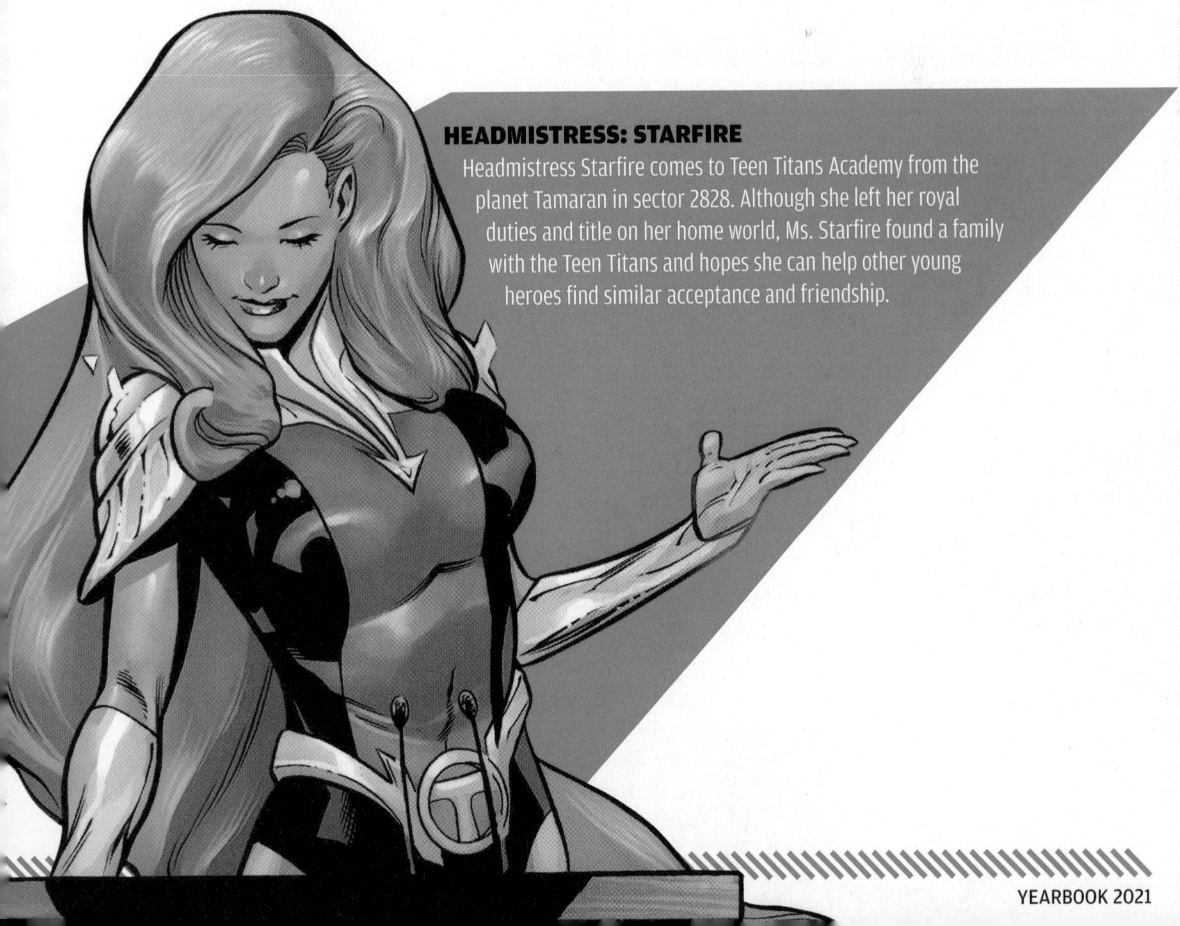

HEADMISTRESS: STARFIRE
Headmistress Starfire comes to Teen Titans Academy from the planet Tamaran in sector 2828. Although she left her royal duties and title on her home world, Ms. Starfire found a family with the Teen Titans and hopes she can help other young heroes find similar acceptance and friendship.

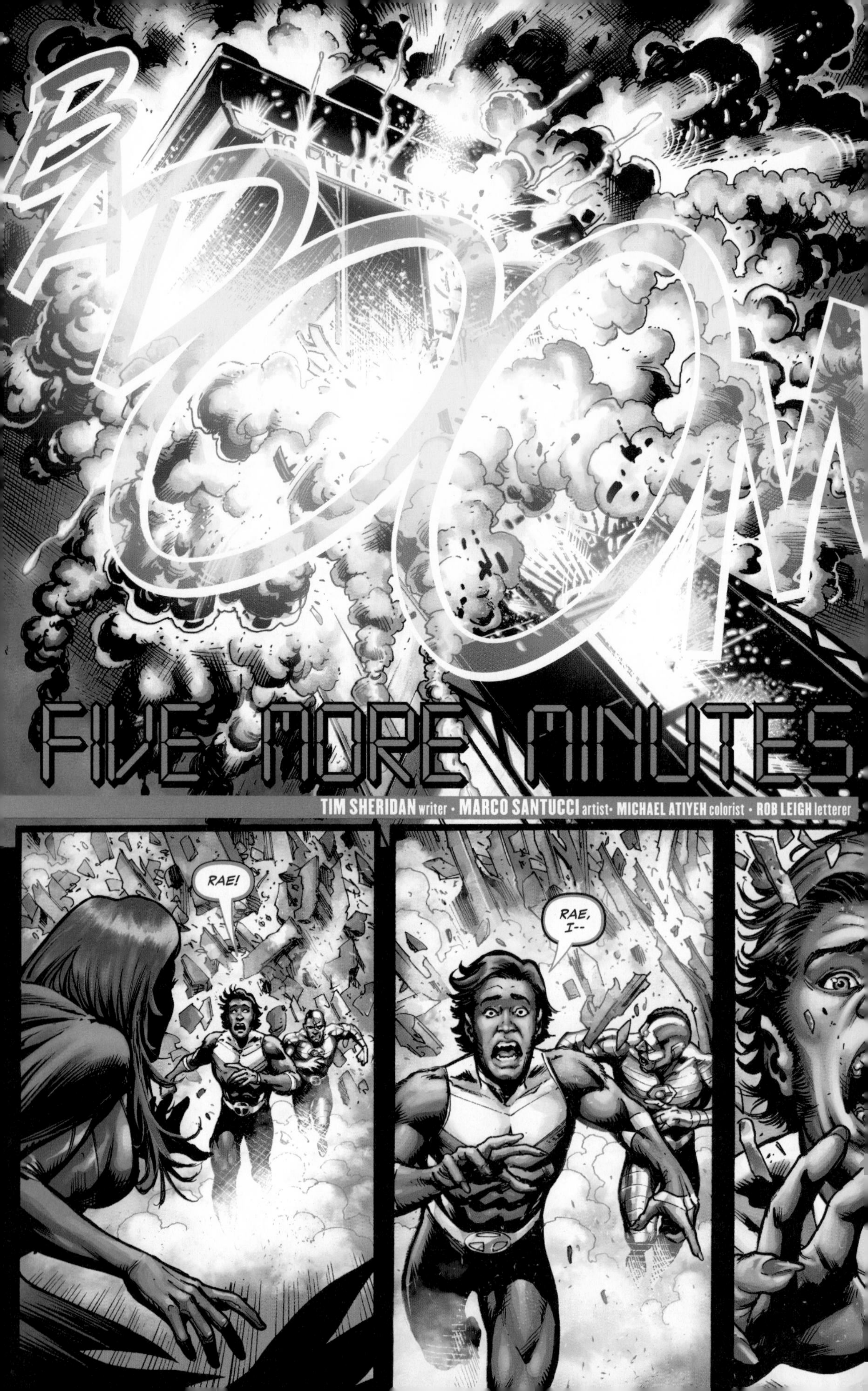
BADOOOM
FIVE MORE MINUTES
TIM SHERIDAN writer • MARCO SANTUCCI artist • MICHAEL ATIYEH colorist • ROB LEIGH letterer
RAE!
RAE, I--

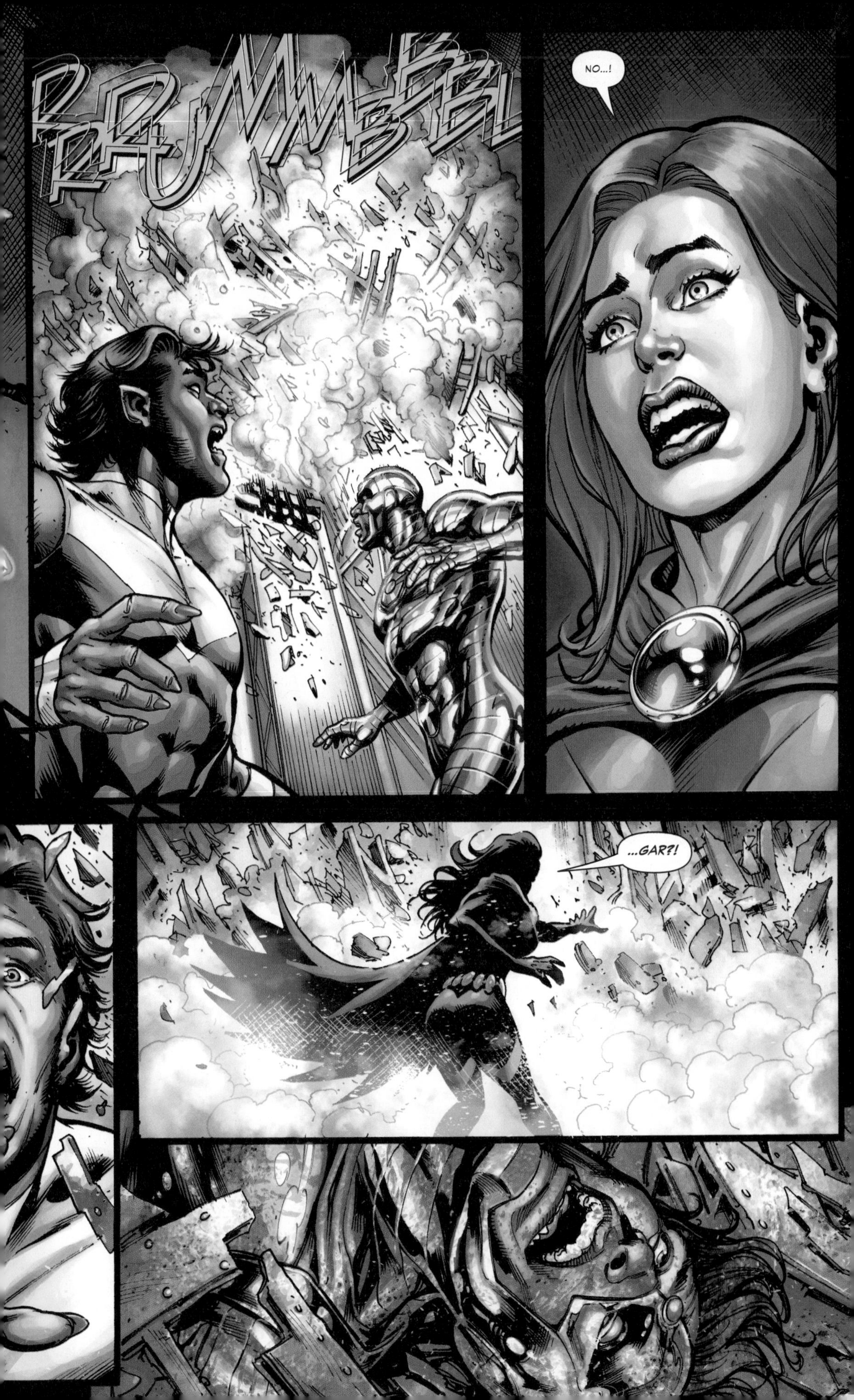
RRUMMBBL
NO...!
...GAR?!

CANDID *Campus*

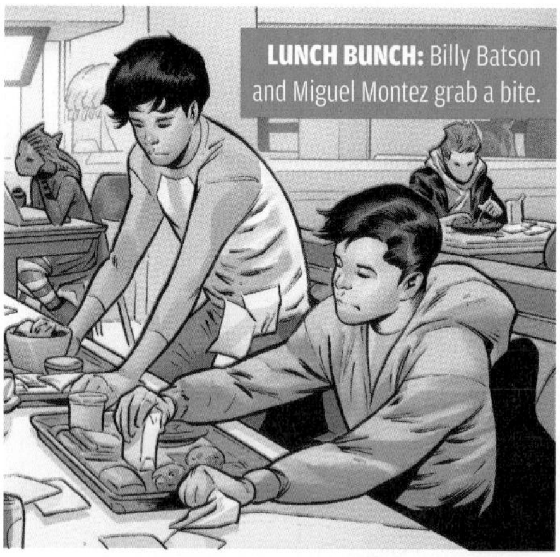
LUNCH BUNCH: Billy Batson and Miguel Montez grab a bite.

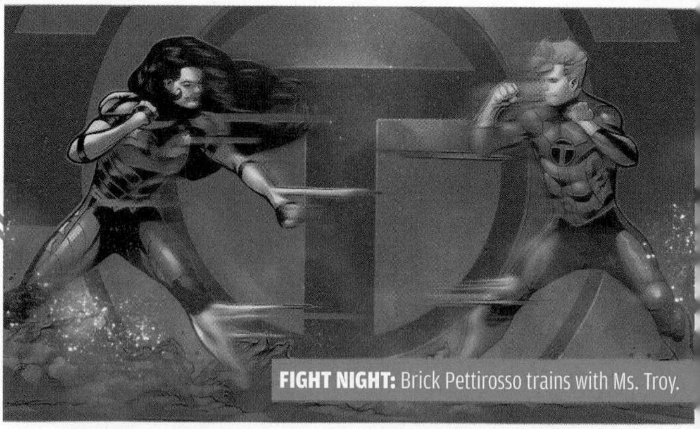
FIGHT NIGHT: Brick Pettirosso trains with Ms. Troy.

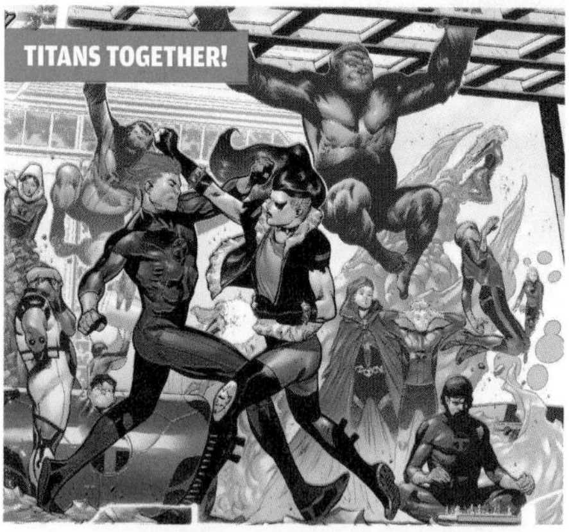
TITANS TOGETHER!

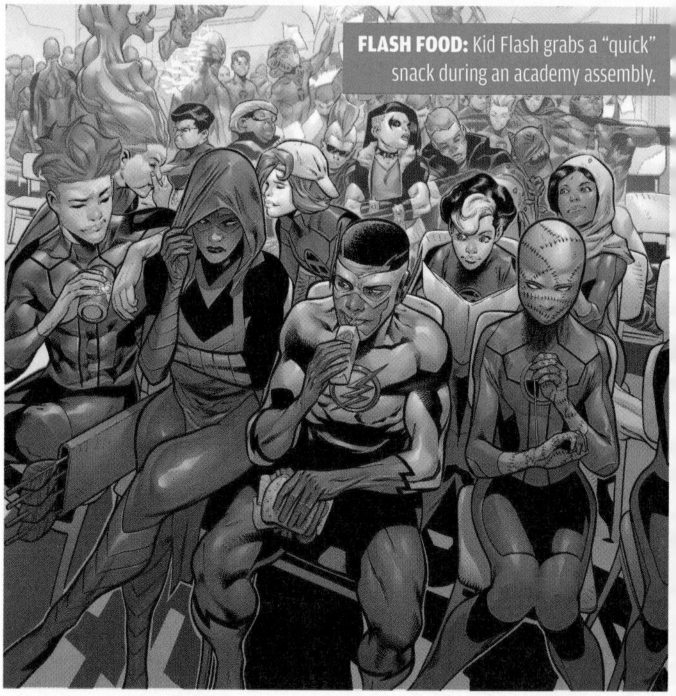
FLASH FOOD: Kid Flash grabs a "quick" snack during an academy assembly.

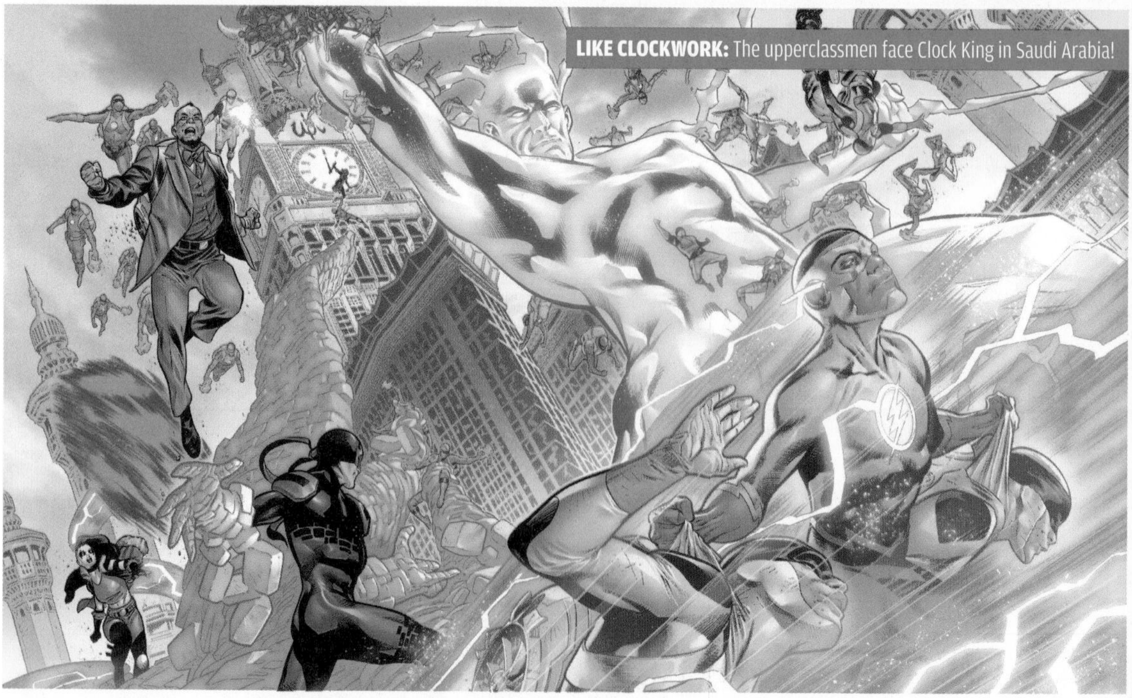
LIKE CLOCKWORK: The upperclassmen face Clock King in Saudi Arabia!

CLASS
Superlatives

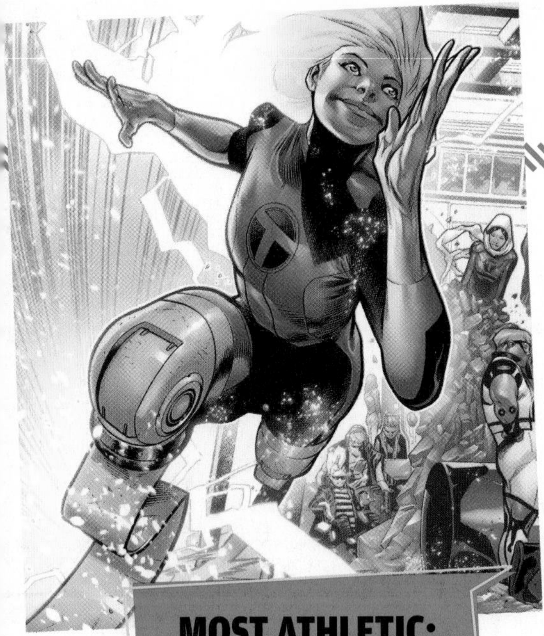

MOST ATHLETIC:
Bolt

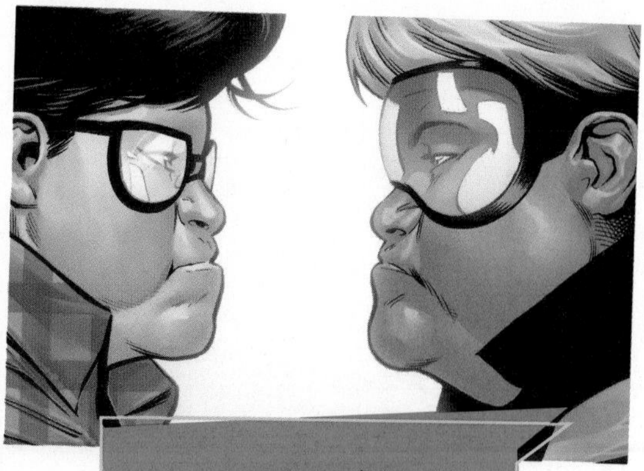

FRIENDS 'TILL THE END:
Tooby & Roundhouse

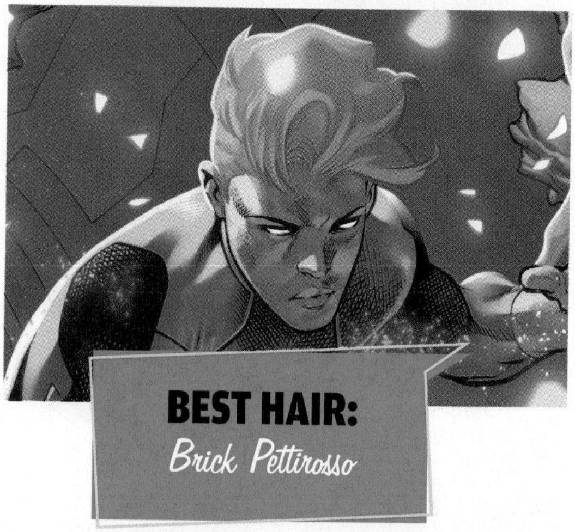

BEST HAIR:
Brick Pettirosso

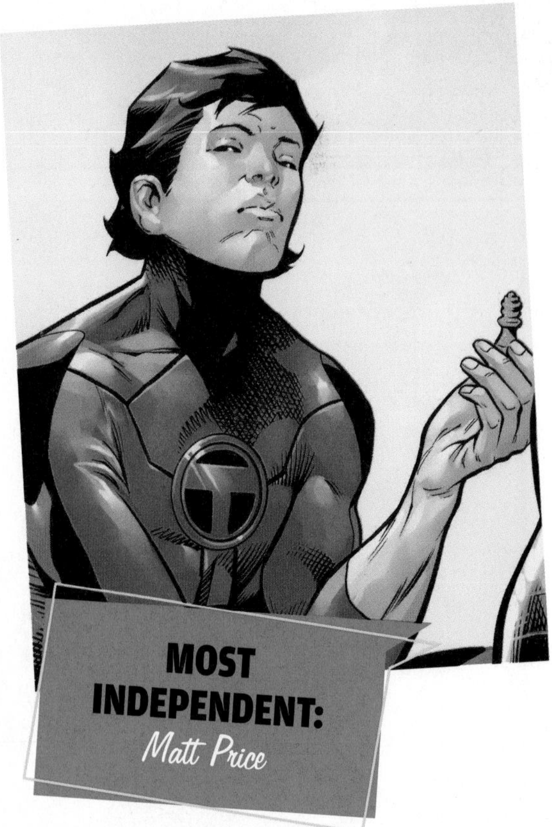

MOST INDEPENDENT:
Matt Price

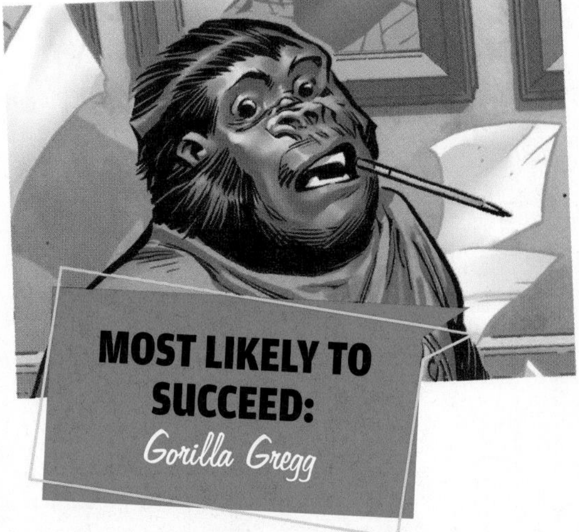

MOST LIKELY TO SUCCEED:
Gorilla Gregg

GOOD HUSTLE, GOOD HUSTLE!

HEY, ARE YOU SURE MATT'S OKAY?

YEAH. I JUST WONDER IF IT BOTHERS HIM WHEN HE HEARS ABOUT OTHER KIDS HEADING HOME ON WEEKENDS LIKE THIS.

I THINK SO. HE USUALLY KEEPS TO HIMSELF.

THE ACADEMY IS HIS HOME. AND WHO KNOWS WHAT MATT HEARS...

SOMEBODY HELP!

TOOBY?

TOOBY'S NOT HERE, SUPERMAN-BOY.

HE'S AT HOME THIS WEEKEND-- UPSTATE.

NOOO!

UPSTATE?

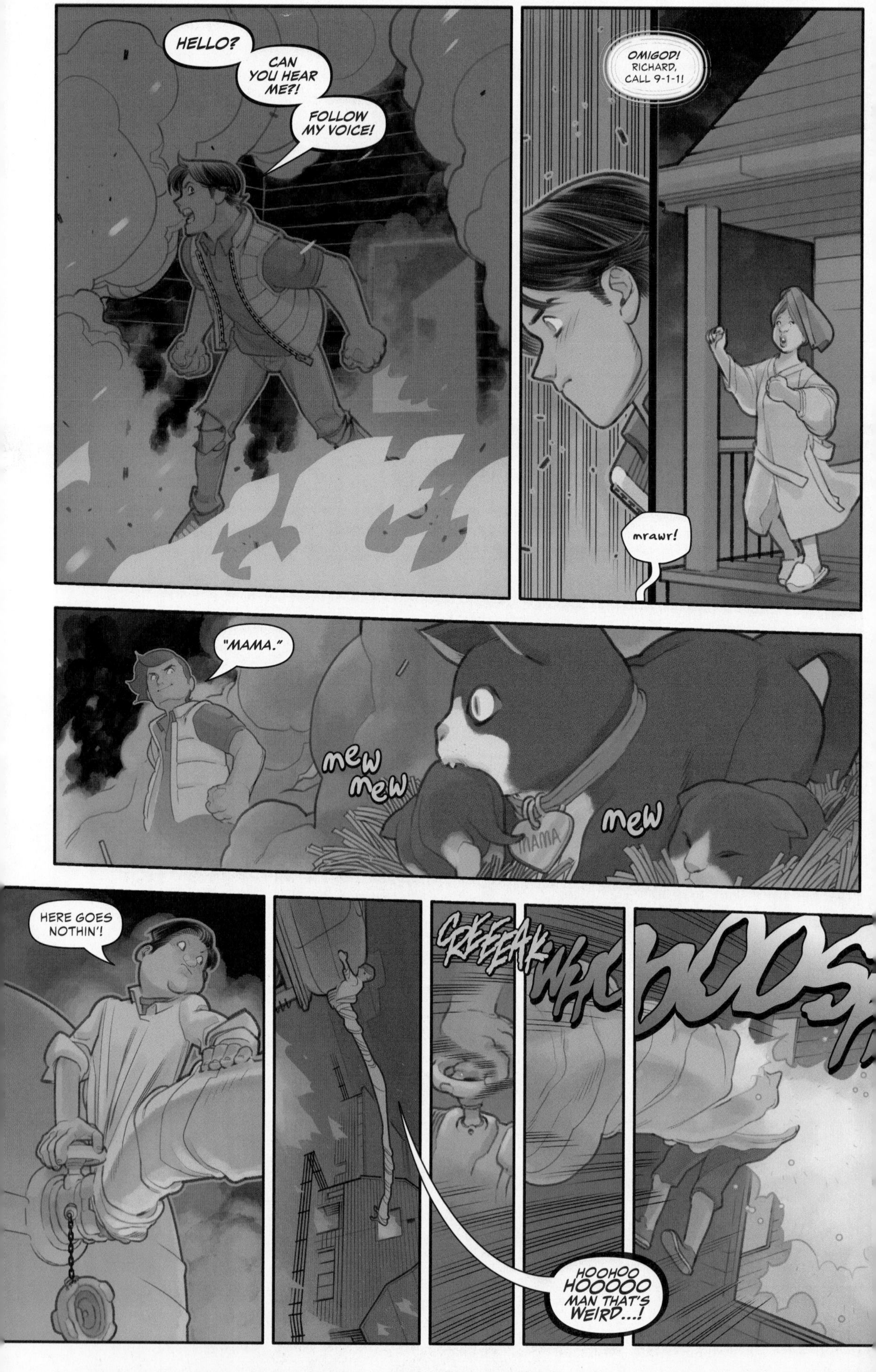
HELLO?
CAN YOU HEAR ME?!
FOLLOW MY VOICE!
OMIGOD! RICHARD, CALL 9-1-1!
mrawr!
"MAMA."
mew mew
mew
MAMA
HERE GOES NOTHIN'!
HOOHOO HOOOOO MAN THAT'S WEIRD...!

HEROES. EVERY ONE.

ESPECIALLY YOU BOYS.

I DON'T KNOW WHAT WE WOULD'VE DONE IF MAMA AND HER BABIES...

VERY HAPPY... TO HELP... MA'AM.

OW! TINY NEEDLE CLAWS!

"OW"? THEY'RE NOT KRYPTONITE KITTENS, MATT.

I TOLD YOU, I'M-- ≫sigh≪--NEVER MIND.

mew!

I DON'T UNDERSTAND HOW THIS COULD HAVE HAPPENED.

JUST BE GRATEFUL WE DON'T DEAL IN LIVESTOCK... AND THAT, THANKS TO OUR SON, THE FIRE DIDN'T SPREAD TO THE FIELDS.

WELL, THAT BARN'S NOT GONNA REBUILD ITSELF! WE SHOULD GET STARTED.

...AFTER BREAKFAST, YOU GUYS.

GO GET WASHED UP.

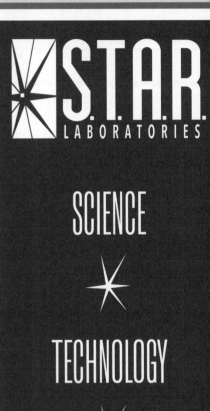

THE ROY HARPER TITANS ACADEMY

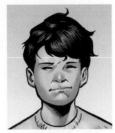

Alinta
Cooper, Merissa
Batson, William
Dane

Gregg, Gorilla
LaPorte, Lucas
Montez, Miguel
Murakami, Marvin "Tooby"

Who is your favorite Titan of all time?

KID FLASH

SUPERBOY
—Dane

ER GIRL
—Matt Price

Perez, Diego

Stitch
Webster, Joely
Zahid, Summer

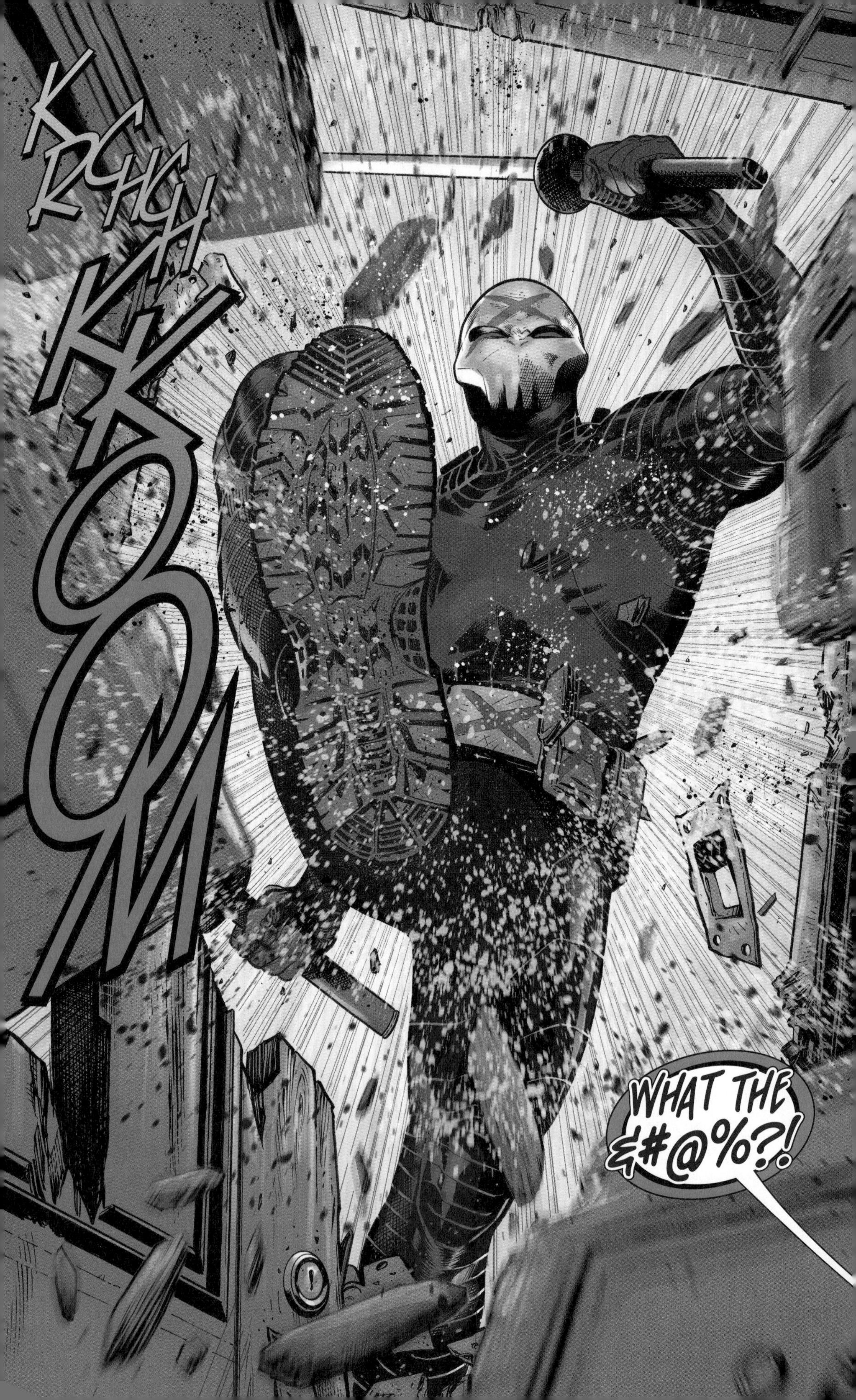
KRCHGH
KROOM
WHAT THE &#@%?!

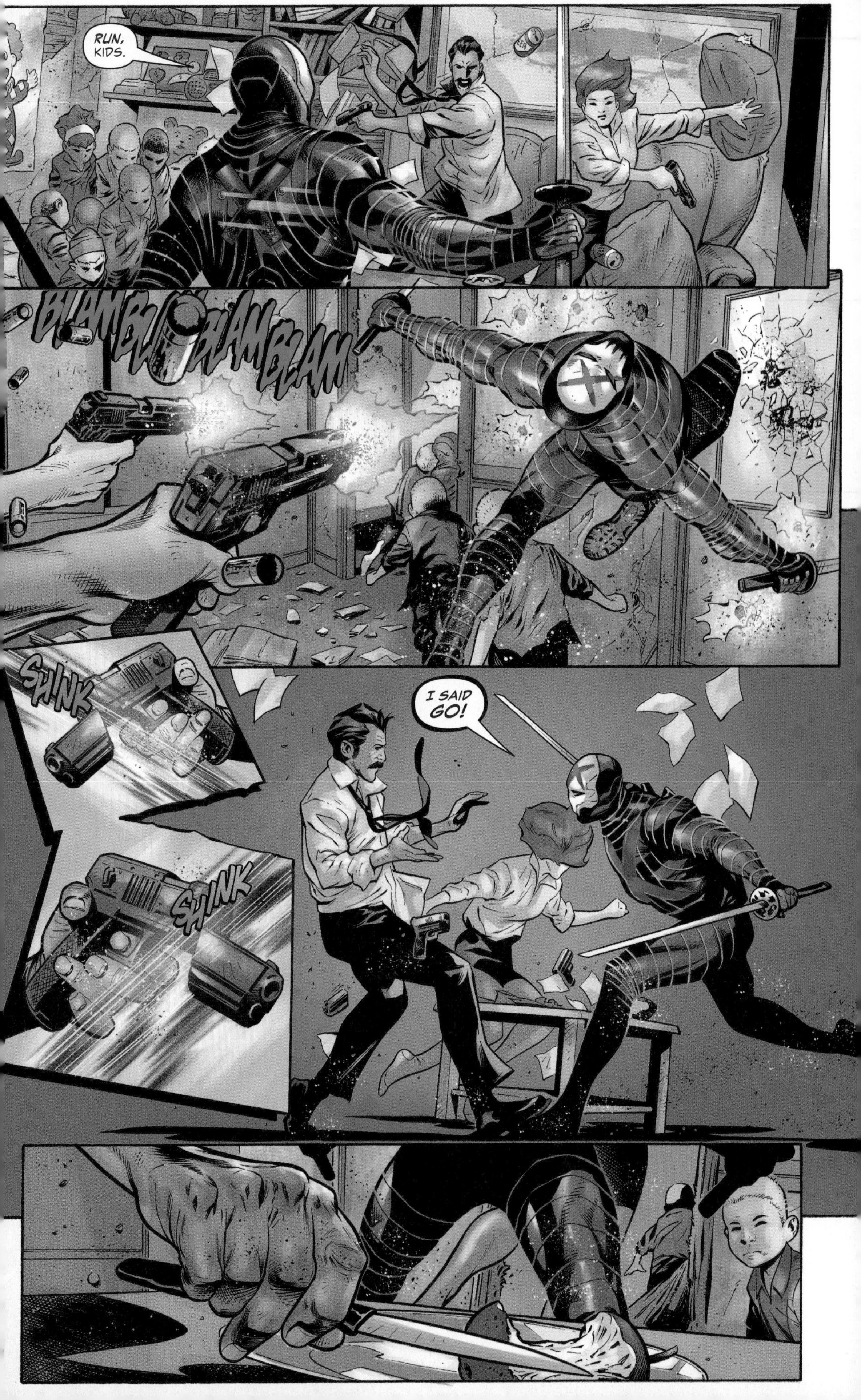
RUN, KIDS.
BLAMBLAMBLAMBLAM
SHINK
SHINK
I SAID GO!

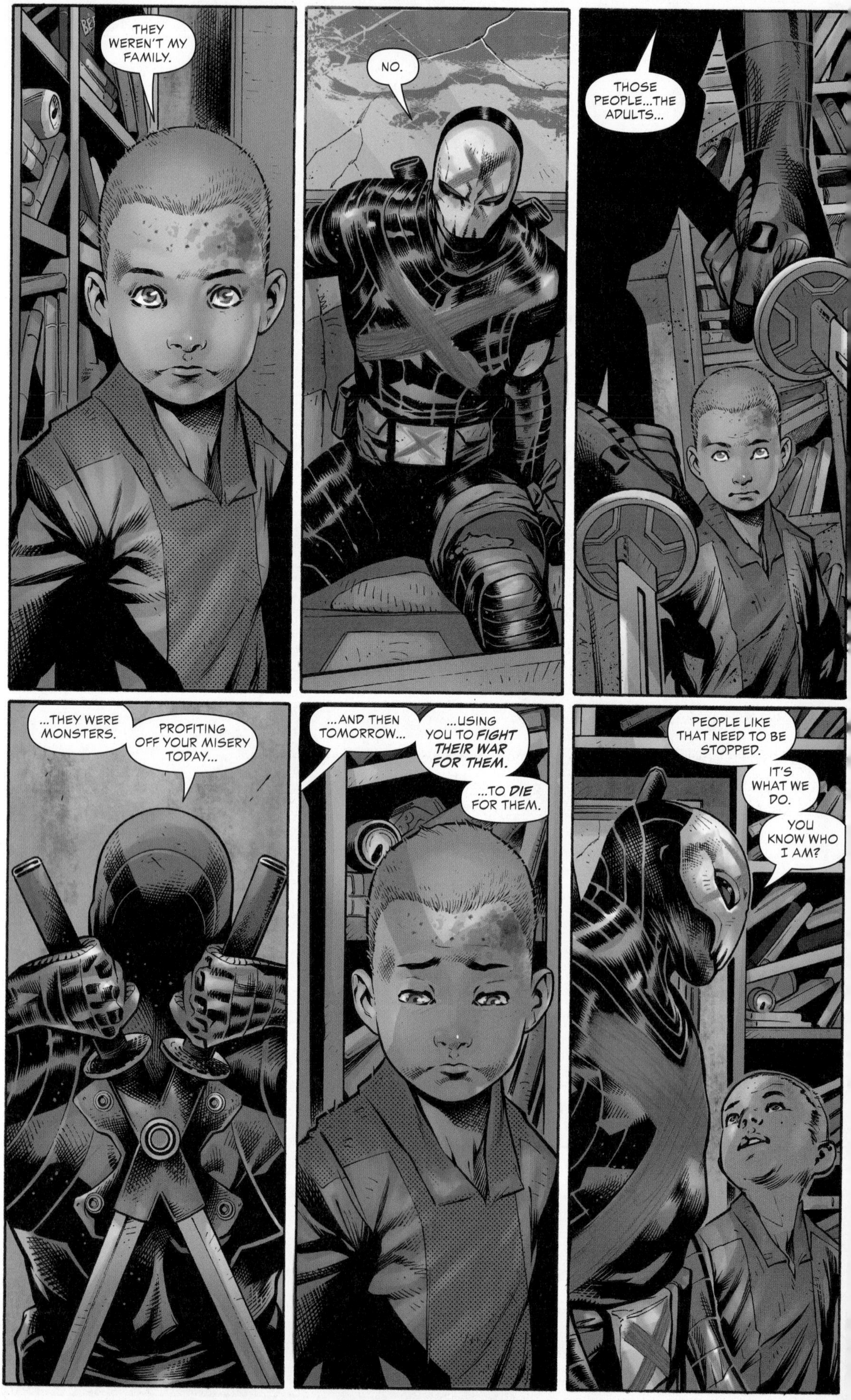

THEY WEREN'T MY FAMILY.
NO.
THOSE PEOPLE...THE ADULTS...
...THEY WERE MONSTERS.
PROFITING OFF YOUR MISERY TODAY...
...AND THEN TOMORROW...
...USING YOU TO *FIGHT THEIR WAR FOR THEM.*
...TO *DIE* FOR THEM.
PEOPLE LIKE THAT NEED TO BE STOPPED.
IT'S WHAT WE DO.
YOU KNOW WHO I AM?

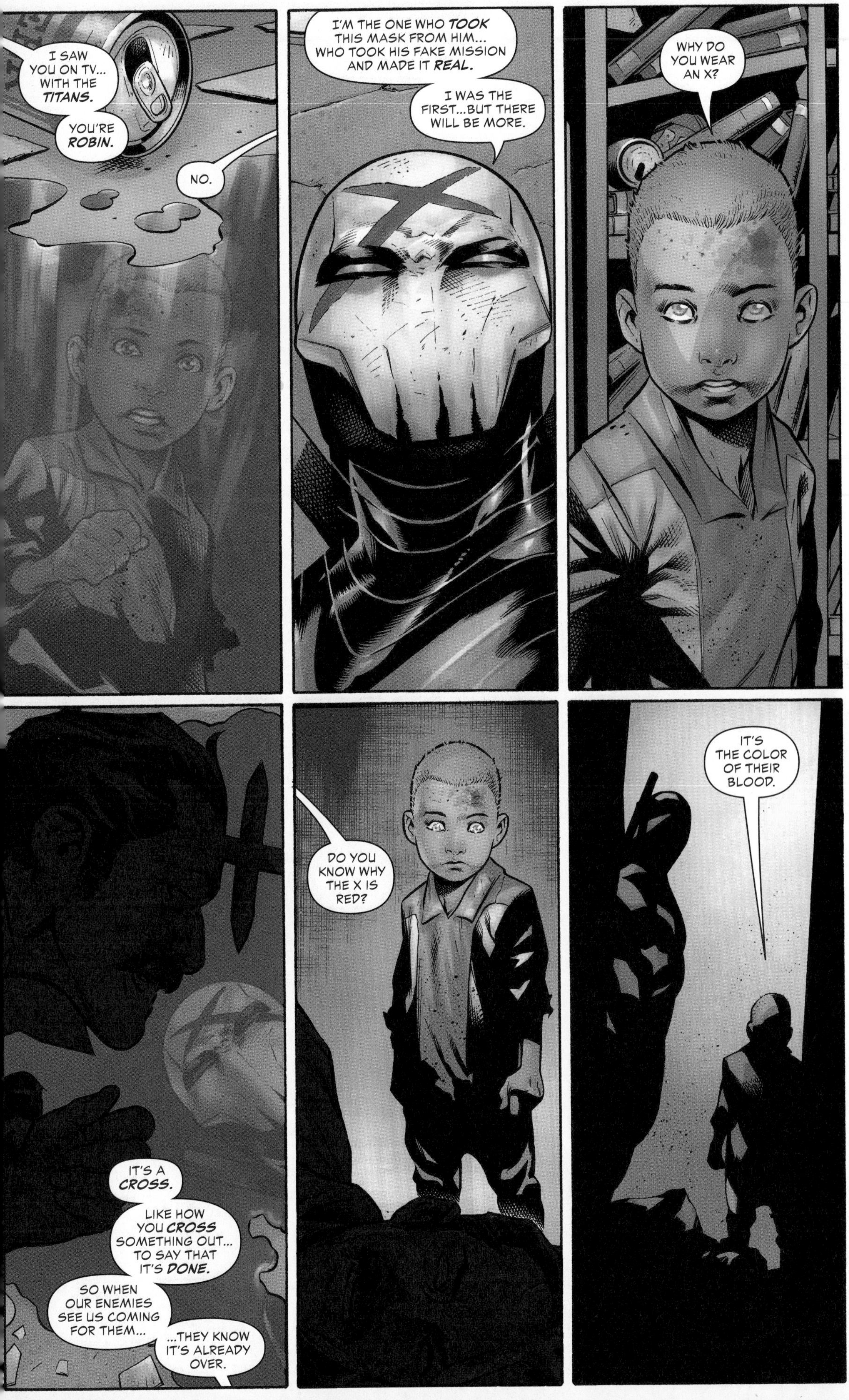
I SAW YOU ON TV... WITH THE TITANS.
YOU'RE ROBIN.
NO.
I'M THE ONE WHO TOOK THIS MASK FROM HIM... WHO TOOK HIS FAKE MISSION AND MADE IT REAL.
I WAS THE FIRST...BUT THERE WILL BE MORE.
WHY DO YOU WEAR AN X?
IT'S A CROSS.
LIKE HOW YOU CROSS SOMETHING OUT... TO SAY THAT IT'S DONE.
SO WHEN OUR ENEMIES SEE US COMING FOR THEM...
...THEY KNOW IT'S ALREADY OVER.
DO YOU KNOW WHY THE X IS RED?
IT'S THE COLOR OF THEIR BLOOD.

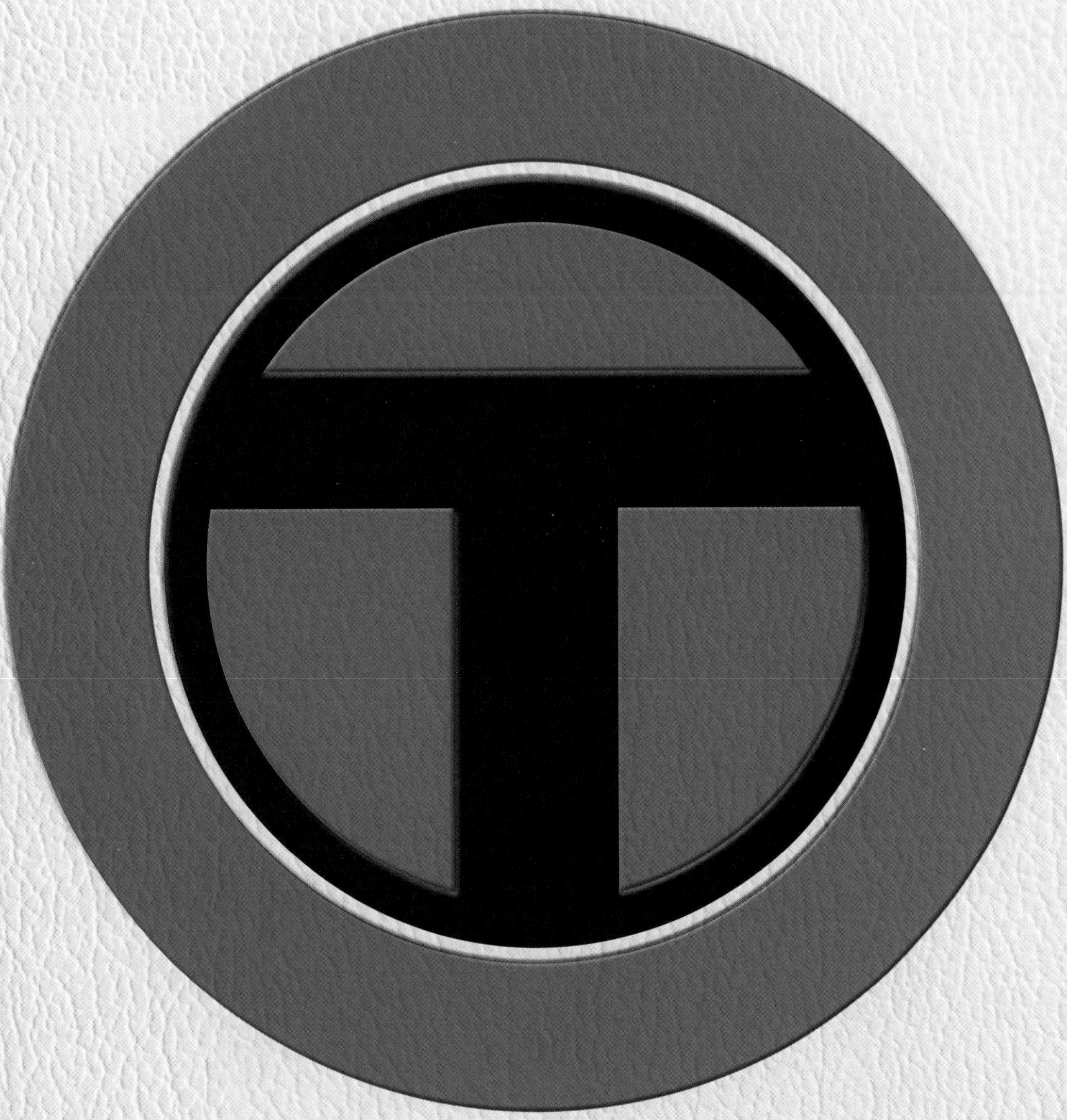

COVER AND SKETCH GALLERY

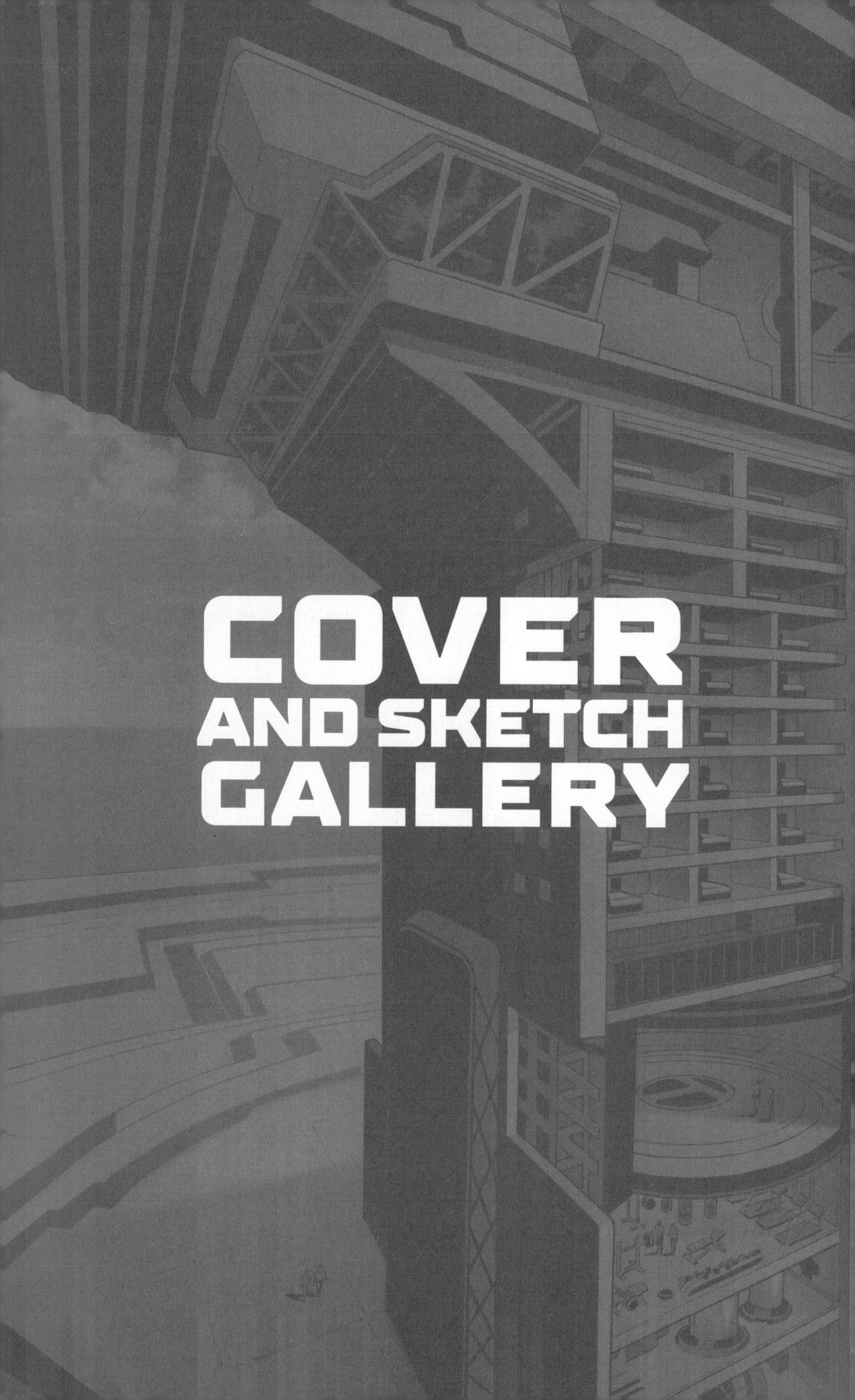

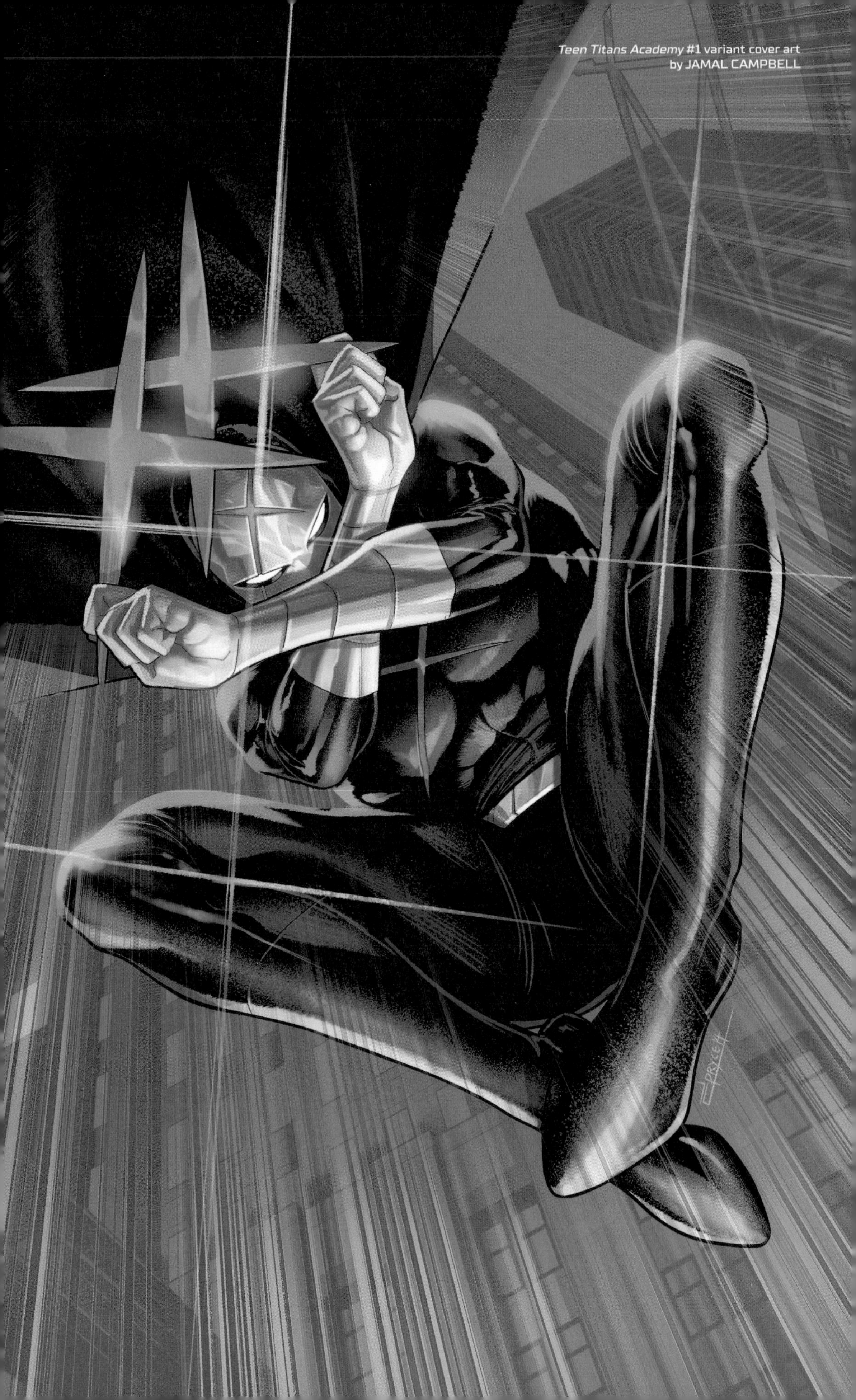

Teen Titans Academy #1 variant cover art
by JAMAL CAMPBELL

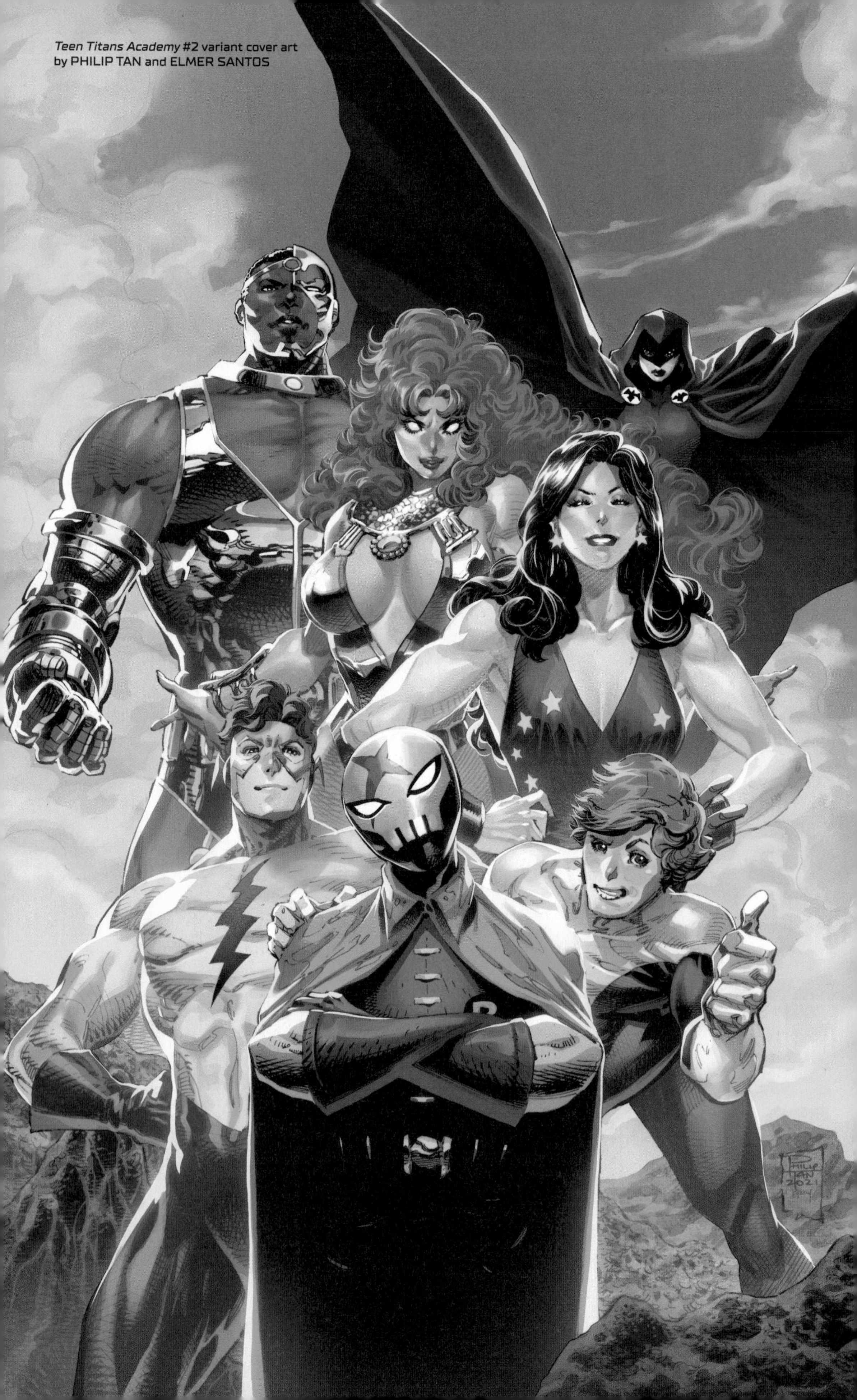

Teen Titans Academy #2 variant cover art
by PHILIP TAN and ELMER SANTOS

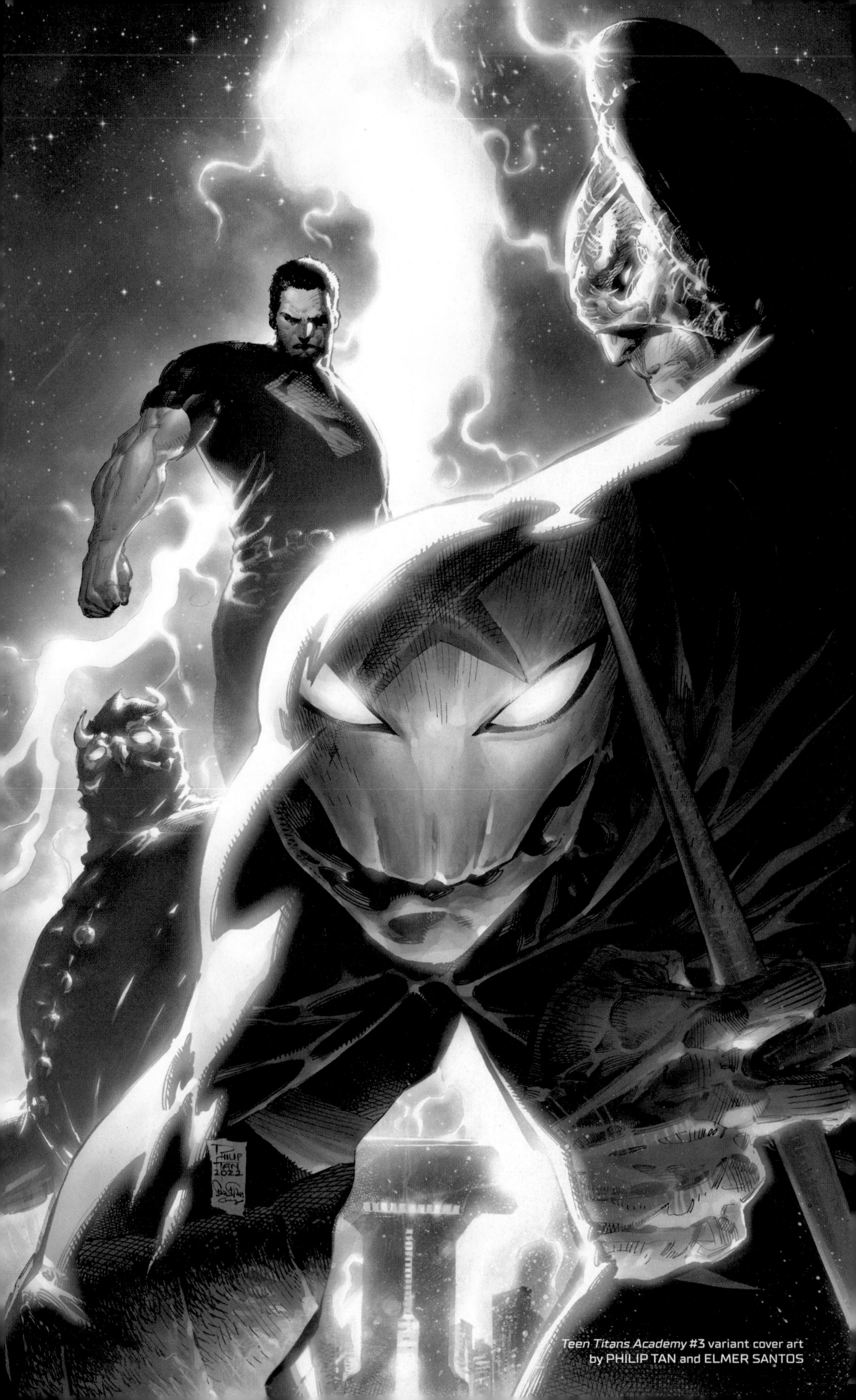

Teen Titans Academy #3 variant cover art
by PHILIP TAN and ELMER SANTOS

Teen Titans Academy #4 Pride variant cover art
by STEPHEN BYRNE

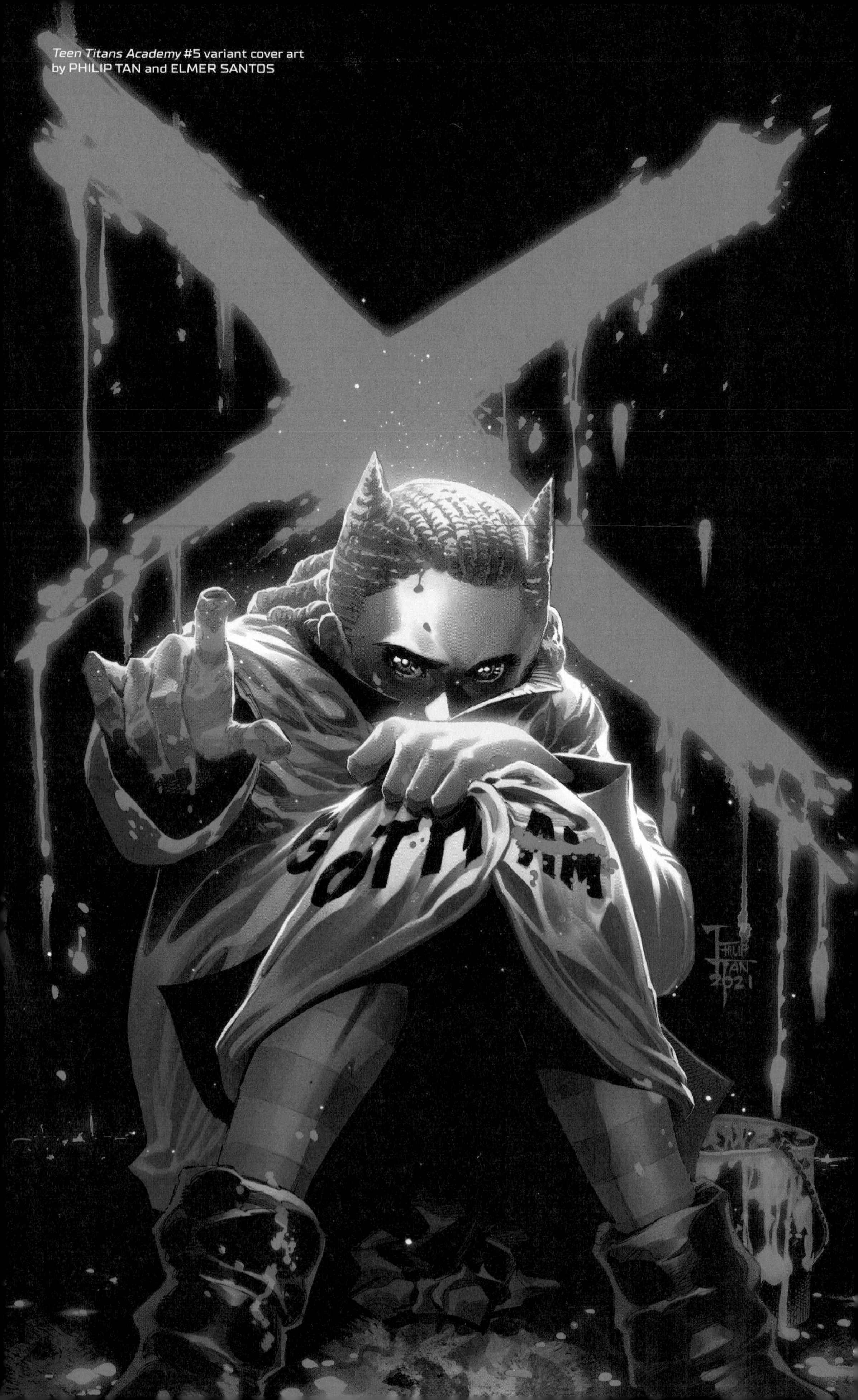
PHILIP TAN 2021

Teen Titans Academy #5 variant cover art
by PHILIP TAN and ELMER SANTOS

Teen Titans Academy 2021 Yearbook Special variant cover art
by RAFA SANDOVAL, JORDI TARRAGONA, and ALEJANDRO SÁNCHEZ

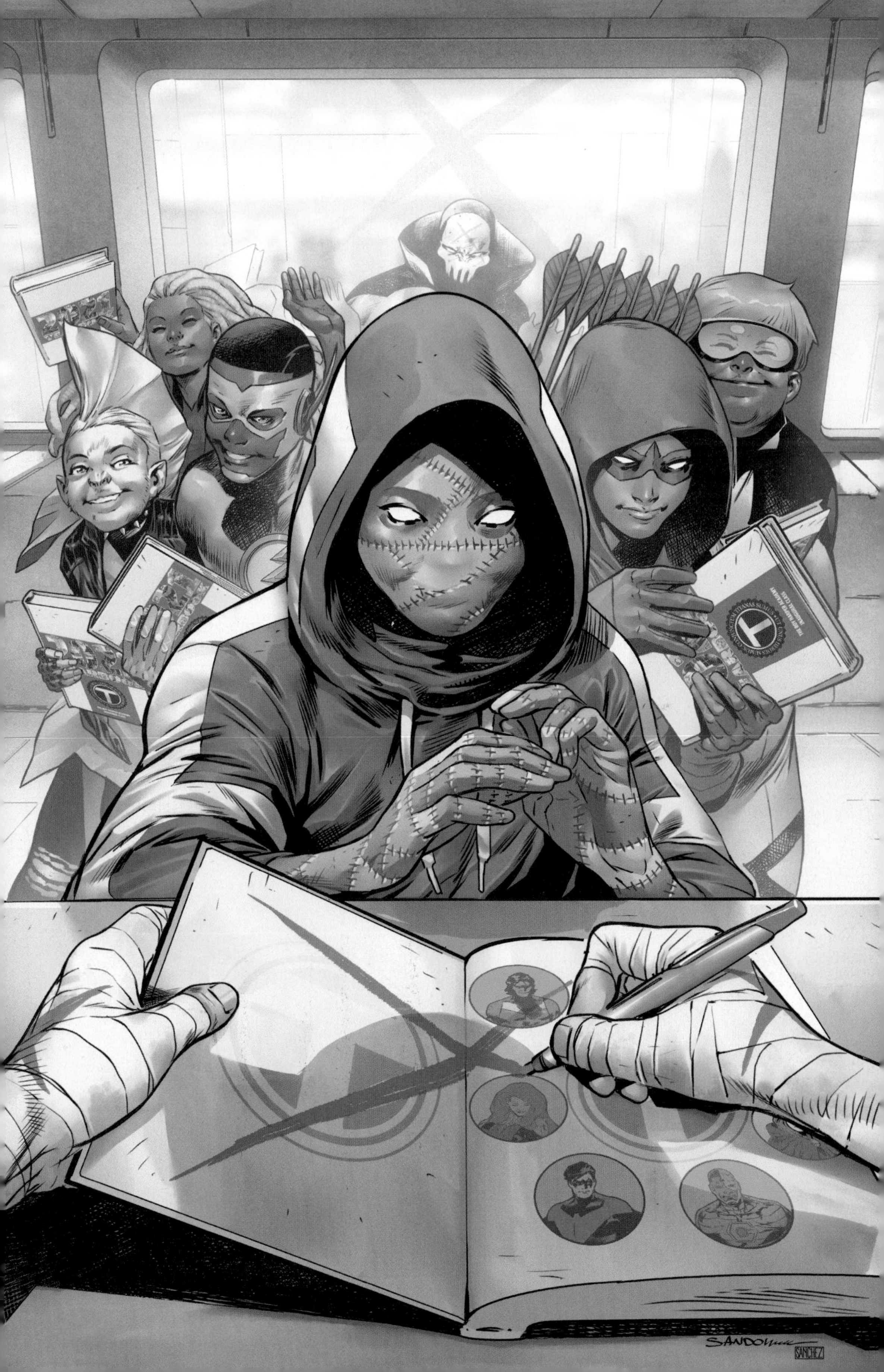

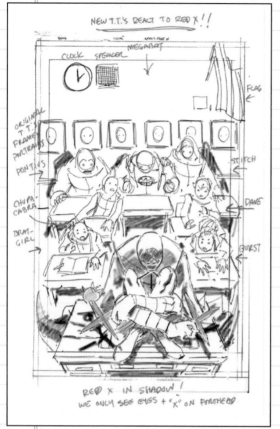

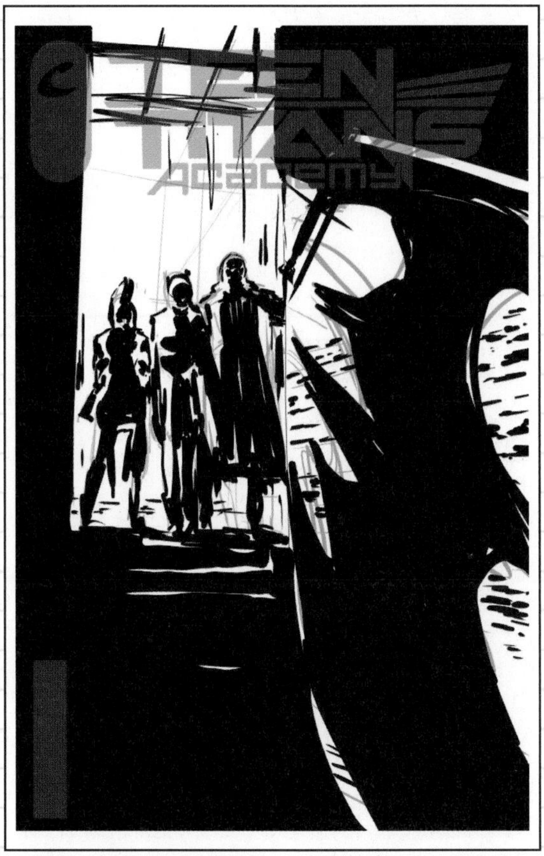
C
TEEN TITANS ACADEMY

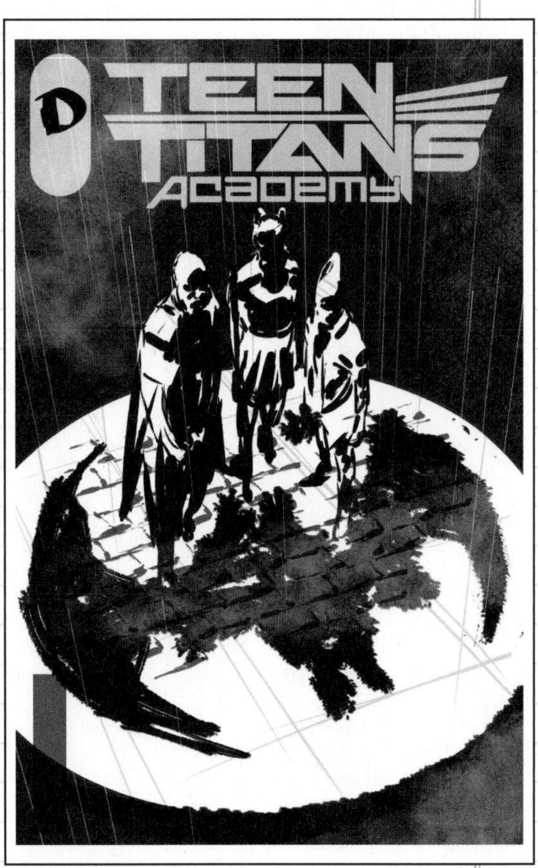
D
TEEN TITANS ACADEMY

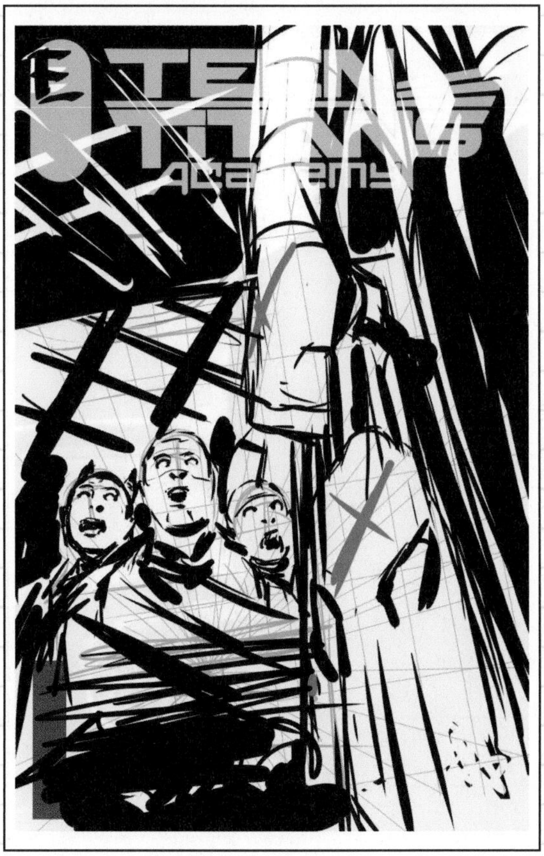
E
TEEN TITANS ACADEMY

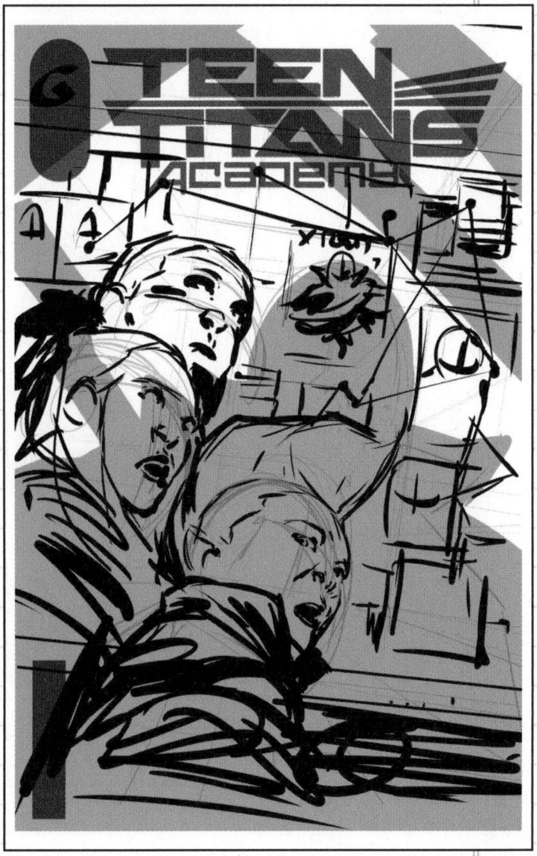
G
TEEN TITANS ACADEMY

Character studies by RAFA SANDOVAL

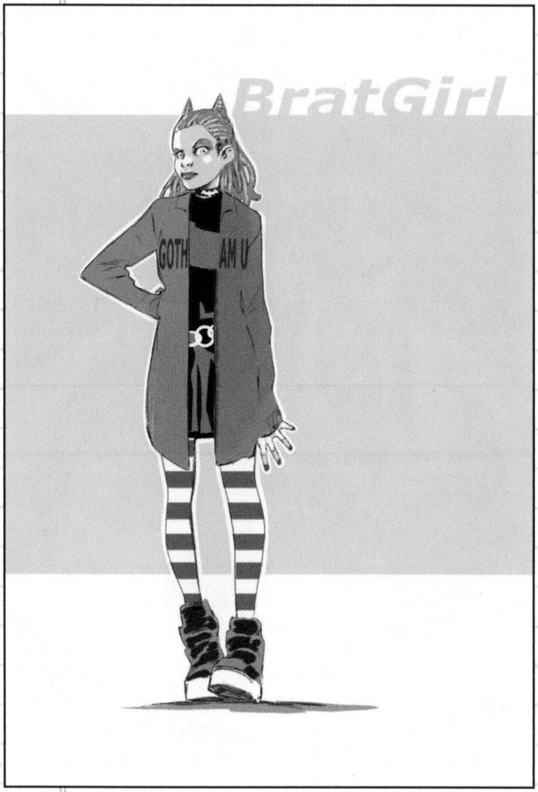
BratGirl
GOTH
AM U

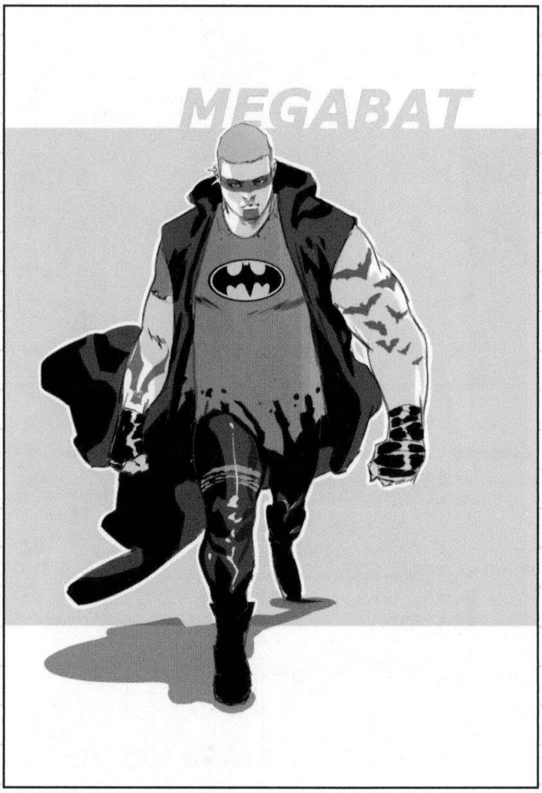
MEGABAT

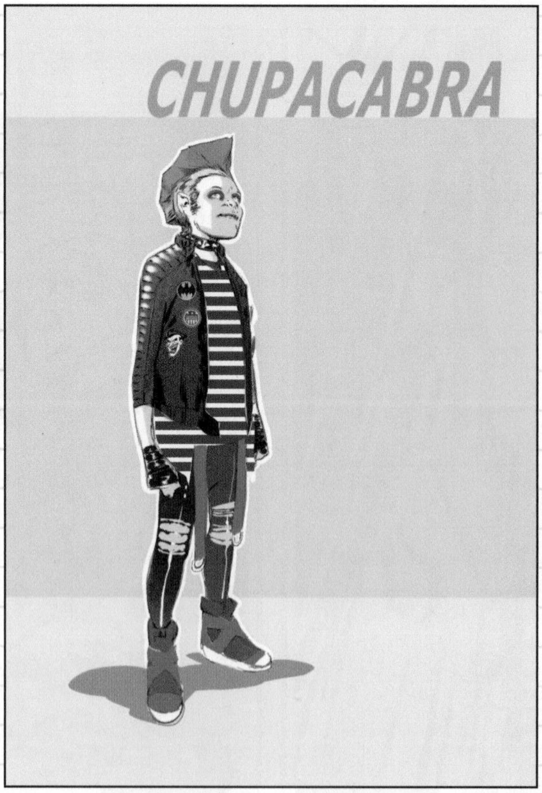
CHUPACABRA

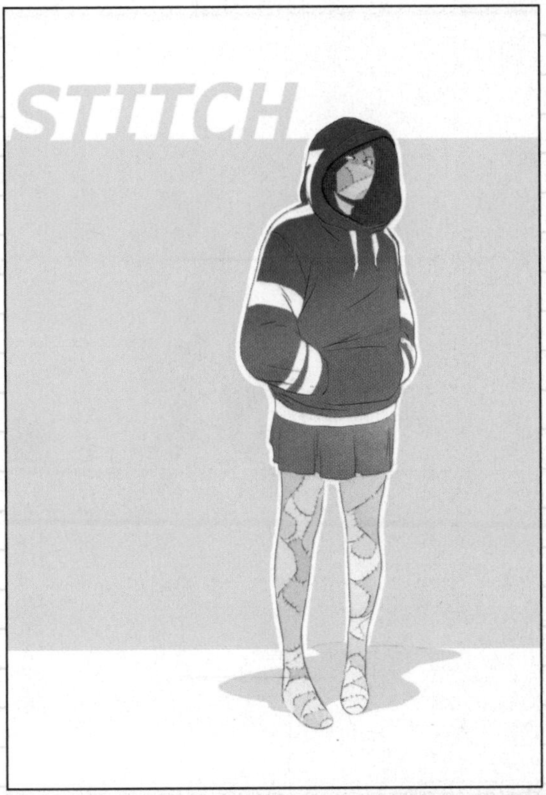
STITCH

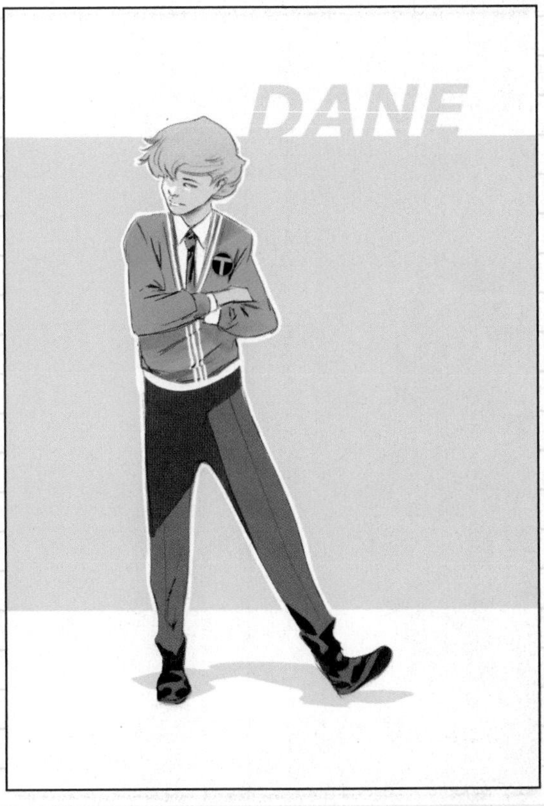
DANE

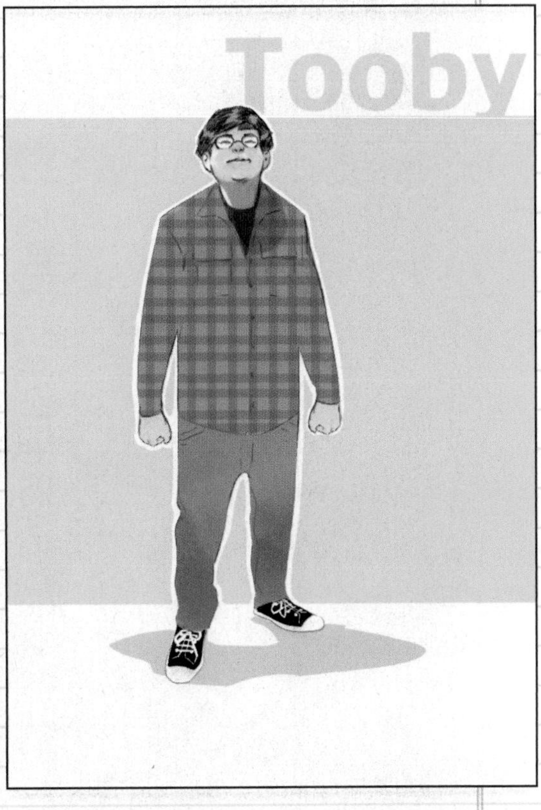
Tooby

BURST

PONTIUS PRIMATE